Shelter

Shelter

Where Harvard Meets the Homeless

Scott Seider

continuum

2010

The Continuum International Publishing Group
80 Maiden Lane, New York, NY 10038
The Tower Building, 11 York Road, London SE1 7NX

www.continuumbooks.com

Library of Congress Cataloging-in-Publication Data
Seider, Scott.
Shelter : where Harvard meets the homeless / by Scott Seider.
    p. cm.
    Includes bibliographical references and index.
    ISBN-13: 978-1-4411-3737-1 (alk. paper)
    ISBN-10: 1-4411-3737-8 (alk. paper)
    ISBN-13: 978-1-4411-8561-7 (pbk. : alk. paper)
    ISBN-10: 1-4411-8561-5 (pbk. : alk. paper) 1. Shelters for
the homeless—Massachusetts—Cambridge. 2. Harvard Square
(Cambridge, Mass.) I. Title.
    HV4506.M4S45 2010
    363.5'8—dc22   2010006798

ISBN: 978-1-4411-3737-1 (hardback)
        978-1-4411-8561-7 (paperback)

Typeset by Pindar NZ, Auckland, New Zealand
Printed in the United States of America by Thomson-Shore, Inc

Contents

Acknowledgments

While this project began in earnest in April of 2008, I have wanted to write this book since I was a volunteer at the Harvard Square Homeless Shelter more than a decade ago. Along the way, I have racked up quite a number of individuals to whom I am greatly indebted.

Seventy-three qualitative interviews required hundreds of hours of transcription. For their contributions to this Herculean task, I am greatly indebted to Alexis Gates, Elizabeth Bernard, Janet Stankiewicz, Lauren Finch, Andrew Barlow, Rachel Paul, Alexa Joki and Meghan Weber. Additionally, Jenna Leavitt played a valuable role in organizing and coding the transcribed interviews; Rachel Paul served as an able proofreader of the manuscript; Alexis Gates did yeoman's work on the index; Brian O'Flaherty an adept copy editor and Sara-May Mallett served as a wonderful project manager. I am also deeply grateful to my colleague, Dr. Lee Indrisano, for turning her editorial eye and graceful touch to this manuscript. Finally, the excellent work of my research assistants, Susan Gillmor and Samantha Rabinowicz, during the summer of 2009 allowed this project to move forward.

This project would never have progressed beyond the planning stages were it not for the enthusiastic support of a number of students and administrators at Harvard University. These individuals include David Dance, Gene Corbin, Adam Travis, Peter Ganong, Jill Stockwell, Shane Donovan and Erin McCreary.

Wholly unfamiliar with the business of publishing, I relied heavily on the wisdom and insights of several mentors: Howard Gardner, Rick Weissbourd, Meira Levinson, Dan Butin, Lee Indrisano and Adam Howard. I am particularly grateful to Continuum's David Barker for his enthusiastic support of this project.

A number of friends and family served as invaluable first readers of this manuscript. They include Ross Seider, Bonnie Seider, Michael Mao, Lee Indrisano and Adam Travis. I am also grateful to Wendy Seider, Gloria Bruce and Selma Seider for perennial encouragement and support.

This project would never have taken place were it not for my opportunity and privilege to join the faculty in 2008 of Boston University. For that opportunity, I feel deeply indebted to Jeanie Goddard, Dan Davis, Stephan Ellenwood, Cathy O'Connor and Charles Glenn. I am also highly appreciative of my incredible students and colleagues at Boston University who make coming to work every day such a genuine pleasure.

Putting together *Shelter* was both an exhilarating and anxiety-provoking process. Joanna Christodoulou allowed me to talk my way through both the exhilaration and the anxiety with patience and generosity. I owe her a significant debt of gratitude.

Finally, there are 53 men and women who generously shared their time and insights with me about their experiences at the Harvard Square Homeless Shelter. Maintaining their confidentiality prevents me from thanking them each by name, but I am hopeful that all 53 will read this book and feel I did justice to their experiences.

Chapter 1

Privilege and Poverty

PREPARATIONS, 6:30 P.M.

The temperature is 20 degrees Fahrenheit but feels colder than that because of the pitch black night sky and three-foot snow banks lining the streets. Pedestrians — businessmen, mothers with strollers, college students — move cautiously along the icy sidewalks of Harvard Square. Many are carrying shopping bags filled with gifts to be wrapped for the Christmas holiday just a week away.

The University Lutheran Church sits dark and quiet a block away from the hubbub, surrounded by a pizza place on one side and a Harvard University dormitory on the other. The church's main entrance for Sunday services sits at ground level, but a nearby set of stairs and handicap ramp lead down to another door. Through that door lies the basement of the University Lutheran Church, which, for the past 26 years, has hosted the Harvard Square Homeless Shelter.

The Harvard Square Homeless Shelter does not open for business until 7 p.m., but the two Harvard students directing tonight's dinner shift are already in the kitchen sorting through a shopping bag of donations dropped off earlier in the day. Nathan Small,[1] a rail-thin junior wearing a T-shirt and a stocking hat, actually grew up in Cambridge just a few miles away. Mae Sarkar, petite and pixie-like, is a sophomore from suburban New Jersey.

The two put away the donated cans of creamed corn, peas and black

1

beans — all useful. They shake their heads over a can of cocktail olives and laugh about a bit of shelter lore — the time someone allegedly donated a bottle of edible chocolate body paint.

The Harvard Square Shelter kitchen holds two large refrigerators, a Hobart machine for washing dishes, a cast iron oven and an island with several sinks. One of the refrigerators is labeled "Church Only." A counter with serving windows opens out into the shelter's large central room that holds a dining area with five small circular tables, a TV area surrounded by several mismatched couches and a long computer table with five desktop computers arranged in a row like a university computer lab. A column of eight-foot-high lockers cordons off one corner of this central space as the men's sleeping area — a tight space that holds ten wooden bunk beds positioned at right angles to each other. Attached to each bunk bed is a laminated card with a large letter on it: "A", "B", "C", etc., so that men staying at the shelter can find their assigned beds.

At quarter to seven, the dinner-shift volunteers start to arrive. Jasper is a blonde Harvard senior wearing baggy canvas pants with numerous pockets. Brianna is a sophomore from Tufts who heard about the shelter through a high school friend. She is short and slender with long dark hair. The third volunteer, Clara, is an Asian American woman in her late twenties, a graduate student in Harvard's Biochemistry Department. These three volunteers have worked together for more than a month now and know how to proceed with little direction from Nathan or Mae. Jasper starts on a pot of coffee while Brianna and Clara begin pulling large trays covered in plastic wrap out of the refrigerator. These trays — leftovers donated the night before by Harvard Dining Services — hold pasta, rice and a tofu concoction. Mae — the director from New Jersey — decides to bake trays of apple and banana crisp to make use of the three wooden crates of bananas and apples stacked in the center of the kitchen, a donation from the previous day.

The Harvard Square Shelter is dark in the way basements are dark, but the Harvard students have sought to bring in some holiday cheer. Construction paper cut-outs of gingerbread men are affixed to each of the lockers that cordon off the men's sleeping area, and green and red Christmas lights frame the swinging door that opens into the kitchen. A picturesque gingerbread house decorated with frosting and gumdrops sits on a tray on the long table in the dining area looking tasty enough that it's surprising no one has succumbed to temptation and broken off a bite.

The security guard, Oscar — the shelter's only paid employee — arrives at five to seven. A South American in his late forties, Oscar comes to the shelter five nights a week for a 7 p.m. till midnight shift at the front door. Oscar's nephew takes the shift on weekends and fills in on the rare nights when Oscar is ill or has another commitment.

Oscar collects the clipboard and metal detector from Nathan. The metal detector resembles the black-and-gold wands used at the airport on people who have set off the walk-through metal detector. On the clipboard is a spreadsheet with the names of the 25 men and women who will be staying in the shelter this evening, their bed assignments, locker assignments and "nights remaining." The Harvard Square Shelter is an emergency, short-term stay shelter. Homeless men and women can reserve a bed for 14 nights in a row, but then must wait a week before reserving a bed for another 14 nights. Promptly at 7 p.m., Nathan tells Oscar, "You can start letting people in." The Harvard Square Homeless Shelter is open for business.

A STUDENT-RUN SHELTER

Every winter night the Harvard Square Homeless Shelter brings together society's most privileged and most marginalized groups under one roof: Harvard students and the homeless. Located in a modest church basement a few blocks from Harvard Yard, the shelter provides a nightly refuge for 25 men and women contending with homelessness. What makes this homeless shelter unique is that it is operated entirely by Harvard College students. It is the only student-run homeless shelter in the United States.

For more than 25 years, nearly 100 college-aged volunteers have worked to keep the Harvard Square Shelter open seven nights a week from November through April — the coldest months of the year in Boston. The majority of these volunteers come from Harvard College, but the shelter also draws on university students from Wellesley College, MIT, Boston University and Tufts.

Approximately 75 of these volunteers sign up for a weekly dinner, overnight or breakfast shift. The dinner shift runs 7–11 p.m., the overnight shift 11 p.m.–6:30 a.m. and the breakfast shift 6:30–8:30 a.m.[2] Volunteers choose a particular shift — say, the Friday breakfast shift — and commit to working that shift for the entire winter. If they need to miss a shift for one reason or another, they are expected to find a substitute to take their place. Jasper, Brianna and Clara are all volunteers on the Wednesday dinner shift.

The other way for students to get involved with the Harvard Square Shelter is by taking on a leadership role as a director. There are 14 directors in total, so that they can cover the seven nights of the week in teams of two. Nathan and Mae are working the Wednesday night director shifts. Additionally, each director takes on a particular set of responsibilities for keeping the shelter operating. There is a volunteer director who ensures there is a sufficient number of volunteers for every shift; an administrative director who communicates with the leadership of the University Lutheran Church and the Massachusetts Housing and Shelter Alliance; a supplies director who keeps the shelter fully stocked; a food director; a fundraising director; a maintenance director; a computers director; and an in-kind donations director. There are also directors in charge of the Harvard Square Shelter's Work Contract, Resource Advocacy and Street Team programs.

These 14 student-directors meet together on Sunday afternoons to report on their various responsibilities and to make decisions about dilemmas and challenges that have sprung up over the past week. Dr. Aaron Dutka, a shelter director during his undergraduate years in the early 1990s, characterized these weekly meetings as critical to the success of the shelter:

> "The shelter had no president, no chief executive. It was really ruled by committee . . . where everyone has a say and everyone sort of counts equally and brings their own expertise. I think it made it possible for the shelter to really be run by the students. Because the judgment of any single 20 or 21 year old is probably not up to the challenge of running an organization like that. But the collective judgment of that group, I think, really did make that possible."

This opening chapter offers a vivid picture of precisely what this collection of Harvard students makes possible. Drawing on detailed field notes from a single night at the Harvard Square Homeless Shelter in December of 2008, I offer a narrative of the incidents, interactions and conversations that took place from the arrival of the student-directors at 6:30 p.m. to the departure of the last homeless man at 8 o'clock the next morning.[3] In so doing, I seek to paint a picture of the Harvard Square Homeless Shelter in action and to capture the rhythm of a typical night there.

Interspersed within this narrative is an overview of the ensuing nine chapters. In the chapters that follow, I draw on more than 70 qualitative interviews with Harvard students, Harvard alumni, professional stakeholders and the homeless themselves to demonstrate how the interactions taking place inside the Harvard Square Homeless Shelter prove transformative for both the homeless men and women taking shelter there and the Harvard students volunteering at the shelter.[4] These transformations offer a window into the nature of both privilege and poverty in America as well as the powerful effects that can result when members of these opposing groups come together.

DINNER, 7 P.M.

The security guard, Oscar, begins letting in one by one the homeless men and women waiting in line outside. Each person must sign the intake sheet, be brushed with the metal detector and answer four questions:

1. Are you sober?
2. Do you have any weapons?
3. Do you have any drugs or alcohol?
4. Do you have any medication?

The Harvard Square Shelter is a dry shelter, which means no one who is intoxicated or high is allowed inside. The security guard or student-directors — tonight, Nathan and Mae — can give a breathalyzer or drug test to anyone whose behavior or appearance calls their sobriety into question. They keep on hand the same easy-to-use tests popular with high school principals for school dances and football games.

By 7:30 p.m., the Harvard Square Shelter already holds a dozen homeless men and women. The Harvard students refer to them as "guests." Upon entering the shelter, most of these men and women head straight for their respective lockers to shed the many layers of clothing they have donned to fight off the cold. Other men and women seek out the student-directors to add their names to the laundry sign-up sheet. Still others head for the showers. Both of the shelter's bathrooms are equipped with two stalls, two showers, two sinks and tile floors. Their doors are propped open at night to discourage covert smokers.

In the kitchen, Brianna and Clara are still working on dinner, but Jasper brings out to the dining area a pot of coffee, a pitcher of Kool-Aid and a tray of pastries left over from breakfast. A number of homeless men sit down at one of the small tables, drinking coffee, thawing out and chatting quietly. "Hello, my young damsel!" one of them — a middle-aged man with a pot belly and bushy mustache — calls out to Mae when she rolls up the window grates separating the kitchen from the shelter's main area. Mae waves from the kitchen.

While Jasper is arranging the coffee and Kool-Aid, he engages in conversation with Fayad, a slim older man with a foreign accent in his early sixties. When Jasper inquires about his accent, Fayad explains he is of Armenian descent but was raised in Turkey. He has been in the United States for 30 years, mostly in Florida, and makes his living as an artist painting icons for Eastern Orthodox churches. He speaks Turkish, Armenian, English, and a little bit of Arabic and Greek. "Yes, Istanbul is beautiful," he notes in response to Jasper's query, but adds that "They don't treat Armenians well there."

Fayad and Jasper's conversation is cut short after ten minutes when Nathan asks Jasper to accompany Clara to one of Harvard's undergraduate dining halls to pick up the leftovers that will constitute tomorrow night's dinner. Jasper and Clara, familiar with this drill, pull a supermarket shopping cart out of a janitor's closet that was likely swiped years ago from a nearby grocery store and greatly facilitates this process of food retrieval.

As Jasper and Clara are wheeling the shopping cart up the ramp that leads out of the shelter, Mae issues a "warning" to a homeless man in his early twenties who has jumped the laundry list queue by simply throwing his dirty laundry into the washing machine. An email summarizing this warning and other important events will be sent out by Mae and Nathan at the end of the shift to the shelter's 12 other student-directors. Three warnings to a particular individual result in a two-week bar from staying at the shelter.

Dinner is served a few minutes before 8 p.m. Nathan, Brianna, and Mae stand on one side of the kitchen counter with ladles and tongs and serve cafeteria-style the spaghetti, rice, salad, and tofu to a line of waiting men and women. These men and women then take their trays either to the small tables in the dining area or to the television area where the news is on. Over the next hour, Nathan, Brianna and Mae are kept busy filling up the plates of new arrivals and doling out seconds to the early birds. Additionally, more than a dozen men, women and teenagers *not* staying at the shelter come to the shelter's front door to request plates of food. The security guard, Oscar, conveys the request back to the Harvard students in the kitchen who spoon spaghetti, rice and salad into carry-out Styrofoam containers, then ferry the containers back to the front door. "You guys kept me waiting 20 minutes," an Indian man with a goatee complains to Nathan upon receiving his carry-away container. "How long does it take to go plop plop?"

Meanwhile, the potbellied gentleman with the mustache has returned to the serving line for seconds but dawdles in front of the kitchen window chatting with Brianna across the counter. He tells her about growing up in Somerville, Massachusetts, lingering on a story about his high school girlfriend. They are still talking 15 minutes later when Nathan comes into the kitchen to take phone calls for emergency beds. Each night at 9 p.m., if the shelter has any available beds — due to no-shows — the student-directors give away those open beds to homeless men and women calling in for them. Tonight, Nathan has six beds to give away. Two men have failed to show up to claim their beds, and, additionally, on nights like this one when the temperature has dropped below freezing, the directors set up four World War II era cots around the periphery of the dining area and take in another four people in search of shelter. At precisely 9 p.m., the phone starts ringing. "Hello," Nathan says. "Okay, Arnie, you're in cot number two." In just ten minutes, all six beds have been claimed.

Immediately following the emergency bed phone calls, Nathan enlists Jasper to change the sheets on the two beds in the men's sleeping area that tonight will be turned over to new occupants. Mae and Clara drag the four cots out from under one of the bunk beds in the overnight volunteers' room and start assembling them. The cots are a dark green, military canvas stretched out across a metal frame. When Clara accidentally drops one of the metal legs, the loud clang reverberates throughout the entire shelter. At 9 p.m., while Nathan was taking phone calls for emergency beds, Mae had turned off the overhead lights illuminating the shelter's central room in deference to two-thirds of the shelter's occupants who had finished their dinner and gone straight to bed. The rest of the men and women staying in the shelter this evening are evenly distributed across the dining, television and computer areas. A chubby White man in his thirties sits at a table in the dining area with a laptop computer. At a table nearby, another man in his mid-twenties plays solitaire with an air of intense concentration. Two more men sit at the shelter's computer terminals. One, a White man in his twenties with a crew cut and weightlifter's physique, is on Facebook. Two other men, and one of the few women in the shelter, sit in the TV area watching *Gossip Girl* at a nearly inaudible volume.

POWERFUL EFFECTS FOR THE HOMELESS

The Harvard students volunteering at the Harvard Square Shelter are transitioning out of adolescence and into emerging adulthood. A number of the characteristics of this developmental period — the college years — allow these young adults to provide support to the homeless in ways that older professional service workers cannot. One such characteristic is an unmatched level of energy and optimism. Developmental psychologists characterize emerging adulthood as the peak period of optimism in the lifespan and also a period in which individuals possess relatively few commitments and responsibilities.[5] As a result, the Harvard students volunteering at the shelter are able to throw themselves into their volunteer work with high levels of energy and idealism.[6] Take, for example, the founding this past winter of the Harvard Square Shelter's "Street Team." Street Team was the brainchild of several Harvard students who sought to bring the resources offered *inside* the Harvard Square Homeless Shelter to the homeless men and women spending the night on the streets of Harvard Square. Though already providing shelter and support to 25 homeless men and women each night, the energy and optimism characteristic of emerging adulthood led these Harvard students to believe they could do more, and to push themselves to increase the number of homeless men and women to whom they offer support and sustenance.

The Harvard students volunteering at the shelter also possess a deep desire to *connect* with the homeless people staying at the Harvard Square Shelter. According to psychologist Erik Erikson, the final step of adolescence entails seeking out peers, mentors, organizations, and literature that can offer a deeper understanding of the world.[7] One of the most effective ways for Harvard students to carry out their identity exploration is by *listening* to the homeless men and women staying at the Harvard Square Shelter.[8] There, under one roof, are 25 individuals who can describe experiences and perspectives that are often very different from those offered to Harvard students by parents, relatives, professors, and friends.

As enthusiastic listeners, the Harvard students volunteering at the shelter also provide an important opportunity for the homeless men and women staying at the shelter to talk about themselves and their lives. Moreover, the students' genuine enthusiasm gives these conversations a very different flavor than those between the homeless and professional social workers. Seasoned professionals are rarely available for long blocks of time to sit and listen to one of their homeless clients, and, on the occasions that they can engage in such conversation, their years of listening to nearly identical stories make some level of skepticism and guardedness inevitable.[9] The Harvard students volunteering at the Harvard Square Shelter, on the other hand, are honored to be seen as confidantes and genuinely engaged by the stories which they experience as fresh and eye-opening. Also, because the Harvard students are typically many years younger than the homeless men and women with whom they are speaking, this difference in age and experience gives the shelter's homeless guests an opportunity to play the role of teacher or mentor — even if the advice they have to offer these Harvard student is simply to avoid particular mistakes and temptations.[10]

The youth and inexperience of the Harvard students leading the Harvard Square Homeless Shelter also leads them to be fearless in trying out new strategies and approaches to combating homelessness. Psychologist Robert Evans has found that young adults associate the word "change" with growth, development, and enhancement while older adults associate "change" with risk, loss, and challenges to their competence.[11] Several of the dramatic adaptations the Harvard students made this past year in order to combat homelessness more effectively included increasing the number of homeless men and women the shelter could accommodate; changing the procedure by which homeless men and women reserve a bed at the shelter; and raising an astounding $130,000 to "endow" the shelter's annual budget. Towards the end of the winter, the Harvard students began contemplating raising the funds to buy an apartment building and turn it into transitional housing units for the homeless men and women who come to the Harvard Square Shelter. There is an old adage that the young are "often wrong but never in doubt."[12] Certainly, not all of these changes panned out for the Harvard students running the Harvard Square Shelter, but their fearlessness about making changes gives the shelter a flexibility and nimbleness unlike nearly any other organization serving the homeless.

EVENING, 10 P.M.

Kelly Parker, the supplies director, stops by the shelter with eight gallons of milk and a dozen loaves of bread. Kelly is a Harvard senior, majoring in biochemistry, and probably five feet two inches tall on her tiptoes. Having grown up in a nearby Boston suburb, she borrows her parents' car once or twice a week to make shelter shopping trips to Costco. Nathan and Jasper help her transfer the milk and bread from her car to the shelter kitchen.

Mae is manning the kitchen when Fayad comes to the kitchen window looking for bread. "Do you want bread with sesame seed?" Mae asks him. "I know how much you like sesame seed." She fetches Fayad a piece of homemade bread that Darwin's, a local sandwich shop, donates to the Harvard Square Shelter several nights a week. The potbellied man with the mustache comes up to the serving window to join the conversation.

"You look tired, girl," he tells Mae. "You been running around all day?" The three chat for the next few minutes across the serving counter that divides the kitchen and dining area. At one point, Mae notes that the potholders hanging on the refrigerator are magnetic. She playfully tosses them at the refrigerator. One "sticks," the other doesn't. Both men cheer her on. "One more try!" Fayad calls out, referring to the potholder that failed to adhere to the refrigerator.

The six men and women awarded one-night emergency beds arrive one by one. One of the six, Andre, has never stayed at the Harvard Square Shelter before. He is an African American man in his thirties wearing jeans, a heavy camouflage Army jacket and construction boots. He asks which cot is his and immediately lies down to go to sleep. The cot is only a few feet away from the television area where several men are now watching the news. Andre shuts his eyes and pulls the blanket up over his head.

In the kitchen, the supplies director, Kelly, finishes unpacking the milk and bread. The bread has arrived just in time, as the night's meal — rice, pasta, and tofu — is now completely gone. For the rest of the evening, if anyone inside the shelter is hungry or someone comes to the shelter door looking for a meal, the only option is a grilled cheese sandwich. Although this, too, is a luxury as far as homeless shelters go. As Frank Green, a homeless man, explained, "At other shelters, you can't eat. Down there, you can knock on the kitchen door and ask whoever's in there, 'Can you get me a sandwich or something I can munch on?'

And they'll say, 'Sure, no problem. Give me a few minutes, and we'll get you a grilled cheese sandwich or something.' At other shelters, they feed you between this time and this time and that's it, they're done."

Just as Kelly has finished stocking the refrigerator full of milk, Lance Mitchell, another student-director who is not on duty tonight, suddenly appears in the kitchen. A junior at Harvard, Lance was heading back to his dorm from the library and decided to stop in on Nathan and Mae, with whom he is friends. He, Nathan, Mae, and Kelly loiter in the kitchen chatting and laughing. In his tight polo shirt and skinny jeans, Lance has a European look to him. He teases Mae, saying he's not wearing as tight a shirt as usual for her.

At 11 o'clock, the dinner volunteers — Jasper, Clara, and Brianna — are done for the night.[13] They collect their backpacks and bags out of the overnight volunteer room and bid goodnight to Nathan, Mae, and the few men and women still awake. A few minutes later, one of the overnight volunteers, Steven, arrives. Steven is a Harvard junior with glasses and dark curly hair. He goes out to retrieve dirty plates and utensils from the dining area and immediately becomes engaged in a long conversation with Allen, the crew-cutted homeless man in his mid-twenties who had spent an hour or two on Facebook earlier in the evening. "You weight lift?" Allen asks Steven.

"On and off," Steven answers, but that's all Allen needs to launch into a description of different types of nutritional supplements Steven should consider taking: amino acids, whey protein, etc.

"I had a problem with steroids," Allen admits at one point in the conversation. "Back when I was really into it." He still works out every day at Planet Fitness in Boston, which is cheap at $20 a month. "The only problem," he confides in Steven, "is too many fags are there." Steven flinches at the slur but doesn't object out loud, and the conversation rolls forward. Allen grew up outside Boston and joined the army after high school. He did a tour in Iraq and is still a member of the National Guard. "Just spent a week out in western Mass dealing with that ice storm," he tells Steven. Steven asks a few questions here and there, but Allen is happy to keep the conversation going. He asks Steven what he studies and is impressed that Steven is a biology major. "I'm taking computer classes now at Roxbury Community College," he admits, "but it's hard to juggle work and school." He explains he'd been working as a plumber's assistant up until a few months ago when he asked his boss to cut back on his hours so he could put school first. His boss stopped giving him enough hours, and he got evicted from his apartment.

While Steven and Allen are talking, the other overnight volunteer, Juliet, arrives. Juliet is a Harvard sophomore from France who speaks English with an appealing accent. She has blonde hair and is wearing a stretchy black dress, black tights and black Ugg boots.

Now that the two overnight volunteers have arrived, Mae writes out the on-duty schedule for the night on a dry-erase board in the kitchen.

> 12–2 a.m.:   Steven
> 2–3:30 a.m.:   Juliet
> 3:30–5 a.m.:   Nathan
> 5–7 a.m.:   Mae

One of the student-directors always takes the latest shift, as that is the period of the night where the largest numbers of men and women are awake. Mae also adds a couple of important tasks to the dry-erase board:

> Midnight: Au Bon Pain
> 3:45 a.m.:   Coffee
> 4:00 a.m.:   Wake up Andre (cot 2)
> 4:30 a.m.:   Wake up Lee (Bed H – bottom)

Now that the remainder of the night has been partitioned, Nathan, Mae, and Juliet head out into the darkened dining area to join Steven, Allen, and the handful of other men and women still awake. "This is a good place," Allen — the weightlifter — notes at one point. The conversation jumps around, mostly fed by Allen's chattiness, from Las Vegas to the military to graduate school. "My girlfriend has a master's degree," Allen notes at one point.

Meanwhile, Juliet and Fayad start talking about Turkey. "I went to Istanbul once," Juliet tells him. They begin to talk about whether Turkey should be allowed to join the European Union. "I'm against it," Juliet tells Fayad. Later in the conversation, she notes that the government in France has recently banned smoking in cafés and bars. "I like it because I'm not a smoker," Juliet tells Fayad.

At midnight, the two overnight volunteers — Juliet and Steven — head out to Au Bon Pain, a local bakery, with the pilfered shopping cart. The security guard, Oscar, leaves with them. He has been standing by the entrance for the past five hours, checking in new arrivals and allowing the men and women already inside the shelter to step out for a smoke. Now that Oscar is gone, no one else can be admitted into the shelter, and anyone who leaves for a smoke cannot return. This policy can be a challenge for some of the more nicotine-dependent men and women who stay at the shelter — going seven hours until morning without a cigarette, leading some to sneak cigarettes in the bathroom as if they were back in high school.

Oscar heads off to the subway station while Juliet and Steven wheel noisily towards the Au Bon Pain a few blocks away in the heart of Harvard Square. Every evening, at closing time, Au Bon Pain donates to the shelter its leftover pastries and baked goods, which are then served for breakfast the following morning. Some nights, the shelter's overnight volunteers return from their Au Bon Pain run with literally 20 pounds worth of pastry: croissants, scones, bagels, muffins. Pastries that just minutes before were selling for $2.50 a pop are suddenly free to the homeless men and women staying at the Harvard Square Shelter and the college students volunteering there.

POWERFUL EFFECTS FOR THE HARVARD STUDENTS

The developmental stage of the Harvard students volunteering at the Harvard Square Homeless Shelter also turns their volunteer work into a transformative experience *for them*.[14] Nearly all of these young adults characterized their volunteer work as an opportunity to break out of the "Harvard bubble" — though this phrase turned out to hold different meanings for different students.[15] For some students, breaking out of the Harvard bubble entailed interacting with a more diverse group of people than their classmates and professors. Other students characterized it as doing work that felt more purposeful than problem-sets and lab reports.[16] Still other Harvard students described their volunteer work at the shelter as a means of staying connected to a pre-Harvard conception of themselves — a way of proving that they hadn't turned into the stereotypical Ivy League snob.[17] In all of these different ways, the Harvard students volunteering at the shelter utilize the shelter as a mechanism for identity exploration and as a "shelter" from some of the academic, social, and personal pressures that are a part of the college years and young adulthood.[18]

Volunteering at the shelter also offered valuable *but different* takeaways for this past winter's 75 weekly volunteers and 14 student-leaders.

For the shelter's 75 weekly volunteers, their experiences at the shelter dispelled misconceptions and stereotypes about homelessness by introducing them to a diverse group of men and women contending with homelessness.[19] The Harvard Square Shelter's 14 student-leaders, on the other hand, came away from their volunteer experience with a much deeper understanding of the complex and varied routes by which people *become* homeless.[20] The factor that seemed most responsible for the different takeaways of these two groups was the heavy responsibility that accompanied the shelter's leadership positions.[21] In taking on the responsibility to bar an intoxicated homeless man from entering the shelter; to sit and console a homeless woman ill with HIV/AIDS; and to make difficult policy decisions about who is and is not eligible for the shelter's Work Contract Program, the Harvard Square Shelter's student-leaders developed a deeper understanding of homelessness, of the wider world, and of potential roles they could play within this world.[22]

Volunteering at the shelter also provided Harvard students with tremendous opportunities to develop as leaders.[23] As noted by Harvard alumnus Dr. Aaron Dutka, there is no chief executive among the Harvard Square Shelter's 14 student-directors. As a result, these student-leaders gain valuable experience working in a collaborative team and engaging in vigorous debate at their weekly meetings about the shelter's policies and practices.[24] Hotly debated topics this past winter included the maximum number of homeless men and women the shelter could accommodate each night; whether or not to run criminal background checks on men and women staying in the shelter; and whether or not homeless men and women with poor hygiene should be required to take a shower. Such debates played an important role in the leadership development of these Harvard students by forcing them to articulate — both to themselves and their peers — the beliefs, values, and objectives with which they approach service work and social action.[25] A number of Harvard students who led the Harvard Square Shelter in the 1980s and 90s cited the dilemmas they debated as student-leaders as having deeply influenced their approaches to leadership and social justice as professionals.

OVERNIGHT, 1:30 A.M.

Steven is the only student still awake, along with three homeless men. Mae, Juliet, and Nathan are asleep on the two bunk beds crammed into the tiny volunteer room near the shelter's bathrooms. Now that laundry hours for the shelter's homeless guests are done for the night, Steven begins working on the mountain of shelter laundry, throwing sheets and towels into the washing machine. While the sheets and towels spin, Steven sits down on a couch in the TV area with a textbook for his political theory class. He reads for a few moments until Lee joins him. Lee is a large African American man with dreadlocks held in place by a do-rag, and wearing camouflage army pants. He could be anywhere from his late thirties to his late forties. Lee explains to Steven that he is a musician — a song writer, mostly funk. "Kurt Cobain was a genius," he tells Steven. "He killed himself because he didn't like what was happening with his music." He adds that he hasn't been writing that much music himself recently because he has been playing so much chess. Long, all-day chess matches. "There are a couple of guys who play over at Au Bon Pain," he tells Nathan, referring to the outdoor chess matches that can attract crowds of tourists, "and watching them is like watching art."

A few minutes later, Lee asks out of the blue, "Steven, what do you think happens when we die?"

Steven pauses, surprised. "Well, I'm pretty pessimistic about these things," he says finally, "so I guess I just think when you die, that's it."

And then Lee is off and running. "You know what's so amazing about Jesus, dude? He was saying things that no one else was saying. Ever. Jesus got me off crack-cocaine. I was addicted, and then 13 and a half months ago, I asked Jesus to help me stay away from the crack, and just like that I quit. The addiction was gone. So I know Jesus was helping me." The conversation rolls forward, and Lee expresses delight at the discovery that Steven is Jewish. "The Jews are the chosen people, dawg. Jesus was Jewish, and the Disciples were Jewish. The Jews, they just keep doing their thing. They haven't changed it up at all." Lee contrasts his respect for Jews with his suspicions about Muslims. "I probably sound kind of prejudiced against Muslims, and I guess I am. But Muhammad, he didn't perform one miracle. Not one miracle. I'm always asking the Muslims who hang out at Wendy's, give me one miracle Muhammad performed!"

Juliet, the volunteer from France, relieves Steven at 2 a.m. She turns on the television and stares sleepily at a black-and-white movie starring a young Katharine Hepburn. Only one other person is awake now, a homeless woman in her forties with long brown hair. She sits transfixed at one of the computer terminals. The shelter is nearly still except for an inconsistent cacophony of snoring and coughing from the men's sleeping quarters. At one point, Andre — the first-timer in the camouflage army jacket — sits up from his cot complaining he is cold. Instead of going back to sleep, he heads over to one of the computer terminals and opens up a Yahoo! email account. "Excuse me," the woman a few terminals down asks. "What's your name?" Her voice pierces the quiet of the shelter.

"Andre," Andre answers instinctively. Then he checks himself. "Why? Why do you ask?"

"Why shouldn't I ask?" the woman responds in a shrill voice. "Should I ask you about the weather instead? Your name is the first thing you're given. Is it a secret?" There is something a little crazy-sounding about this woman's response. She sounds angry. Juliet sits up straighter, watching for any trouble. Will she need to go wake up Nathan and Mae?

"What's your name?" Andre asks the woman. She huffs, but doesn't respond. Andre shakes his head and turns back to his computer.

POWERFUL EFFECTS FOR SOCIETY

The National Alliance to End Homelessness estimates that nearly three-quarters of a million people go homeless on any given night in the United States.[26] The replication of the Harvard Square Homeless Shelter's student-run model in major cities across the United States could allow thousands more Americans contending with homelessness and thousands more college students to have a transformative influence upon each other. Equally important would be the effect upon America of these college-aged volunteers ultimately taking their place in communities and professional spheres all across the country. Such educated young adults would be in a position to serve as powerful advocates for a constituency — the homeless — to which the majority of Americans respond with disgust. In fact, Princeton psychologist Susan Fiske has found that showing photographs of the homeless to individuals placed inside an fMRI scanner reveals a sequence of reactions in the brain similar to when people are shown photographs of trash.[27] Moreover, these photographs of homeless people failed to activate areas of the brain that typically activate when people think about other people or themselves. From this research, Fiske concluded that many Americans, when they think about homelessness, do not conceive of homeless men and women as real-life human beings.[28] Imagine a town hall meeting or local ballot initiative, then, where issues affecting the homeless are up for debate. In such settings, educated Americans who can speak to the humanity of the homeless and debunk misconceptions about homelessness are sorely needed.

Moreover, a number of scholars have reported that a dangerously small proportion of young Americans now express interest in pursuing careers in government or public service.[29] Yet, many of the talented young adults involved in leading the Harvard Square Homeless Shelter credited this volunteer work with redirecting their career aspirations towards these very sectors rather than more lucrative careers in finance or banking. This is already the case for dozens of Harvard Square Shelter volunteers from the 1980s and 90s. For these young adults, volunteering at the shelter has highlighted the rewards of doing meaningful work, helped them to identify professional arenas where they can continue to do so, and honed the leadership skills that they will bring with them into these professional arenas. Imagine the impact upon society of dozens more student-led homeless shelters graduating thousands of civic-minded college students each year. The infusion of *empathy* into America's cities and towns and *talent* into America's public sector could be transformative.[30]

BREAKFAST, 4:30 A.M.

People are starting to wake up. With only four showers for the entire shelter, a number of homeless men and women have determined that the only way to ensure a spot in the shower is by waking up ahead of the crowd. Nathan — working the 3:30–5 a.m. shift — has brewed a fresh cup of coffee and put out some pastries, and a number of men sit quietly, sleepily, in the dining area drinking and eating. An elderly African American woman wearing a beret and a large flannel shirt is packing pastries away into a Tupperware container for later.

The first man heads for the exit at ten minutes to six in the morning. He is an older man in his fifties who piles on several layers of clothing and then straps on an overstuffed backpack. "All right guys, if I don't see you before Christmas, have a happy holiday!" he tells Nathan and

Mae who are up to help with breakfast. "Don't eat too much!"

The breakfast shift volunteers arrive a few minutes later. Tye is a young-looking Asian male, a Harvard freshman, who could easily be mistaken for a 14 or 15 year old. Lisa is a Harvard junior with red hair, green eyes, a nose ring and a Gothic aesthetic. "Let's do chocolate chip pancakes," Lisa declares. Tye refills the coffee and starts working on a vat of oatmeal. Their fresh energy stands out in sharp contrast to Mae, Juliet, and Nathan, who are dragging.

At 7 a.m., Mae turns on the overhead lights throughout the shelter's main room, and virtually everyone is up and moving. Piling on clothing, eating breakfast, drinking coffee, watching the TV news, searching through a bin of donated clothing. An older man in his sixties who resembles the farmer in *American Gothic* zips up his coat and walks out without saying a word to anyone. A long-haired man missing several of his front teeth hangs a sign around his neck that's really a spiral notebook with a string tied to it. "Happy holidays to you and yours from me and mine," the sign reads. The student-directors, Nathan and Mae, are busy opening lockers for men and women who are preparing to face the wintry day.

Mae starts taking calls for 14-day beds at precisely 7:30 a.m. Only one man is finishing his stay this morning, so she has only one bed to give away. "I'm sorry, we don't have any more 14-day beds. You can call tonight for an emergency bed at 9 p.m.," she tells nearly a dozen dejected callers.

Nathan asks Tye to start reminding everyone they need to be out of the shelter by 8 a.m. "Fifteen minute warning!" Tye calls out several times, as he walks through various regions of the shelter. "Closing up in fifteen minutes!"

"Tell me when there's 14 minutes left," complains a bald-headed man with tattooed arms. He is sitting at one of the computer terminals showing two other men a YouTube clip of his daughter in a cheerleading competition. She is 12 years old but appears to be a foot shorter than all the other girls on her squad.

The older black woman wearing the beret complains to Mae that one of the male guests made inappropriate sexual comments to her. Mae promises to alert the other directors and listen herself for this type of talk.

By 8 a.m., only the students remain in the shelter. Nathan, Mae, Steven, and Juliet have been here all night, and Tye and Lisa for the morning. Familiar with the shelter's cleaning routines, they spread out across the shelter: mopping the floor, folding laundry, dismantling the cots, and, least popularly, cleaning the two bathrooms. A clock radio from the kitchen blares a Bruce Springsteen rendition of "Santa Claus is Coming to Town" as Juliet mops the dining area in her Uggs and rumpled black dress. Nathan sits on a bottom bunk in the overnight volunteer room, typing up a summary of the night's happenings on the shelter's laptop computer. He will email the summary to the other student-directors for their perusal and comments.

By 8:30 a.m., Nathan has flipped off the lights, locked the shelter's front door, and followed Mae, Steven, Juliet, Tye, and Lisa up the steps that lead out to the snowy Cambridge streets. The day is sunny but very cold, and the five young adults jocularly compare notes on who can go to sleep, who has class, who has time for breakfast, and who has the most work before the Christmas break. Several are heading straight to classes in Harvard Yard while others peel off towards their respective dormitories. Busy days await all of them. For the next ten hours, the Harvard Square Homeless Shelter will sit dark and quiet until tonight's student-directors — Mark and Leo — arrive at 6:30 p.m. to flick on the lights and begin sorting through the most recent donations. They will be joined by fresh teams of dinner, overnight, and breakfast volunteers, but the majority of the homeless faces will be the same. They will begin lining up around quarter to seven, waiting for Oscar, the shelter's security guard, to let them inside.

SYMBIOSIS

Philip Mangano, who served from 2002 to 2009 as director of the federal government's Interagency Council on Homelessness — effectively the 'homeless czar' for the United States — is a long-time supporter of the Harvard Square Homeless Shelter. Mangano has observed that, in the interactions between the homeless men and women and Harvard students at the shelter, "There's a certain beauty to that transaction that exceeds the normal governmental response or even the usual non-profit response."[31] The beauty that Mangano refers to lies in the *symbiosis* of the Harvard Square Homeless Shelter.[32]

The homeless men and women staying at the Harvard Square Shelter benefit from the passion and idealism, desire to connect and outside-the-box thinking of the Harvard students volunteering there. These struggling Americans can work with educated young adults to connect to resources to which they are entitled and also describe recent challenges and happier times to engaged and empathetic listeners. Harvard Professor Julie Wilson has noted that "One of the worst parts about homelessness is being invisible, and you are not invisible at the Harvard Square Shelter."[33] Simultaneously, the Harvard students volunteering at the shelter are engaged in processes of growth and development that are enriched and deepened by the opportunity to listen, converse, and learn from the homeless men and women staying at the shelter.

There are few other places in America like the Harvard Square Homeless Shelter where night after night America's most privileged and most marginalized citizens break bread together. As demonstrated in the chapters that follow, however, this juxtaposition of privilege and poverty offers powerful effects for the homeless men and women who stay at the shelter, the Harvard students who volunteer there, and the wider society into which both groups will emerge. In chronicling these powerful effects, I also seek to paint an intimate portrait of privilege and poverty in America through two intriguing groups, Harvard students and the homeless, and the basement shelter in which these groups come together each winter night.

Chapter 2

The Cadillac of
Homeless Shelters

Ｔhe first seeds of the Harvard Square Homeless Shelter were
sown on a wintry night in 1982 when leaders of nearly a dozen
different churches in Cambridge, Massachusetts met to discuss
the surge in homelessness occurring right before their eyes in Harvard
Square.[1] Since taking office in 1980, the Reagan administration had
dramatically reduced the production and maintenance of public housing while simultaneously removing incentives for private developers to
build low-cost housing.[2] As a result, tens of thousands of Americans
who had been living in public housing, low-cost housing and single
room occupancy (SRO) hotels now found themselves out on the
streets.[3] Like many urban centers, Cambridge's Harvard Square began
filling with scores of newly homeless men, women, and children.

After much discussion, Cambridge's faith leaders decided to establish a weekly dinner for anyone in need of a free meal. Concerned with
further dehumanizing an already demoralized population, the pastors
agreed there would be no intake procedure, referral system or eligibility
requirements for this free meal. Anyone who wanted to could come
in off the streets for a hot dinner. Each congregation would take turns
preparing the meal itself, but the site of this weekly dinner would be
the Christ Church, founded in 1759 and sandwiched in between the
Harvard and Radcliffe campuses. There seemed something fitting about
opening up to struggling Americans a church that had played host to
George and Martha Washington during the Revolutionary War, and

where President Theodore Roosevelt had once taught Sunday School.[4]

Today, churches and community centers across Boston have teamed up to offer a hot meal for the homeless most nights of the week throughout the year. In the early 1980s, however, the Thursday night meal at Christ Church was one of the few resources available to an exploding homeless population. Almost immediately, the pastors found themselves serving dinner to nearly 150 people a week in search of a hot meal. It was like catering a moderate-sized wedding every Thursday.

What bothered University Lutheran Church Pastor Fred Reisz was that, when the Thursday night meal ended, virtually all of the men, women, and children who had filled up Christ Church went right back out to the streets. A few stayed at Cambridge's lone homeless shelter and a few more at Boston's Pine Street Inn, but most had no better option than an alleyway or heating vent. Pastor Reisz realized these men, women, and children needed more than a hot meal; they needed shelter — particularly during the harsh Boston winters when temperatures routinely dropped down into the teens and single digits. On those freezing cold nights, spending the night outside could be deadly. And, in Puritan Boston, even the subway system closed at midnight. The rapidly expanding population of homeless men and women truly had nowhere to go.

Stewart Guernsey was equally troubled by the lack of options for the homeless men and women he encountered at the Thursday night meals program. In 1982, Guernsey was a first-year graduate student at the Harvard Divinity School. He had been born and raised in rural Mississippi where he began practicing civil rights and poverty law after college and law school.

In the early 1980s, Guernsey grew dissatisfied with his work as an attorney and began to consider the possibility of entering the ministry. After being accepted to the Harvard Divinity School, he arrived in Cambridge in the fall of 1982 to begin training for a career in ministry. Coming from rural Mississippi, Cambridge was a shock to Guernsey's system. As he explained, "In the first few weeks of Divinity School, I encountered homelessness for the first time. I had never been in a city where there were homeless people."

Guernsey learned about the Thursday night meals program at Christ Church and began volunteering for the program. Taken aback by the growing number of homeless men and women in Harvard Square, he wanted to talk to these men and women in order to find out more about them. The meals program, for its part, was happy to take on a volunteer with five years of experience in poverty law. The church leaders running the meals program put Guernsey to work connecting the homeless men and women coming to the meals program with the few resources available to them. As Guernsey recalled, while the meals were being served, "I was on the phone trying to find shelters for people." However, there were so few shelter beds available in Boston and Cambridge that Guernsey's efforts were often futile. A number of times he invited homeless men and women he met at Christ Church to sleep on the floor of his room in a Harvard Divinity School dormitory.

For Guernsey, his difficulty finding shelter for homeless men and women turned from frustration to outrage one night in late October of 1982. A homeless man named Bobby had asked Guernsey for help finding a shelter bed. Over the course of multiple conversations, it had become clear to Guernsey that Bobby was suffering from schizophrenia as well as physiological brain damage from having been beaten a number of times out on the streets of Boston. As Guernsey explained:

> "On this cold, rainy October night, I simply could not find a shelter for this guy. And it broke my heart. I mean, there was no excusing that. And the wealth, the incredible wealth, that surrounded me. And I strongly considered taking him to stay in my room, but the fact that he was incontinent and really did not like to shower or bathe, I thought I probably would have raised all kinds of hackles, so I didn't take him. And I had to say, 'I'm sorry. I just can't.' And that was a turning point for me."

Later that week, Guernsey approached the ministers running the Thursday night meals program and expressed his desire to start up a homeless shelter in Harvard Square. He found a willing partner in Pastor Fred Reisz.

The two men began to discuss the possibility of setting up an emergency homeless shelter in the basement of Reisz's church, the University Lutheran Church, for the coldest months of the year, approximately, November through April. As they discussed this possibility in greater detail, Pastor Reisz and Guernsey grew more and more convinced of its feasibility. Pastor Reisz would provide the space for the shelter in his church's basement; Guernsey would solicit volunteers to staff the shelter from Harvard's undergraduate and graduate communities; and Harvard Square restaurants and businesses could donate food and supplies. Of course, before any of these plans could be put into effect, there were two important bodies that needed convincing: the University Lutheran congregation and the city officials running Cambridge.

The University Lutheran congregation came around first. Julie Wilson, a Harvard professor and long-time University Lutheran congregant, recalled that many congregants initially expressed reservations about the plan because the church basement — where the shelter would be located — currently housed the church's Sunday school classes. How would a religious-school-by-day and shelter-by-night work out? Would that be safe? University Lutheran Deacon Selma Brooks remembered others' reservations as well. Setting up a homeless shelter that ran seven nights a week all winter long would curtail a number of church events held in the basement space. Was such a disruption worthwhile?

Stewart Guernsey recalled one of the early meetings about the proposed shelter in which a number of University Lutheran congregants raised legitimate and sensible concerns about the plan. But then an older man stood up to speak. According to Guernsey:

> "I'll never forget an old guy standing up and saying, 'Isn't this what we're supposed to do? Isn't this what Jesus taught?' And that was the turning point. I mean, there were six huge reasons that we shouldn't do it that had been put before the congregation, and this one old fella standing up and saying, 'Yes, all of that's true, but isn't that who we are? Isn't that what we are called to do?' It was a Eureka moment. I'm sure there were still huge reservations, but essentially everybody said, 'Yes, you're right. How can we do anything else?'"

Long-time University Lutheran congregant Terry Tebow was also present at those early meetings of the University Lutheran congregation regarding the proposed shelter. In Tebow's words, the congregation decided the obstacles that accompanied giving up their basement space were "a relatively small price to pay for something that needed to happen." Of course, Tebow also acknowledged that "We all truly believed that this was a temporary condition [and] that if we could put up with it for a winter or two, the government would get this turned around and would do something intelligent to solve the homelessness." Few congregants in 1982 would have guessed that, nearly 30 years later, the emergency homeless shelter in their basement would still be there.

The city of Cambridge — or, more specifically, Cambridge's city manager — found Pastor Reisz and Stewart Guernsey's arguments less persuasive. To be fair, the shelter's basement was in no way equipped for habitation. There was a large central room, but sleeping areas for men and women would have to be cordoned off using dividers. There were already men's and women's restrooms in the basement, but neither came equipped with a shower. Pastor Reisz figured they could turn four of the urinals in the men's bathroom into shower stalls using garden hoses, and that he or one of the volunteers could "sort of stand guard" outside the bathroom door while women staying in the shelter took turns showering.

Cambridge's city manager listened to Pastor Reisz and Guernsey's shower plans, along with their larger goal of taking 30 people off the streets each night, feeding them dinner and breakfast, and then closing the space down during the day. Reisz and Guernsey explained they would like to offer dinner to more than 30 people, but figured they could only squeeze about 30 mattresses into the designated sleeping areas. Cambridge's city manager listened carefully to all of these plans and then noted, "You don't have enough parking spaces for housing that number of people." Pastor Reisz's jaw dropped.

"I'm not sure you understand," he recalls himself exclaiming, "We're dealing with homeless people, most of whom do not have cars. They're right off the street."

"I'm sorry," the city manager told them. "Our regulations say that if you're going to house this number of people, you have to have this number of parking spaces. That's what the regulations say."

Shot down by the Cambridge bureaucracy, Pastor Reisz and Guernsey reconvened with the University Lutheran leadership, then with the larger congregation, and came to a decision. They felt a moral imperative to open this homeless shelter, and so they were going to open up as planned. If the city felt compelled to shut them down, so be it. "I mean, we won't resist," Pastor Reisz said of this plan-of-action. "We will put stuff in the newspapers and stuff, but we will close if they close us."

Looking back on the chain of events, Stewart Guernsey expressed gratitude that the city of Cambridge had chosen to focus its objections to the Harvard Square Shelter on such a trivial regulation:

> "If it had been one of the more sensible ordinances, the congregation probably would have bought in and said, 'You know, we can't be illegal because it's not safe.' But happily, since it

was such a ludicrous reason, the congregation could get past that and say, look, yeah, we'll commit civil disobedience in this fashion."

Reisz and Guernsey invited Cambridge's fire and police departments to come tour the basement of the University Lutheran Church in case they ever had to come in for a fire or to break up a fight, and opened the shelter in February of 1983 without any sort of permit or permission. Then they held their breath and waited. But Cambridge didn't close the shelter down. None of the city's officials or administrators said a word. Homeless men and women were starting to overwhelm Harvard Square, and the politicians running Cambridge had decided not to get in the way of a church trying to do something about it.

HAPPY CHAOS

The Harvard Square Homeless Shelter opened on the evening of 17 February, 1983, and Stewart Guernsey described that very first night of operation as a "nightmare." In his words:

> "We had half a dozen drunks. Everybody wanted to get in a fight. We had far more people than we could possibly accommodate. And of the people we let in, two or three of them were intensely mentally ill and kept ruminating around the room all night talking and keeping everybody else up. And so I threw my arms up and said, 'What have I gotten myself into?' But I did come back the next night, and we opened again."

Fortunately, Guernsey and Reisz learned quickly from their mistakes and began to establish routines that smoothed out those initial challenges.

The Harvard Square Homeless Shelter circa 1983 opened for dinner seven nights a week, and anyone who wanted to could come inside to eat the meals donated by restaurants all over Cambridge. Sometimes 60 or 70 people would pass through the shelter for a meal. Guernsey recalled:

> "We had some very odd dinners. We started shopping at the Boston Food Bank, which got odds and ends at different

times, so I remember we ran through a string one January of frozen pheasant. And we got to the point where the homeless people would come in and say, 'Oh, not pheasant!'"

Getting a bed at the Harvard Square Shelter was strictly first come, first served. Homeless men and women lined up single file outside the steps leading into the shelter, and the first 30 in line received beds for the night. The only criteria for coming inside was that you had to be sober, though Stewart Guernsey admitted that "We were not very good on that point, really. We didn't allow a couple people in, but then there were other folks who got past us." Neither Guernsey nor Reisz were particularly skilled at identifying insobriety. They stood at the entrance of the shelter and asked men and women coming inside to breathe on them. If they smelled alcohol, that individual was turned away. It was not a perfect system.

That first winter, Guernsey and another divinity student stayed at the shelter virtually every night of the week. Pastor Reisz stayed on hand from dinner until midnight four or five nights a week. They also enlisted seven volunteers — mostly graduate students from Harvard Divinity School — to commit to one overnight a week as overnight supervisors. The thinking was that, between Guernsey, Reisz and these seven overnight supervisors, there would always be two volunteers in the shelter to keep things running smoothly. Shortly thereafter, Harvard's undergraduate community service organization started sending over volunteers, and the adult members of the University Lutheran congregation pitched in as well. As congregant Julie Wilson explained, "It was very much a family-centered affair, so families volunteered with their kids. . . . Certainly for my kids and the children they grew up with, the shelter was a huge part of their lives."

Lucy Draper, who ate dinner at the Harvard Square Shelter several times in the late 1980s during her two years of homelessness, described the happy chaos she encountered there: "People were wandering in and out. Students were hanging out with us on the stairs. People were going downstairs. They were letting people take showers. It was very casual. People that didn't use shelters used the Harvard Square Shelter because it was a place everyone was treated with respect."

Ward Welburn, who volunteered at the shelter as an undergraduate in the late 1980s, described the shelter in nearly identical language. Similar to Draper, Welburn commented that the first image that comes to mind when he thinks back on his volunteer work at the Harvard Square Shelter is that staircase leading down into the shelter:

"It was always filled with a million people, and they would be sitting on every step all the way up and down. And everything would be wet and smelly, and it was a funny combination of very direct, clear parameters, and yet this incredible freedom for people to be their own individual, funky selves in that environment. . . . It was charcoal drawings in the corner; it was having a debate about Wittgenstein with a graduate student. These people were talking about films and so forth. And there were so many people, that I would climb the stairs vertically, so I'd climb through the railings, with my feet slipping, and I'd think 'God, I can't believe we're doing this,' and be juggling plates of food to feed people who couldn't stay but had to move on."

Looking back on those opening days of the Harvard Square Shelter, Pastor Reisz acknowledged that "We really were lucky as hell, or God was looking over us or something." With a shudder, he recalled student-volunteers washing the bloody feet of homeless men in basins of water, ignorant at that point about HIV or AIDS. Congregant Julie Wilson noted that they learned the hard way that letting 80 people inside the shelter for dinner, but then only allowing 30 to spend the night, led to conflict. When they changed the rules so that people coming for dinner could sit and eat in the stairwell but not come down into the shelter, another student-volunteer from the mid-1980s, Dennis McGonagle, remembered that "Keeping people crammed in a small space created more conflict than the other [system], so there were ways in which it was a tough, somewhat dangerous space, but really no more so than high school."

FILLING THE VOID

Divinity student Stewart Guernsey had played a leading role in getting the Harvard Square Shelter up and running, and then seeing the shelter through its first year of operation. By 1984, however, Guernsey was ready to move on. In his words, "My whole approach to sheltering and working with homeless people was changing and evolving into an intentional community-based approach." Guernsey had come to believe that people became homeless because they lacked a community or network to fall back on and, thus, the most effective way to combat homelessness was to "supply the networks that people had fallen out of." He envisioned building communities which could offer to homeless men and women "the same benefits extended families have: somebody to talk to when you need it, resources that you may not have, different strengths and weaknesses, division of roles, all of that." A makeshift winter shelter in a church basement wasn't designed to be the type of community Guernsey envisioned. As a result, he shifted his attention away from the Harvard Square Homeless Shelter and began petitioning Boston and Cambridge to provide property for the establishment of these intentional communities for homeless men and women. Guernsey formed three such communities over the next eight years; however, his involvement with the Harvard Square Homeless Shelter dropped dramatically.

As for Pastor Fred Reisz, he remained intimately involved with the Harvard Square Shelter, but he was also a married man with young daughters. Even spending three or four evenings a week at the shelter became infeasible, much less whole nights. Likewise, the majority of the University Lutheran congregation had always conceived of itself as playing a supportive role, rather than a primary one, in the shelter's operation. Yet the homeless population in Boston and Cambridge had only increased, and the federal government showed no signs of solving the problem anytime soon.[5]

Harvard College students stepped forward to fill the void. As Stewart Guernsey said, "After the first year, the undergrads more or less took over." He recalled that "I wasn't needed that much by the second year. Certainly, I was there if they had questions or if they needed money I could usually find somebody to throw a few bucks their way. But by the second year, it was their ballgame, and they took it and ran." This transition inadvertently turned the Harvard Square Homeless Shelter into the first and seemingly *only* student-run homeless shelter in the country.

An exceedingly simple management structure evolved to keep the shelter operating seven nights a week from November through April. Two undergraduates served as the shelter's "directors." One or both worked the shelter's dinner shift, 7 p.m.–midnight, seven nights a week. Lana Zielinski, who graduated from Harvard in 1989, served as one of the Harvard Square Shelter's first directors. She described her nightly director's shifts as exhausting but also energizing. "You had to go in and get everything done and get everyone fed and get everyone in a bed, get the lights out, so it was a high energy environment, and you felt as if you were immediately getting something done for a community." "High energy" may have been an understatement. In her five-hour shelter shifts, Zielinski would let in the homeless men and women one by one, ask if they were sober or high, and then request that they hand over any medication or weapons (to be returned to them the next morning).

While Zielinski worked the front door like a bouncer, the undergraduate volunteers working the shift with her would cobble together dinner from the contributions of local restaurants and businesses and the leftovers donated each night by Harvard Dining Services. They aimed to serve dinner each night by 9 p.m.

Outside of the nightly dinner shifts, Zielinski and her co-director divided up the shelter's administrative responsibilities. She managed the volunteer schedule and coordinated the food donations. Her co-director communicated with the church leadership, the city of Cambridge, and Massachusetts' department of social services. Both co-directors met with Pastor Reisz every few weeks to smooth out the wrinkles that came from two profoundly different organizations sharing the same space. This was especially the case in those early years when the University Lutheran basement still housed the church's Sunday school. Congregant Julie Wilson recalled that "The kids were really tolerant unless the homeless people moved their pictures on the wall or moved their crayons."

At midnight, Zielinski and her volunteers would turn over the shelter to the overnight supervisor. There were seven undergraduates who served as supervisors — one for each night of the week — and, sometimes, a volunteer to divide up the night with them. These students communicated with each other via a spiral-bound logbook kept in the shelter's kitchen. Recall that cell phones didn't start showing up on college campuses until the early 2000s and that Harvard did not provide students with email accounts until 1995. All the way through the 1980s and 90s, the most efficient way to keep everyone running the shelter on the same page was with pencil and paper. As co-director Lana Zielinski explained:

> "It was just sort of a wonderful thing because there were both stories about what had happened during the night, just little anecdotes, and also some people would be very brief and just sort of write this is what happened, 'easy night, no issues.' Other people would sort of go on, but really describe anecdotes in a wonderful way, and some people were very

funny in fact. Other people would just talk a little bit more about either things we should think about doing, not doing, how we could improve things."

Nearly 30 years later, the Harvard Square Shelter's directors still utilize a modernized version of the logbook. At the end of each shift, the director on duty sends out an email to the Supervisor/Director Listserv detailing the main events of the shift. Other supervisors and directors can respond to comments or questions raised by the email, and sometimes a single email will trigger numerous responses (and responses to those responses). All of those emails are archived and stored electronically just as many of the shelter's spiral-bound logbooks from over 20 years ago can still be found at Harvard's community service center.

ADAPTATIONS

The Harvard Square Shelter's logbook isn't the only facet of the shelter to have adapted to changing times. Fast forward to 2009 when the Harvard Square Homeless Shelter now engages 14 Harvard College students as directors. Stewart Guernsey left Boston in 1991 to do anti-poverty work in his native Mississippi. Likewise, Pastor Fred Reisz left his position as leader of the University Lutheran Church in 1992 to assume the presidency of the Lutheran Theological Southern Seminary in South Carolina. Their departures cemented the shift towards giving Harvard undergraduates full responsibility for the day-to-day operations of the shelter. As congregant Julie Wilson remarked:

"It feels like it's not our shelter any more in some ways. Obviously, if they needed people, we would be right there, but my sense is that it's their shelter, and they want to be running their shelter, and our role [now] is to create the scaffolding around that so that they can do it."

Though certainly the church and its congregants have remained involved. Congregant Selma Brooks runs a program in which church members prepare and serve dinner at the shelter one evening a month. One of Pastor Reisz's successors, Pastor Donald Larsen, sponsors a similar program involving monthly breakfasts, and each year the children in the University Lutheran Sunday school bake a cake for the men and women staying at the shelter. Dozens of University Lutheran congregants pitch in to keep the shelter running through Christmas vacation and spring break when large numbers of students leave Cambridge. Particularly around the Christmas holiday, congregant Selma Brooks explained, "The outpouring of the congregation for gifts is unbelievable, and so a lot of things that people give are the practical things like gloves, socks, razors, toothpaste, playing cards."

Perhaps most importantly, in 1997, the University Lutheran congregation embarked upon a capital campaign to raise the $800,000 necessary to transform a makeshift basement into a safe, functioning homeless shelter.[6] The garden hose showers that Pastor Reisz had jury-rigged in 1983 had been upgraded, but not by much. Certainly, the shelter could never have passed any sort of fire-code or health inspection. If the city of Cambridge had decided at any point in the 1980s or 90s to stop averting its eyes to the wildcat shelter in the University Lutheran basement, that would have been that. Congregant Terry Tebow recalled that "The situation was pretty primitive, literally."

In embarking upon this capital campaign, the University Lutheran leadership and congregants were acknowledging that, despite their expectations in 1983, homelessness was not proving to be such a temporary or short-term problem.[7] And in going ahead with the renovation, the church membership renewed its commitment to playing a role in addressing this social ill. Rusty Sadow, a community organizer in Washington DC, was a student-director at the Harvard Square Shelter in the late 1990s during the renovation. Sadow, a Jewish American, expressed deep admiration for the University Lutheran Church's commitment to social justice:

> "The University Lutheran Church sets the bar high for the type of synagogue that I would join. I mean, here is a church that has a limited congregation, not a huge budget. And they had a million dollar capital campaign to renovate the basement so it would be a better facility for the shelter. And when they failed to raise the full amount of money, they took out a second mortgage on the building so they could do it right. And at the end of the day, they left their worship space untouched. And when you think of most religious congregations — synagogues, churches, whatever — when they raise a million dollars, they spend that money renovating their sanctuary."

The renovations took place after the shelter had closed for the season in April of 1999. Modern bathrooms, showers and laundry facilities were installed as well as a handicapped-accessible entrance and café-style dining area. A separate sleeping area was created for women staying at the shelter, and new furniture was purchased for the shelter's sitting and eating areas that brightened the space considerably. As congregant Selma Brooks observed, "I think that it helps the guests feel privileged that they are there. Would I rather have them in a house or a room? Yeah, sure, but at least it is welcoming." You might say the University Lutheran congregation put its money where its mouth was in renewing the commitment to combating homelessness that their old pastor, Fred Reisz, had made nearly 20 years earlier.

AMENITIES

The Harvard Square Shelter's new amenities are not lost on the homeless men and women who stay there. As Frank Green, who stayed at the shelter this past year, explained, "When I got in there, I said, 'Wow, it is really comfortable, and a nice little seating area for TV, nice dining area. It's a pretty comfortable place.'" The bulk of the shelter's food now comes from un-served leftovers collected each night from Harvard's undergraduate dining halls. Whatever Harvard students think of their meal options, the men and women at the Harvard Square Homeless Shelter are highly appreciative. Green, for example, noted, "The food is excellent. Mostly from Harvard, so you eat pretty good. I gained thirty pounds there this winter." Joe Presley, who stayed at the shelter in the early 1990s, remembered that the students would even make you a lunch to take with you during the day, which he described as "unheard of." As Presley remarked, "It was like, wow. They really cared."

Also highly appreciated by the men and women staying at the Harvard Square Shelter is the opportunity to do laundry. "What's nice down there, too," Green said, "is that they have laundry which none of the other ones have. They have a washer and dryer, and some people stay up half the night doing that because they're hard to get." Ralph McGann, who stayed at the shelter in the early 1990s and then again in 2002, added that "It was great. You could do your laundry, get a nice clean shower, because sometimes the biggest shelters, [in] the shower they get razor blades from other people using them." McGann also claimed that, at a lot of Boston's bigger homeless shelters, "You take a shower, your underwear would be gone."

Lucy Draper praised the Harvard Square Shelter's fleet of five networked computers: "There is no other shelter where someone can just get up in the middle of the night and go up and use a computer." Nineteen-year-old Mike Andretti, who stayed at the shelter this past winter, expressed his appreciation that "they actually take the time to clean the place." Ralph McGann said: "It's human, it's civilized, you know. . . . That's why people like the Harvard Square Shelter." And Kaye Wild, the Vice-President of the Massachusetts Housing & Shelter Alliance, described a recent trip to the Harvard Square Homeless Shelter in which one of the men staying there described the shelter to her as the "Cadillac of homeless shelters." Clearly, a homeless shelter in a church basement is never going to be mistaken for Club Med, but the majority of the men and women staying at the Harvard Square Homeless Shelter are thankful for the opportunity to eat, shower, do laundry, and send an email.

SAFETY

Far more important than these "amenities" to the men and women staying at the Harvard Square Shelter is their sense of safety inside the shelter. At the beginning of her two years of homelessness in the late 1980s, Lucy Draper spent five nights in one of Boston's largest homeless shelters. On her very first night there, she got held up at knifepoint in the shelter's bathroom for her driver's license and shoes. This experience left her so emotionally scarred that she refused to step foot inside another shelter until another homeless friend literally dragged her into the Harvard Square Shelter to be fed. Other men and women described similar feelings of danger in Boston's larger homeless shelters. Ralph McGann, speaking of another one of Boston's larger homeless shelters, explained that "There are people shooting up in the bathroom and drinking outside by the gas station. I mean they have prostitution over there. It's ridiculous." Likewise, Frank Green remarked of the Harvard Square Shelter: "You're very safe in there. There were a few theft problems this year, but you go into some of the other shelters, you'll be sleeping, and someone will smack you in the head and make sure you're sleeping and take your sneakers right off your feet."

To be fair, the Harvard Square Shelter, as a dry homeless shelter, has some advantages over Boston's larger ("wet") homeless shelters. While a wet homeless shelter will offer a bed to any homeless individual in any condition, the Harvard Square Shelter now enlists a security guard to screen out men and women who are intoxicated or high. The student-directors even reserve the right to breathalyze or drug test anyone staying with them whom they suspect to be under the influence of alcohol or drugs.

But men and women who have stayed at the Harvard Square Shelter also described additional factors that contribute to their sense of safety. Frank Green referenced the two directors and three or four volunteers working every shift: "It's the kids. There's so many of them. Other shelters, at night, they're down to a skeleton crew. And down there, they've got eight, ten people floating around all night. I think people can't get away with as much." Rather than an organizational structure where a lone employee leafs through a magazine at the front desk, the Harvard students volunteering to work the overnight shift are constantly moving about the shelter, talking to the night owls, doing laundry and keeping an eye on things. Having chosen to spend their night at the shelter, the last thing these young adults want is to be left alone.

Moreover, Ralph McGann talked about being able to trust the students who volunteer at the Harvard Square Shelter. In his words, "The students, you can trust them emphatically. They're not going to touch any of your stuff. They'd give you a locker, [and] only they knew the combination." Another formerly homeless man, 19-year-old Lex Obain, offered a similar perspective. An immigrant from the Ivory Coast, Obain alternated between the Salvation Army Shelter and Harvard Square Shelter during his year on the streets. At the Salvation Army, Obain explained that "I was sleeping with my wallet, my bag with me. I didn't want anyone to take my stuff because I know how it is." Especially as an immigrant to the United States, Obain lived in fear of losing the documents that proved his status as a legal immigrant. At the Harvard Square Shelter, in contrast, Obain appreciated the personal locker assigned to him and trusted the Harvard students that his belongings would be safe there.

A number of Harvard students described the homeless men and women themselves as contributing to a sense of safety within the Harvard Square Shelter. Amelia Ginsberg, who worked as a shelter director in the late 1990s, noted: "I don't really remember ever not feeling safe there. I felt like the security guard was there, and I also felt there were enough male guests who would protect me if something had gone down." Anusha Ghosh, the shelter's volunteer director in the early 2000s, echoed this sentiment in explaining that "A lot of the men in particular would be protective of some of the women volunteers. I never felt unsafe in the shelter." Dr. Kristin Sommers, who worked as a shelter director in the mid-1990s, said:

> "I felt that the guests protected all of the volunteers because they knew we were there because we wanted to help. Before we had security, if there was a commotion at the door, guests would come up and make sure everything was okay and make sure no one was getting into a fight or being harmed, so they would be there just to watch. They would also check in and make sure everything was okay if an argument or disagreement happened. Certain guests always had their eyes open all the time to make sure everything was safe inside because they also felt safe in there and didn't want to lose that either."

Here, Sommers' description mirrors almost word for word the explanation by Helen Van Anglen, who served as a Harvard Square Shelter director nearly a decade earlier. According to Van Anglen:

> "Someone would ring the bell, and we would have to say, 'You can't come in, you've been drinking.' Or whatever. And often at night the guys would follow me upstairs and see who was at the door. Sort of keep an eye out and make sure I was safe and okay and nobody took advantage of me. And I think that says a lot."

One of the current student-directors, Amanda Mooney, offered a recent example of what both Sommers and Van Anglen describe. According to Mooney, "There was this one night where I was supervising and these two guests, it was like two in the morning, got into this very scary verbal argument, and I just didn't know how to handle it, and basically Lex diffused it and saved my skin. And that's something I'm really grateful for." The "Lex" that Mooney is referring to is Lex Obain, the 19-year-old immigrant from the Ivory Coast referred to earlier. When asked for his take on this incident, Obain recalled:

> "I just kind of calmed the situation down, and then they put the guys out for a couple days or something like that. You

know, I didn't want anything to happen in that place because I didn't want them to close that place because that would be bad for me, and I didn't want anyone to be hurt."

In these words, Obain suggests that former shelter directors Kristin Sommers and Helen Van Anglen were right to believe that the homeless men and women staying at the Harvard Square Shelter had their backs if ever trouble arose.

RESPECT

Safety may be the paramount concern for any homeless person contemplating a night in a homeless shelter versus an alleyway, but preservation of dignity isn't far behind. Meghan Goughan, the Assistant Director of Cambridge's CASPAR Homeless Shelter, characterized the shelter system as often "demoralizing" for the men and women it serves. A 2007 study of homeless people's experiences in homeless shelters found that *all* of the homeless men and women in the study felt like they were "being ignored, rushed, brushed aside, or treated rudely."[8] Fred Slomiak, who spent three years on the streets in the mid-1990s, explained further:

> "There is one basic fact [about homeless shelters] that bothered the hell out of me, more than anything else, why I just couldn't deal with it. I am not a child, and I don't like being treated like a child. And to elaborate on that a little bit more, here I was in my forties being told when to go to bed like a command, and what I could and couldn't do . . . Yes, some [people] need that kind of structure, but I think you should be able to earn more personal responsibilities, especially if you're in recovery."

Slomiak's perspective on the infantilizing nature of homeless shelters might lead one to expect the venture set in motion by Pastor Fred Reisz and Stewart Guernsey in 1983 to have failed spectacularly. After all, what could be more frustrating for homeless men and women than to step into a shelter run by teenagers? Perhaps the only thing worse than being treated like a child is being treated like a child *by a child*. As former volunteer Helen Van Anglen remarked, "If I were a homeless person under stress, and there was some 18 or 19 year old who had say over whether or not I could stay inside on a really cold night, my God I might be kind of pissed." Fred Slomiak admitted that when a counselor at another Boston homeless shelter told him about the Harvard Square Shelter and suggested he try to get a bed there, "I thought they were going to be a bunch of nerdy, nitwit Harvard students." Leo LaSala, one of the Harvard Square Shelter's current student-directors, acknowledged that "I wouldn't want to be on the other end of a situation where a 19 year old was telling me when I had to wake up."

Perhaps former homeless czar Philip Mangano described the concerns about the Harvard Square Shelter most eloquently. Mangano was working a breadline for the homeless in downtown Boston in the early 1980s when he first heard about the shelter:

> "I think a lot of the homeless folk that I met were just put off by the whole idea that they would be going to a student-run program. . . . Maybe not so much spoken was the idea that 'Wait a minute, I'm an adult, I want to be treated like an adult. How can students treat me like an adult?'"

Looking back, Mangano characterized such a response as a legitimate concern:

> "One of the things that we've done over the years is dumb down homeless people. 'Oh they don't know what they need, they don't know their social security number, they couldn't maintain housing, they can't maintain a job.' So that dumbing down, which of course affects the morale of the homeless person him or herself, that in some ways was supported in the notion that just students in a church basement would be good enough for our homeless neighbors. So I think that was a legitimate concern on the part of homeless people."

Here, Mangano described what would seem to be the Achilles' heel of a student-run homeless shelter: that homeless men and women don't want to be directed by a small army of young adults. What makes the Harvard Square Homeless Shelter the "Cadillac" of homeless shelters, however, are all of the reasons why this assumption about what homeless men and women do and do not want turned out to be wrong.

Former shelter guest Joe Presley characterized the Harvard students running the shelter as "friendlier" and "more engaging" than the staff at a typical homeless shelter. He thought that the Harvard students "didn't seem to look down on you. At most homeless shelters, people see it as just a job. These kids, it seemed like more than a job, more like this was a concentrated concern, that they really wanted to help." Presley described the Harvard students as taking the time to really talk to people, "you know, asking them how their day is. Sitting down and talking to people and watching TV. Engaging people. I thought that was really different. . . . I think a lot of homeless people are genuinely shocked that students would take that much interest. That they genuinely care." Another former guest, Ralph McGann, rejected the idea that the unprofessionalism of the Harvard students is problematic. According to McGann, "They don't have to be. They're just human. They're young, and they're actually a lot more ingratiating because they're not looking to get over on anyone or anything like that."

The CASPAR Shelter's Meghan Goughan offers an important perspective on what the Harvard students running the Harvard Square Shelter have to offer the homeless. Goughan believes that, because they are new to working with homeless people, the Harvard Square Shelter volunteers are less likely to come across to their homeless clients as jaded or judgmental:

> "I think just the nature of who staffs many homeless shelters, you have a lot of folks who are in recovery who have been homeless before. And I think sometimes that's a barrier. Because sometimes I think some of our clients think, whether real or not, the people are thinking, 'I did this, this way, and you can get out of it.' And they feel like they're being judged. . . . My sense of the Harvard Square Shelter kids is that they don't try to pretend to be things they're not or understand things they don't."

Goughan describes here the possibility that the youth and inexperience of the Harvard students actually facilitates their ability to connect with the homeless men and women staying at the Harvard Square Shelter. In this possibility, Goughan unintentionally repeated the observation of nineteenth-century composer, Hector Berlioz, who famously said of a rival, "He knows everything but lacks inexperience." In both Berlioz and Goughan's estimation, there is value in a fresh set of eyes and ears.

Goughan's point about the Harvard Square Shelter volunteers not pretending to know more than they do is evident in the words of volunteers such as Harvard freshman Nancy Mellor and junior Nathan Small. Mellor thought that she feels "sympathy" for the men and women she meets at the Harvard Square Shelter, but, "I'll never say I can empathize with them because that would be kind of disrespectful to them." Likewise, Nathan Small said, "You know, we're young kids, and these are people who've been through a lot. And there are so many levels at which we can't connect. We can't say we understand, and so I think I try to listen. I try to be that source of someone you can talk to." Mellor and Small's acknowledgment of what they *do not* know is integral to their respectful interactions with the homeless men and women staying at the Harvard Shelter.

Perhaps the people who can speak most eloquently about the students' ability to treat the homeless with dignity are Lucy Draper and Fred Slomiak. Lucy Draper was a suburban wife and mother working in a biology lab at Harvard when the combination of divorce and mental illness catapulted her into two years of homelessness from 1989 to 1991. One of her strongest recollections from that period of her life is a feeling of shame: "I would duck down, run into doorways rather than see people that I worked with for 20 years." Nonetheless, Draper still expected to be treated by social services professionals like an adult. In her words:

> "I have a master's degree in biology, I ran a lab for a major professor, I have got a lot of experience, I have done a lot of things, and I expected to be treated like an equal. Even though I was crazy I still expected to be treated like an equal, and that is not part of the established practice at a large shelter. I mean you are off in a corner, [and told to] be quiet, stand in a line."

At the Harvard Square Shelter, in contrast, Draper encountered college students who treated her with a sense of respect and dignity that, 20 years later, she still described as "a life-changing experience." She recalled in vivid detail stepping into the Harvard Square Shelter "and just sitting and talking and that experience of suddenly walking in there and not being a walking crazy woman, but being someone that someone felt valuable enough to sit down and have a conversation with." According to Draper:

"It was a life-changing experience . . . going in there, looking like someone who lived in the streets and subways because that was what I was doing, and just having someone treat me like they respect my intellect, [which] had nothing to do with how I was dressed, or because I was homeless. They didn't dwell on my homelessness. We talked about food, cooking, food salvaging, and then it went kind of from there to other stuff like books, so that was really special."

In her description of stepping into the shelter, Draper went out of her way to note that "the students weren't picking my brain. We weren't talking about homelessness." In so doing, she alluded to her gratitude that the Harvard students volunteering at the Harvard Square Shelter treated her like a full-fledged human being rather than a statistic or a project to be solved. Fred Slomiak told a similar story about the atmosphere of respect and dignity he encountered at the Harvard Square Shelter nearly a decade later.

Fred Slomiak ran a successful restaurant for more than 20 years before alcoholism and mental illness drove away his wife and daughters and propelled him into homelessness in the mid-1990s. Looking back on that period of his life, Slomiak recalled that "I was kind of just existing, trying to sort something out like a puzzle, like a Rubik's Cube that I was incapable of solving." Over the course of three years on the streets, Slomiak described himself as "getting so beat up" by the various social services agencies purporting to help him that he began rejecting assistance of any kind. He described being assigned a psychiatrist who barely spoke English and then, despite a problem with alcoholism, being placed in a clinic for crack cocaine abusers. According to Slomiak, "It just deepened my resentment towards any type of system, or dealing with the government, or the agencies." As he began to turn away from the offerings of social service providers, a counselor at one of Boston's larger homeless shelters suggested that he give the shelter in the University Lutheran basement a try. "If you won't go into an organized place," the counselor told Slomiak, "there is a shelter in Harvard Square, and it's run by college students, and they are not the system. They are just a bunch of college kids that are interested, that want to be helpful, [and] aren't there to fix you or save you, but just care." Slomiak decided to give the Harvard Square Shelter a try.

Interestingly, two of the Harvard Square Shelter's current student-directors, Leo LaSala and Kathryn Tobin, described the shelter's merits

15 years later in nearly identical terms. According to LaSala, "A lot of people come to our shelter because they walk in the door and they don't feel like they're being herded from professional to professional who are giving them paragraphs of advice on how to fix their lives without even getting to know them." Likewise, Kathryn Tobin, another student-director, observed:

> "If someone was frustrated and disillusioned with the system, I would not feel much better or feel much more empowered if someone just told me that they could fix my situation, that it was easy, that all I had to do was fill out various forms or find the right agency. Because it's really not easy. It's really hard. And I don't think our role is to belittle the difficulty of that condition."

Both of these students seemed to understand intuitively that homeless men like Fred Slomiak are certainly in need of support, but are not looking to be "fixed."

During his first week staying at the Harvard Square Shelter, Slomiak met a student whom he credits with changing his life. A Harvard sophomore named Maggie asked Slomiak to teach her how to play chess and, later, asked if he would mind her writing a paper about that experience. As Slomiak recalled:

> "In this paper she wrote about me, about how I taught her chess, she described it as Fred maneuvered chess in some ways as a master, his way of teaching and communicating. And she went on to write other things, and that instilled — I had two daughters I was separated from — and that instilled in me [a sense of] contributing. That was the moment, the definitive moment, where after all of that despair, that someone as bright as this used terms like that in the way that I communicated and taught."

Here, Slomiak described the powerful effect of seeing himself through the eyes of an admiring young person. Buoyed by this reminder that he still had something to contribute to the world, Slomiak began the process of controlling his alcoholism, seeking treatment for bipolar disorder and getting his life back on track.

Today, 15 years later, Slomiak has worked with the United Way and Home Start to combat family homelessness all across the United States.

Reflecting on his time at the Harvard Square Shelter, he explained that "I feel like those students changed how I perceived life. They saw the dignity within me, and one of the things that happens when you become homeless is a severe blow to your dignity. You almost blame yourself for an un-blamable situation." Similar to CASPAR's Meghan Goughan, Slomiak suggested that what turns the Harvard Square Shelter into the "Cadillac" of homeless shelters is the students' ability to "see us past our homelessness." Or, even more simply, Slomiak said, "The number one thing for me is they would listen to what I had to say and thought it important." Not yet cynical or jaded, what the Harvard students volunteering at the Harvard Square Shelter have going for them is inexperience.

As Philip Mangano admitted, many individuals within Boston's homeless community were initially put off by the idea of a student-run homeless shelter. Mangano himself saw these concerns as legitimate ones. However, as he went on to note:

> "I think it's to the credit of the students and to Fred Reisz, and to the members of the Uni-Lu church, that they were able to overcome that perception of homeless people and that in fact rather than being a place where you went to be ostracized and exiled from the center of the community, that the people experienced a form of welcome and hospitality and dignity that perhaps they weren't receiving in some of the larger shelters in the area."

What, on its face, seemed like the Harvard Square Shelter's greatest liability turned out to be its greatest asset. Or, as the University Lutheran Church's current pastor, Donald Larsen, asserted, "That's part of what makes these sorts of places Cadillacs because the non-professionals recognize the humanity of this other person and want to respect it." Larsen's perspective is underscored by sociologist Alisa Lincoln who has investigated the factors that encourage homeless men and women to take advantage of programs and resources. According to Lincoln:

> Homeless people are looking for a place that respects them as fellow human beings and adults; a place that feels like home and offers some privacy; and a place that doesn't have too many rules and restrictions. The theme of respect popped up in interviews over and over again.[9]

Although short on privacy, the rest of Lincoln's description fits the Harvard Square Homeless Shelter to a T.

NOT A UTOPIA

Despite singing its praises, none of the homeless men and women staying at the Harvard Square Homeless Shelter would ever mistake the shelter for paradise. Virtually every man and woman who has ever spent the night there would have preferred to be somewhere else and in different circumstances. And while the Harvard students running the Harvard Square Shelter strive to preserve the respect and dignity of the men and women who stay there, 30 people spending the night together in a church basement are bound to experience some irritation, frustration and tension. Frank Green expressed his frustration with the naivety of the Harvard students he encountered at the shelter this past winter. Green noted first and foremost that the students running the Harvard Square Shelter "are great kids, all of them," but that "they've just lived sheltered lives, and they don't know enough about the real world to be making adult decisions." According to Green, the students' naivety means that plenty of the men and women staying at the Harvard Square Shelter can "con them out of stuff" and that "these kids with no experience in the real world, living sheltered lives, get the wool pulled over their eyes."

Frank Green was by no means the only homeless person this past winter to express frustration with the Harvard Square Shelter and its students. Harvard junior Lester Pearsons offered the following observation of several of the homeless men and women he encountered during his weekly dinner shift at the Harvard Square Shelter:

> "I can't help but feel there must be some antipathy on their part because sometimes they have made a few remarks. There was one guy who was saying, 'Harvard kids, they're just people, they're not better than anyone else, they're just people.' He's not the only one who feels that way, I think."

Wellesley College sophomore Charlotte Wu offered a similar perspective: "Some of the guests are very friendly, but there are others who don't come there as often who are a little more put off.... And whenever even the smallest thing goes awry, they go, 'Oh Harvard students. Blah,

blah, blah.'" Both Wu and Pearsons had picked up on some sensitivity among the men and women staying at the Harvard Square Shelter regarding Harvard students putting on airs.

Another volunteer, Harvard senior Elyse Margolis, expressed her surprise that "some people are not as grateful as other people." On her weekly dinner shift, Margolis made a point of noticing which of the men and women staying at the shelter did and did not say "thank you" as they came through the serving line for dinner. Harvard junior Amanda Mooney said:

> "There's a certain few guests who give kind of a lot of flak for being a Harvard student . . . It's like, 'Oh, if you're so smart, then why can't you figure this out? You're a Harvard student!' Or, 'You think that you're better than me!' You know, not in those plain of terms, but that is definitely the gist. Either it's you think you're better than me or you should be able to do this. Kind of like a mocking type of thing. Most people aren't like that."

Clearly, the pressures of homelessness, the tight quarters of the church basement, and the natural tensions between different individuals sometimes lead to moments of tension. That said, these moments occur with far less frequency and vehemence than one might expect. Harvard alumnus Ward Welburn suggested that the shelter generally attracts a particular segment of the homeless community. In his words, "I think people who are hard core and you know just sort of wouldn't be able to put up with these idealistic students wanting to talk to them for two hours would go down to Central Square, into Boston, and so forth." As a result, the homeless men and women who *do* come to the Harvard Square Shelter are generally those interested, or at least willing, to contend with the strengths and weaknesses of a homeless shelter operated by young adults.

A TWO-WEEK BAR

The greatest animosity between Harvard students and the homeless typically involves dissension over a "bar." The Harvard Square Shelter's 14 directors must occasionally bar individuals from the shelter as a result of behavior that violates shelter policy. The length of the bar is proportional to the severity of the violation. For example, an individual found to be intoxicated or high inside the shelter automatically receives a two-week bar, but may return to the shelter after those two weeks have passed. On the other hand, physically threatening behavior typically results in a permanent bar from the shelter. Virtually all of the Harvard students who serve as directors expressed their dislike for this aspect of the job. Harvard senior Leo LaSala talked about the difficulty of "the first time you have to tell someone they can't stay, for whatever reason." Another senior, Robert Vozar, explained that "One of the most sad and frustrating experiences for me last year was that I had to bar one of the guests that I was closest with for testing positive for drugs. It sucked."

As might be expected, homeless men and women at the Harvard Square Shelter will oftentimes disagree with the rationale behind a particular bar. Frank Green was barred twice this past season for two weeks apiece. The second bar occurred the weekend before Harvard's Spring Break. According to Green, he was chatting with three other men in the shelter's dining area when he noticed another homeless man lurking by his locker. In Green's words, "I'm looking down, and I say, jeez, this guy looks like he's in my locker. But he must have the one next to mine. From this distance, I guess looks can be deceiving." As Green watched, the individual moved over to another wall of lockers and started tinkering around with the locks. Green alerted Lissette McDonald, one of the directors on duty, that someone was rifling through people's lockers. While McDonald confronted the alleged locker thief, Green stood nearby checking on the contents of his locker. In his words, "So I opened my locker, and I said, 'That fucking goddamn faggot was in my fucking locker. All my shit is turned upside down. I have a heart condition. My fucking medication better be here, or someone is going to fucking get killed.'" Ultimately, Green found nothing missing from his locker, but remained certain its contents had been rifled through.

McDonald and her co-director first worked to sort out the actions and consequences for the alleged thief, but later returned to Green with concerns about his behavior and language. As Green recalled:

> "They said, 'We have to give you a write-up because you were swearing at the guy.' I said, 'Fine, write me up, I don't give a shit. So what? I swore at the guy. I was pissed off. The guy was robbing me. I had every right to be pissed off!' And they said, 'You called him a faggot, and we can't tolerate that. And that's a hate statement.' And I said, 'I don't give a shit, just write me

up!' So they give me a write up . . . and then three days later, their policy board supposedly meets, and they come back to me when I go in that night. Now it's three days later, and they say, 'Oh, the policy board met because you called that guy a faggot and swore at him. We changed the policy, so now the new policy is you get a 14-day bar, so we have to bar you.' I said, 'You can bar me three days after the fact? There's something not right with this picture . . . you people got your friggin' priorities wrong.'"

From Green's perspective, receiving a bar for his response to nearly being robbed was ridiculous. He believed the Harvard students should have focused their efforts entirely on the alleged thief rather than worrying about his harsh language. From Green's perspective, "Swearing at somebody isn't a very serious crime."

Perhaps not surprisingly, Lissette McDonald — the student-director who had the responsibility of sorting out the situation — viewed Green's language through a different lens. She had observed the effeminate mannerisms of the homeless man later accused by Green of rifling through his locker, and literally the night before the confrontation had warned her fellow directors in an email to "watch out for any homophobic things going on." As a result, McDonald argued strongly for Green's language to result in a two-week bar. She faced some pushback from her peers who believed a warning was sufficient given the circumstances and, in her words, "There was a lot of debate about whether or not when we barred this guest if it was too harsh."

Another of the student-directors, Amanda Mooney, admitted that she initially believed the situation required a warning rather than a bar but that "Lissette made a strong case for this being hate speech." As Mooney said, "While, had I been the director on the ground, [I] would have given a warning, I do very much support the bar. Because if that big of a majority on staff feels that it was hate speech, then I agree that should not be tolerated."

In the end, the student-directors decided to upgrade Green's consequences from a warning to a two-week bar, of which he was notified three days after the incident itself had taken place. In this conflict, one can certainly see the source of Frank Green's belief that the Harvard students operating the Harvard Square Shelter are both naive and inconsistent. Interestingly, however, Green also noted that the four weeks he was barred from the shelter this year were the only 28 days all winter long that he did not stay there. In response to a question about the frustration of putting up with such naivety and inconsistency, Green responded, "They're good kids. I just think it's lack of experience." In fact, Green added that the Harvard Square Shelter remains the only shelter he is willing to stay in. If he couldn't have a bed there this past winter, "I had a tent set up if I needed to. 'Cause I could sleep in sleeping bags. You can stay outside all winter if need be. I don't like other shelters."

"THE LAWSUIT"

While Frank Green expressed substantial frustration over his two-week bar from the Harvard Square Shelter, another homeless man, Tony Ventrone, actually took the shelter to court in the spring of 2009 over *his* two-week bar. Harvard senior Leo LaSala noted that the lawsuit "might be a first. There's been a lot of people that have threatened to. We've even gotten complaint letters, 'If you don't do this, I will sue you,' but we've never actually been taken to court." According to LaSala, Ventrone was barred after receiving three warnings from shelter directors for a variety of infractions: taking photographs of other people in the shelter without their permission, missing the shelter's 9 p.m. curfew, and getting into a yelling match with another man staying at the shelter. According to Ventrone, in issuing these warnings, the Harvard Square Shelter wasn't adequately accommodating for his clinically diagnosed mental illness, and so he filed suit. Interestingly, Ventrone was not seeking financial compensation, but rather a guaranteed shelter bed at the Harvard Square Shelter for the remainder of the shelter season.

A hearing was held in April of 2009 in Cambridge's Middlesex Superior Court. A year earlier, the students operating the Harvard Square Shelter had secured permanent pro-bono counsel from Mintz Levin, a large Boston law firm, and were represented by an associate from the firm. Ventrone represented himself and spoke first. Harvard senior Robert Vozar attended the hearing on behalf of the Harvard Square Shelter and offered the following description of Ventrone's testimony:

> "He spoke first, and he told a very compelling story. . . . He said, 'You know sir; it's a small shelter. But, it's really an excellent shelter Your Honor.' And, we were just like this is so

beautiful. This guy who is suing us is telling the judge about what a great shelter we are. You know and then he said, 'Well, you know I got warned for coughing. And I got warned for yelling, and I don't think that's fair.' And then we said our piece. And then the judge said dismissed.

The entire hearing lasted only last a few minutes, but, again, it is notable that one of the Harvard Square Shelter's most vocal critics might well have been the same homeless man who characterized the shelter to MHSA Vice-President Kaye Wild as "the Cadillac of homeless shelters." Ventrone was suing, in large part, because he wanted so fervently to maintain his stay there.

THE HOW AND THE WHY

Philip Mangano believes that the Harvard Square Shelter's birth story plays an important role in making the shelter a welcoming place for the homeless men and women who stay there. As Mangano noted, Pastor Fred Reisz and his congregants "extended a beautiful sense of hospitality to the students, who then transferred that and extended that same hospitality to the guests, and that's a big difference from being a non-profit organization which rents a building and then places people in the building." According to Mangano, what makes the Harvard Square Shelter so special is embedded deep within the circumstances of its creation.

In offering *their* perspective on what makes the Harvard Square Homeless Shelter the "Cadillac" of homeless shelters, a number of the homeless men and women who have stayed at the shelter focused on the amenities such as a washing machine and computers; a sense of safety within the shelter; and a culture of dignity and respect. Clearly, the Harvard students operating the shelter are not perfect, and, in several of the incidents of this past winter, one can glimpse the drawbacks of an organizational structure entirely reliant on non-professional young adults. That said, in the eight chapters that follow, I draw upon more than 70 interviews with current and former volunteers, homeless men and women, and professional stakeholders to suggest that the Harvard Square Shelter's "Cadillac-ness" is *because*, rather than in spite of, its student-run structure.[10]

In making this case, I respond to important challenges to the existence and viability of a *student-run* homeless shelter. These challenges were explicitly given a voice in my follow-up interview in March of 2009 with Harvard freshman Ashwin Ganguli, who had just finished his first winter of volunteering at the Harvard Square Shelter. In this interview, Ganguli described an upsetting exchange with another Harvard student who had questioned the wisdom of his volunteer work at the shelter. According to Ganguli:

> "She had some very fundamental questions about why the shelter existed at all, and unfortunately that shook a lot of my own beliefs. Her question exactly was, 'You're eighteen years old. You're a college freshman. What makes you think you are capable of doing something like this? What makes you think you are a good person to put on the line for people you don't know, [and] who you probably will never see two years from now? Why can't you just raise funds and employ professionals to deal with this?'"

The next eight chapters respond to these challenges. While it would be absurd to suggest that all homeless shelters should immediately be turned over to the leadership of college students, I demonstrate that there are attributes and qualities possessed by these young adults that make them uniquely suited to working with marginalized communities such as the homeless. More than just stepping up to fill a void as the shelter's founder, Pastor Fred Reisz, originally envisioned, the Harvard students operating the Harvard Square Homeless Shelter alter the dynamic of the traditional provider–client model in ways that are deeply beneficial to the homeless men and women staying there; the Harvard students themselves; and the communities into which both groups will emerge.

Chapter 3

Doing Passion Well

Twenty-one-year-old Lex Obain spent much of the past two winters at the Harvard Square Homeless Shelter. Born in the Ivory Coast, Lex moved to France with his mother and younger siblings when he was six years old and grew up in a working class neighborhood outside Paris. Upon graduating from high school, Lex spent his savings on a one-way plane ticket to the United States with the goal of playing college basketball but no clear plan about how to proceed.

After arriving in Boston, Lex enrolled in courses at Boston's Bunker Hill Community College where he also found part-time work as an English as a Second Language tutor and office clerk. For shelter, he relied on the hospitality of several distant relatives and, later, different members of Boston's tiny community of Ivory Coast immigrants whom he met through his church.

Lex spent nearly eight months sleeping on people's couches, staying at one house until he had worn out his welcome and then moving on to the next house. But on a Friday night in January 2008, the last of Lex's friends in Boston informed him that he had to move out the next day. With no "next house" to go to, Lex was homeless. His mother offered to wire him the money for a plane ticket back to France, but, as Lex explained, "I said I would never come back to France like that. I have younger brothers; they need to have a model. We don't have a father, so I need to be like a grown man and show them some things."

A Google search for Boston homeless shelters alerted Lex to the existence of the Harvard Square Homeless Shelter, and he figured that anything associated with Harvard couldn't be all bad. That said, Lex described the walk through Harvard Square towards his first night at the Harvard Square Shelter as the longest walk of his life. In his words:

> I stood still, 30 yards away from the shelter, and I stared at the three homeless men around the main door. It was freezing cold and I was emotionally hurt because I felt lonely and helpless. . . . Prejudgments filled my mind, but I was so hungry and cold, the bottom of my pants so wet from the snow, that my feet started moving instinctively. I hid in my hooded sweatshirt like a child in his bed, and before I knew it or could stop myself I found that I was inside the shelter sitting at a table next to the television with a big plate full of food from Au Bon Pain. In one hour, my life had been physically and spiritually changed. I had admitted to myself, and the world, that I was homeless.[1]

That first night at the Harvard Square Shelter, Lex stayed hidden and alert inside his hooded sweatshirt, but he also took advantage of the shelter's abundant food and networked computers. He also began talking to the Harvard students on duty.

Over the next few weeks, Lex came to know the students running the shelter, and he confided in them his own dream of attending an American university. Fortunately for Lex, if there is one topic about which elite college students are virtual experts, it is the college admissions process.[2] Amanda Mooney, a Harvard junior, began meeting Lex at six in the morning to help him study for the ACTs, and another student worked to prepare him for the SATs. Harvard senior Robert Vozar bought Lex a suit for admissions interviews, and Nathan Small and several other students began helping Lex put together his applications. The above description of Lex walking towards the Harvard Square Shelter comes straight from the personal statement that accompanied his application to 12 different universities. As Lex recalled:

> "During that time, I was meeting with Robert on Sundays, I was meeting with Nathan, I was meeting with them, and we were going over the applications. And one night Nathan called me during the day and said we have to look over all the applications and then my financial application, my financial

papers, my essays, so they were good . . . I think I had to send my stuff by the next Monday. It was a Saturday, and I had one day to fix up all the things and send it to all the schools. I was working in an office at Bunker Hill, and I was able to mail my stuff. So from there I mailed in all my applications to the 12 schools."

Because he had no mailing address of his own, Lex listed Harvard senior Robert Vozar's dormitory mailbox as his own on each of the 12 applications.

The night in November on which the first of the admissions decisions arrived, Lex received a text message from Vozar alerting him that a letter from Hamilton College had arrived. Lex hurried the mile and a half to Vozar's dormitory and then offered the following description of what unfolded:

"So we were there — Nathan, Achira and Robert — and they said, 'Okay, Lex, this is it. So let's do it. Let's open the letter.' So I said, 'Okay, Robert, you open the first half, and I'll open the second half. We did this together, so let's go.' And then I looked at it, and I see the word, 'Congratulations.' I was like, 'Oh my God!' I just let everything out. And everyone was happy, but then Robert was like, 'Oh wait, let's look at the financial aid first.' I almost was yelling, screaming I was so happy. But then I was like, 'Oh, let's see what they said.' And they gave me a full scholarship with $1600 for pocket money or something like that. So basically I was homeless for a year from January twenty-first until that day where I got the letter at Robert's dorm."

Several of the Harvard students operating the Harvard Square Shelter had played crucial roles in Lex's college admissions process, so perhaps it was only fitting that four of these students rented a mini-van and drove Lex to college. As Harvard senior Robert Vozar tells it: "We drove Lex to Hamilton College to drop him off for school with all his stuff. And, that was really fun. You know it was a day-long road trip, and it felt like suddenly someone's life had begun." Another of the students who made the trip, Leo LaSala, recalled:

"It was a really amazing experience because even something as simple as walking into this new dorm and him realizing that

I have this place to live now after two years of being homeless. You know, all those things we take for granted are really called to mind by that experience."

Now a fellow college student, Lex has kept in touch with a number of the young adults from the Harvard Square Shelter via telephone, text message and Facebook. Senior Robert Vozar recalled getting an excited text message from Lex a week into his first semester in which he reported, "I have this Black Jewish roommate. I went to Trivia Night and Pajama Night. And, I have to take a swim test. And, I'm going to take sociology of this and French Literature and Orgo and — and just sort of being totally wrapped up in college life already."

Lex, for his part, considered that "The nicest people in my life that I've ever met were these guys. These young students . . . and they were like good people, and they were friends. Real friends." In appreciation for all they have done for him, Lex keeps the names of the students on a piece of paper inside his wallet. He described this private homage as "something personal. It's something I want to keep."

At the end of his first semester at Hamilton, Lex reported that he had earned an A– in French, a B in Sociology and C+'s in his two science classes. As a pre-medical student, Lex explained that "I'm kind of disappointed [with the grades] because I want to go to medical school, and I don't know how that will look on my transcript." While it is difficult to imagine a medical school not taking a chance on such an impressive young person, Lex expressed determination to improve his grades in subsequent semesters. His is a tremendous success story, and while Lex's own intelligence and perseverance are staggering, nearly as impressive is the passion with which the college students at the Harvard Square Shelter offered him their support.

EMERGING ADULTHOOD

Each year, the University Lutheran Church hires an intern from the Harvard Divinity School to lead a series of reflection sessions with the Harvard students volunteering at the Harvard Square Shelter.[3] The intern for the 2008–09 academic year was Wendy Burrell. Burrell, just 23 years old, was blonde, bespectacled and a recent college graduate herself. In response to a question about what the Harvard students volunteering at the Harvard Square Shelter do well, Burrell responded,

"I'm not sure if you can do passion well, but I do think they bring a lot of passion to the work."

A number of the homeless men and women who have stayed at the Harvard Square Shelter echoed Burrell's sentiment. A formerly homeless man, Joe Presley, described the Harvard students he encountered at the shelter as motivated by a "concentrated concern" for combating homelessness and that "they really wanted to help." Likewise, Frank Green, a homeless man who spent much of this past winter at the shelter, characterized the Harvard students as "doing it more out of their heart" than the typical shelter employee. Another homeless man, 19-year-old Mike Andretti, stated simply that "They care more. They're there for you." Certainly, this concern and care were evident in the Harvard students' support for Lex Obain and his improbable pathway from a homeless shelter to Hamilton College.

These men and women's descriptions of the passion that the Harvard students bring to their volunteer work at the shelter align with psychologist Jeffrey Arnett's characterization of emerging adulthood.[4] Emerging adulthood is the developmental stage that extends from roughly 18 to 26 years old. Individuals in emerging adulthood are no longer fully beholden to their parents but have not yet assumed responsibility for a family of their own.[5] In short, emerging adults possess "few ties that entail daily obligations and commitments to others."[6] As a result of this relative freedom from commitments, emerging adults are able to direct substantial amounts of energy and attention to a particular project or pastime. More specifically, without the responsibilities that accompany caring for a family of their own, emerging adults are able to invest themselves wholeheartedly into an endeavor such as running the Harvard Square Homeless Shelter (or traveling the world, or writing the Great American novel). As Arnett explains, emerging adulthood is the period "when most people are most likely to be free to follow their own interests and desires."[7] Older, professional service workers, on the other hand, are likely to need to divide their attention and energy (and justifiably so) between their commitment to their work and to their spouses and children.[8] Arnett notes that it is precisely for these reasons that "programs such as AmeriCorps and the Peace Corps find most of their volunteers among emerging adults."[9]

Emerging adulthood is also characterized as the "age of possibilities, when optimism is high, and people have an unparalleled opportunity to transform their lives."[10] As evidence of this optimism, psychologist Jean Twenge reported in 2006 that an astounding 98 percent of college freshmen agreed with the statement "I am sure that one day I will get to where I want to be in life."[11] In their classic study of moral exemplars, Colby and Damon reported that a trait common among their study's exemplars was optimism — "a capacity for finding hope and joy even while frankly facing the dreary truth."[12] The heightened optimism associated with emerging adulthood, then, allows emerging adults such as the Harvard students running the Harvard Square Shelter to believe in Lex Obain's ability to conquer the college admissions process. One might say that emerging adulthood is a developmental period particularly suited for participation in community service and social activism.

And there is evidence to suggest that such optimism and idealism only increase over the course of the college years. In their classic work, *How College Affects Students*, Pascarella and Terenzini reported that "The evidence is abundant and consistent in indicating that changes toward greater altruism, humanitarianism, and sense of civic responsibility and social conscience occur during the college years"[13] Likewise, Tanner noted that "The college environment has the potential, for some, to facilitate explorations, soul-searching, and optimism about one's potential to change the world."[14]

Interestingly, Linda Sax and colleagues found that the increases individuals experience during the college years in their focus on helping others in need, participating in community service and influencing the political structure actually recede again after graduation.[15] Likewise, neuroscientist Ronald Dahl describes adolescence as a time of "ignited passions."[16] By this, Dahl means that during the developmental phase of adolescence, individuals experience a spurt of neuronal capacity that results in a temporary "infusion of energy into whatever captures a younger person's attention."[17]

In short, then, the Harvard students operating the Harvard Square Shelter — on the border between adolescence and emerging adulthood — are in the ideal stage of life to direct their energy and attention towards combating homelessness. This chapter considers the implications for the homeless men and women staying at the shelter of interacting nightly with bright, idealistic young people who are ideally situated to "do passion well."

FRANCINE AND THE STREET TEAM

The Harvard students' passion for combating homelessness can also be seen in the Harvard Square Shelter's Street Team. Street Team was the brainchild of Harvard students Larry Yoon and Mark Lee. It occurred to these two young men that while the Harvard Square Shelter accommodated nearly 30 people every night of the winter, there were dozens of other homeless men and women in Harvard Square *not* taking advantage of the shelter's services. As Yoon explained, "It's not like people don't know the shelter is there; often, it's rather that people don't want to be in a shelter. They've had bad experiences or they have mental illness [or] trust issues."

In the winter of 2007, Yoon and Lee decided they should try to bring some of the shelter's services out into Harvard Square. At first, the two just walked around Harvard Square a few nights a week from 9 to 10 p.m. distributing leftover sandwiches from the shelter's dinner shift. When there seemed to be a demand for the sandwiches and when other shelter volunteers expressed interest, Yoon and Lee decided to make these sojourns into Harvard Square more formalized. Beginning in November 2008, they set up six teams of three to go out Sunday through Friday nights. Then they purchased ostentatious purple backpacks for the Street Team members to wear and in which to carry sandwiches. Their goal was to make the Street Team a recognizable presence in Harvard Square.

In November 2008, as the Street Team was just getting off the ground, Yoon said that the venture was going "kind of as expected. . . . We're meeting people, and we're talking to people, and that's kind of what we're striving for. And at this point it's continuing to converse, continuing to get to know people, and further on connect people to other things that will get them off the streets." The Street Team members also encouraged the homeless men and women they encountered to call for a bed at the Harvard Square Shelter. According to Jerry Chen, another Harvard student involved in the Street Team, the students kept a logbook of their nightly activities and, by the end of the winter, they had distributed 15 pounds of bread in the form of peanut butter and jelly sandwiches, talked to 103 distinct individuals, and referred a few dozen for stays at the Harvard Square Shelter.

Leo LaSala, a Harvard senior and Street Team participant, described his interactions with the homeless during Street Team as even more egalitarian than inside the shelter:

58 SHELTER

"On the Street Team, you're really meeting people much more in their own space, on their level. You say, 'Hey you want a sandwich?' and they say, 'No, get lost,' and you get lost. On the other hand, if you just sit there and talk, you can talk about anything and everything. That also happens inside our shelter, but there's no rules [on the street]. There's no implicit anything, really. It's just having conversations with people."

The mere existence of a Street Team indicates the level of passion with which these Harvard students approached the work of combating homelessness. Not content to sit back and allow those in need of shelter to come to them, these young people were actively combing the streets of Harvard Square with the larger goal of connecting homeless men and women to useful services but, in the short term, simply offering company and conversation. In so doing, significant age, class and often racial borders were crossed.[18]

The students' commitment was not lost on the homeless men and women staying at the Harvard Square Homeless Shelter. Mike Andretti, a 19 year old who stayed at the shelter this past winter, noted that the young adults running the shelter "care more. They're there for you. They even walk around at night and pass out food to people who don't go in there. They come out to talk to people. They come out to get people to go in there." Andretti's praise for the willingness of the Harvard students to "come out" into Harvard Square is underscored by research by epidemiologist Daniel Herman, who investigates resources that can help individuals transitioning from hospitals and prisons to avoid homelessness. According to Herman:

The most effective approaches require some workers — social services workers, mental health workers, outreach workers — to go out to places where these people are. The best thing may not be to say, "Won't you come with me, and we'll get you psychiatric help," because that might not be at the top of their priorities. But you might say, "We can offer you a place to sleep, we can offer you a place to wash up, to see a doctor, to deal with sores on your feet."[19]

In this description, Herman offers what could be the mission statement of the Harvard Square Shelter's Street Team.

The Street Team also became responsible this past winter for the incident that turned the Harvard Square Shelter into the toast of Cambridge's social services community. Street Team got Francine to come inside.

Francine was a homeless woman in her early sixties notable for an enormous, single gray dreadlock that reached down to her waist. She had been a nearly permanent fixture outside the Harvard Bookstore in Harvard Square for more than 20 years. According to other profession-als in Boston and Cambridge working with the homeless, Francine had refused any sort of professional services since at least 1987. Meghan Goughan, the Assistant Director of the CASPAR Homeless Shelter, described her as the "epitome of when you think of a mentally ill home-less woman." She would likely have frozen to death long ago if a local sporting goods store had not outfitted her in winter gear intended for alpine mountain climbers.

At the beginning of the winter, Harvard student Larry Yoon noted that one of the people Street Team had been talking to was "a lady who has been out there for 20 years." Initially, Yoon explained, "She'd X me out and be like, 'Don't talk to me.'" However, Francine became less hostile as she came to recognize the students' faces from their nightly sojourns through Harvard Square. As Francine grew friendlier with the Street Team, a debate arose among the shelter's student-leaders about whether they should try to connect Francine to more professional services. But, as Yoon commented, "Some of us are skeptical about how fruitful that'll be when she's been there for 20 years." The students also feared making any moves that might compromise Francine's growing trust in them.

In late December 2008, Yoon emailed Meghan Goughan and men-tioned that they were making progress with Francine. Goughan recalled that "Of course my cynical side was like, she's probably yes-ing you, tell-ing you what you want to hear so you'll go away. I almost sent an email back that was like, 'Don't get too excited. She's been there 20 years.'" As a dedicated professional with more than a decade of experience working with Boston's homeless, Goughan had experienced disappointment far too many times to let Francine get her hopes up.

A week later, Goughan heard through a buzzing professional grapevine that, on the evening of January 1, 2009 — a bitterly cold night — Francine had gone over to the Harvard Square Shelter to spend the night. While another homeless man had played a role in convincing her to go inside, Goughan noted that Street Team had unquestionably played a "very important part" in Francine's decision, an accomplishment she described as "incredible." Likewise, Lucy Draper, a formerly homeless woman who now runs a non-profit organization in Cambridge, arranged a meeting with the Harvard students to impress upon them the importance of keeping Francine in the shelter.

Francine ended up staying at the Harvard Square Shelter for three weeks before an incident outside the shelter led to her hospitalization. In April 2009, Yoon was working on arranging a time to visit Francine in the hospital; he had heard she was now being seen by a psychiatrist and social worker. It was not clear where Francine would end up — or ultimately how big a role the Harvard Square Shelter will have played in her trajectory — but the sheer act of getting Francine to come inside after 20 years on the streets indicated the impact of the passion and youthful idealism with which the Harvard students operating the Harvard Square Shelter approached this work.

MOTIVATIONS FOR VOLUNTEERING

The transition from adolescence into emerging adulthood can explain the passion and enthusiasm with which the Harvard students provided support to individuals like Lex Obain and Francine, but what explains their focus on homelessness in the first place? Why were these talented young adults not, instead, focusing their efforts on getting 4.0 GPAs, writing for the school newspaper, competing for the debate team, or pledging a fraternity?[20]

In more than 50 interviews with current and former Harvard Square Homeless Shelter volunteers, nearly every volunteer offered an explanation for how he or she got involved with the shelter that touched upon a common theme: the shock of witnessing homelessness in Harvard Square.[21] Harvard freshman Nancy Mellor — volunteering at the shelter this winter for the first time — stated:

> "I come from an area in Ohio that has no homelessness. It's not a utopia, but it's a really small farming town, so there's really no crime, poverty, anything. So this was something I remember when I first got here, that it really struck me, I couldn't believe it, to see someone sleeping on the sidewalk. You hear about it, but it's different to see it. So I think that was my main motivation in going [to the shelter]."

Here, Mellor voiced a recurring explanation: the vast majority of Harvard students volunteering at the shelter came from suburban (or rural) communities where the issue of homelessness was either non-existent or invisible.[22] Melissa Sanguinetti, a Harvard junior, commented that in her home state of South Dakota, "Even though poverty is so prevalent at home, it's not so much on the street. It's not so much in your face. It's very much behind closed doors." Harvard senior Lissette McDonald expressed a near identical sentiment about her hometown of Montpelier, Vermont:

> "I think the other thing that really drew me to the shelter was that coming from Vermont, and from Montpelier, homelessness is prevalent, but it's certainly not as visible there. There might be one person downtown or two people downtown that you kind of know are the downtown people. So to me, freshman fall, coming here, at least once a day, I'd have to walk from the [Harvard] Yard, down JFK Street. And there are people who stand along JFK asking you for money. And every day I was torn because I'd been told it wasn't the best idea to give people money, nor do I really have that much money to give. But every day I was torn about whether I should look away or say hello or say sorry that I couldn't give them anything."

In all three of these students' words, one can hear their emotional response to a social issue to which they were being exposed for the first time. In their functional approach to volunteerism, researchers Clary and Snyder characterized the sentiments expressed by these young adults as examples of a "value expressive function" — a commitment to volunteerism based on "an altruistic concern for others in need, humanitarian values, and/or a desire to contribute to society."[23] In their research on public service motivation, Brewer, Selden and Facer characterized volunteers as Samaritans, Communitarians, Patriots or Humanitarians.[24] It seems likely that these scholars would characterize these three students — Mellor, Sanguinetti and McDonald — as Samaritans, whom they define as individuals who are "moved emotionally when they observe people in distress."[25]

These current Harvard students mirrored the sentiments of many who came before them. For example, Dr. Kristin Sommers, a Harvard Square Shelter volunteer who arrived at Harvard College in 1994

— nearly 15 years ahead of Nancy, Melissa and Lissette — described
the following motivation for getting involved in the shelter:

> "Every day walking to and from class and looking out into the
> streets I could see people living on the streets. Growing up in
> the suburbs it's something that I hadn't experienced before. I
> wanted to get involved in the community and see what was the
> cause and the root of the issue and how I could help."

Likewise, Lana Zielinski, a 1988 Harvard graduate, began volunteering at the Harvard Square Shelter more than 20 years ahead of Nancy,
Melissa and Lissette:

> "I grew up in Northampton, Massachusetts which is a much
> smaller town where we really did not have much of a homeless
> population at that time. And moving into the Harvard dorms
> near the Square, there is a sizeable homeless population, and I
> was very aware of it. And it is a troubling thing, and you feel if
> there's a way to have an impact on that, then you should."

In these words, Sommers and Zielinski offered what might be characterized as both a Samaritan motivation for volunteering but also a
Communitarian motivation — a desire to serve based in part upon
"sentiments of civic duty and public service."[26]

In comparing the words of these Harvard Square Shelter volunteers over a span of nearly 25 years, one is struck afresh by University
Lutheran Pastor Fred Reisz's genius in 1983 in realizing that the
Harvard Square Shelter could take advantage of the replenishing
"reservoir" of bright, idealistic and *passionate* college students popu-
lating Boston and Cambridge. These young men and women are in a
period of life in which they have the freedom, time, and optimism to
dedicate themselves to combating a social issue, homelessness, that
clearly strikes an emotional chord. Of course, it is simultaneously dis-
couraging to realize just how wrong Pastor Reisz, Stewart Guernsey
and the University Lutheran congregants were in their assumption that
the homeless shelter they established in their church basement in 1983
would only be around "for a winter or two" and that "the government
would get this turned around and do something intelligent to solve the
homelessness."[27]

HAPPY TO BE HERE

Although the Harvard Square Shelter volunteers offered weighty explanations for their involvement in the shelter, what also came across in their explanations was how *excited* they were to be volunteering there. Harvard alumna Anusha Ghosh, who volunteered at the shelter in the early 2000s, admitted that the time she spent volunteering at the shelter *did* cut into the time she spent on academics. However, she also noted that prioritizing the shelter was easy "because it was so much more interesting than a lot of the classes that I took. When you have real world issues that you're dealing with and people that you're getting to know, it's hard to cut back on that and work more on other things." This sentiment was echoed by Harvard junior Deanna Galante who admitted: "Today I missed a class so I could keep talking to people in the shelter, and I'm totally happy to do that, which kind of concerns me, but I get more out of it."

Other Harvard students described their decision to prioritize their work at the shelter as well. Junior Melissa Sanguinetti explained that "Because it's the most important extracurricular that I feel like I'm involved with, it sort of takes precedence over everything else, so I don't feel like I'm sacrificing things that I'd rather be doing." Sophomore Antonia Garcia-Brown pledged a similar prioritizing: "Next year I'm just going to chill out about academics and just do what I need to get by . . . so that I can go and do things that actually matter to me." Freshman Anna Robinson — a member of Harvard's varsity crew team — offered the following description of her determination to be involved with the shelter:

> "I do crew which is pretty time intensive. And I was thinking about crew vs. the shelter, and fortunately they're not mutually exclusive, but I did have to talk with my coach and be like, 'Okay, I'm going to be doing an overnight [shift].' It wasn't really a matter of, 'Can I do an overnight?' In the beginning, I was thinking about it and do I have to ask about it, and I decided, I *am* going to do this."

In order to do a weekly overnight shift at the shelter, Robinson was willing to quit the crew team if necessary, and in fact four other Harvard Square Shelter volunteers actually did quit crew prior to deepening their involvement with the shelter — the extracurricular commitment about which they felt the most passionate.

Amelia Ginsberg — who volunteered at the shelter in the mid-1990s — recalled: "It was such an amazing thing to hear [about] these people's lives and just be like, there are so many different worlds right here co-existing that we don't know anything about." Similarly, Harvard senior Lissette McDonald said, "People can be homeless for so many different reasons and I always want to know, 'What's your life story? What are the events in your life that brought you here?'" In both of these women's words, their passion to get to know and learn from the homeless men and women at the Harvard Square Shelter was unmistakable.

Ward Welburn —who volunteered at the shelter as an undergraduate in the mid-1980s — offered the following description of how his religious convictions and volunteer work combined during his college days in a tremendously satisfying way:

> "I would usually sleep at the shelter on Friday and Saturday nights. I gave up my Friday and Saturday nights for a long time, and Sunday morning I would get up, get everyone out of the building, go back to my dorm, take off my stinky clothes, shower, shave, and on the way from home I'd pick up a bagel that I really liked, and then I would go to church. And [Reverend] Gomes would hold forth, and the music, and I was on Cloud Nine. I was so happy I could dance, I could kiss the sky. And it was this combination of the whole thing, you know. The sort of giving all that you felt that you had to give, and then the sort of being open to what God was saying to you through this environment, and I was just through the roof."

Here, Welburn recalled the genuine joy that he experienced, in large part, through his work at the Harvard Square Shelter. In less religious terms, Harvard senior Robert Vozar described a similar experience during his own overnight shifts at the shelter. Specifically, Vozar admitted that one of his initial motivations for volunteering was that "It seemed kind of cool to stay up all night." He also recalled heading back to his dormitory the morning after each overnight shift "with a narrative about how that shift went, but also how I felt about life and the world and other people based on what I learned and saw during the shift . . . I remember always feeling like I was coming home with a world of stories."

Psychologist Erik Erikson characterized adolescence as the developmental period in which individuals are working to understand who they are and what their place is in the world.[28] When Welburn described his joy as a "combination of the whole thing," he meant that both his volunteer work and religious convictions were playing a role in addressing the two questions — Who am I? And how do I fit in? — that Erikson regarded as the central crises of adolescence.[29] Likewise, current senior Robert Vozar described the shelter as filling his head with stories that influenced his thinking "about life and the world and other people." Psychologist Sharon Daloz Parks describes young adulthood as a period for asking "big questions and discovering worthy dreams."[30] One explanation, then, for the enthusiasm and energy that the college-aged volunteers brought to their work at the Harvard Square Shelter is that this volunteer work helped these young adults to consider some of the "big questions" that were central to their transition from adolescence to emerging adulthood.

Perhaps most indicative of these Harvard students' passion for their work at the shelter was the sheer amount of time they spent there. Junior Nathan Small, who began volunteering at the shelter as a high school student growing up in Cambridge, spent three nights a week at the shelter during the 2008–09 academic year. He worked a director's shift from 7 to 11 p.m. on Wednesday nights and then spent Friday and Sunday evenings supervising the teens from his old high school who came in to the shelter to prepare dinner. Small attended the shelter's staff and policy meetings each week, and estimated that he spent another few hours reading and responding to emails sent out by other shelter directors. He predicted that his total time each week doing shelter-related activities amounted to roughly 20–25 hours. In regards to this substantial commitment, Small said, "The shelter is a community I draw a lot of support from, and it's really important to me. So while it takes up time, I think it probably enhances the quality of my life in general and makes me more productive in all sorts of other ways." In this explanation, Small offered a motivation for volunteering that Clary and Snyder characterize as playing a social-adjustive function, or "providing a way of expanding one's social circle."[31] Having volunteered at the Harvard Square Shelter for seven consecutive years, Small was unequivocally one of the college students most committed and invested in the shelter; however, there were numerous other students as well whose passion for their work at the shelter led them to spend more than 20 hours a week there.

ADDICTED TO THE SHELTER

Rusty Sadow is now a community organizer in Washington DC whose work focuses on affordable housing and healthcare. As a Harvard undergraduate from 1996 to 2000, he started volunteering at the Harvard Square Shelter as an overnight volunteer and quickly became one of the shelter's student-directors. Similar to many shelter volunteers, Sadow began volunteering at the shelter because "you would pass homeless people on the street everywhere around Harvard Square." As he observed, "You didn't have to go very far to encounter this social problem, and [here was] this opportunity just three blocks away to learn more about it and figure out what to do about it."

Sadow signed up to work the Friday overnight shift, whose responsibilities he described in the following way:

> "I thought of my job as hanging out in the kitchen all night making sure no one burned down the shelter. And while doing that, playing chess and Connect Four, you just talk to people and learn what their lives were like before the shelter, how they got to the shelter, what their lives were like before they were homeless, what they hoped their lives would be like in the future. That's a whole universe of things I'd never thought about or considered before, and had no other venue to learn them."

Sadow characterized this exposure to a whole new world as incredibly exciting. Volunteering at the shelter came to feel to him like "the most meaningful thing I could be doing with my time. Writing a paper seemed boring; studying for an exam seemed boring. Everything else seemed boring compared to what I was learning at the shelter, what I was doing at the shelter. I was helping other people. I was valuable." In this description of his volunteer work, Sadow offered what Clary and Snyder characterize as a knowledge function; in other words, the Harvard Square Shelter offered Sadow an opportunity to learn about a particular aspect of the world.[32]

Midway through his freshman year, Sadow characterized himself as having grown "addicted" to the shelter. During Harvard's exam period that January, he volunteered to take on the overnight shifts of other exam-crazed students and ended up spending nearly 20 nights in a row at the shelter. When his parents came to visit him during Parents'

Weekend, he refused to go out for dinner to a fancy restaurant "because of all the homeless people in the street who were eating leftover Harvard food." Originally a Near Eastern languages major, Sadow switched to Social Theory. Looking back, he noted:

> "Basically the entire organizing principle around my education was, 'Why do people end up at the shelter?' From a historical perspective, from a social perspective, from an economic perspective, from a political perspective. I took three different classes that had housing or homelessness in the title. My thesis was . . . following 35 young adults into different shelters and drop-in shelters, and [I] wrote about why they were homeless."

In these words, one can see a textbook example of a young adult seeking out experiences and ideologies that can help him to make sense of the world and his place in it. As the psychologist Erikson explained, Sadow was looking for "a system of ideas that provides a convincing world image."[33] According to Erikson, adolescents typically seek out such ideas in "religion and politics, the arts and sciences, the stage and fiction."[34] Sadow sought out this system of ideas through the shelter and his academic courses.

While Sadow's "addiction" to the Harvard Square Shelter ebbed over the course of his college career, his passion for combating the societal issues that contribute to homelessness did not. He regards his current work as a community organizer as having grown directly from his work at the Harvard Square Shelter and noted that the shelter was "one of the most important things I did in my life. I would be a completely different person doing completely different things if it weren't for my experience at the shelter."

In previous writings, I have described the college years as representing an important developmental moment in which young adults are seeking out new influences and experiences to inform their worldviews. The particular influences and experiences they encounter during college can have a powerful influence on the types of adults they will ultimately become.[35] From Sadow's perspective, this was certainly the case when he looks back on his own career trajectory. Moreover, his desire to *seek out* such influences and experiences explains the tremendous energy and passion with which he threw himself into his volunteer work at the Harvard Square Shelter.

Sadow's trajectory and commitment to the Harvard Square Shelter are notable but not unique. Over the course of this year-long study, several Harvard students' commitment to the shelter ballooned to similar heights. Harvard junior Amanda Mooney grew up in suburban Michigan, the daughter of two physicians, and aspired to go to medical school herself. At the beginning of 2008–09 school year, Mooney described her extracurricular time as divided between the shelter and her a cappella singing group: "I spend a lot of time at the shelter, but I probably spend more time singing with the Veritones. And I love those people dearly, and they're my family." By the spring, however, Mooney's commitment to the shelter had eclipsed her other priorities: "If I had to choose between spending time on work or at a gig or at the shelter, it's no contest any more." She admitted to spending "most of my waking hours thinking about the shelter, reading shelter emails, at the shelter studying and doing laundry, and talking to other directors who happen to be there."

Like a number of the other most engaged volunteers, Mooney had also taken to stopping by the shelter at night on her way home from dinner or the library. In her words, "I think it's important to be around. Simply, I think that it really shows people that you care. And, that's how you can build meaningful relationships." Similar to junior Nathan Small, Mooney invoked what Clary and Snyder would characterize as a social-adjustive function to explain her deepening commitment to the Harvard Square Shelter.[36] While still studious, Mooney admitted to spending less time now on her pre-medical coursework "because what I learn in the shelter is so much more pertinent to what I want to do."

There is little doubt that all of Mooney's time at the shelter resulted in deeper relationships with the homeless men and women staying there. One of the homeless men who stayed at the shelter this past winter, Mike Andretti, offered the following description of a conversation with a Harvard student that had stuck in his memory.

> "With a girl named Amanda and [about] music. Well, I like music, and she liked music, so we just talked about a lot of music. And then I told her I made a song for my grandmother when she passed away, and I told it to her, and she said it made her day a lot better. I write a lot of music. That's the only thing that keeps me going through the day is writing."

It was clear that this conversation mattered to Andretti, and, in fact, later in the shelter season, Mooney was able to draw upon her relationship with him to dissuade him from picking a fight with another homeless man, as he was threatening to do.

Another homeless man staying at the Harvard Square Shelter credited Mooney's support with helping him move forward out of homelessness. In Mooney's words:

> "We had this guest. He's not staying with us any more because he got into a transitional program. His name is Mark Mantsur. And he was trying to recover from certain addictions and trying to get back on his feet as a trucker and just rebuild his life. And every day I just talked to him for five minutes about his goals, and [would] be like, 'You can do this!' Like, 'I see how determined you are.' Like, 'I believe in you.' You know? And when he left, I wasn't there, but the directors put in a note, being like Mark Mantsur got into his transitional program, and he wants to thank all of us for what we've done, especially Amanda. And, I was like, what? I didn't do anything. But that really made me realize that encouragement is enough. And believing in someone is enough if you can be genuine about it. That's what I think that we have to offer."

Clearly, Mooney's commitment and passion for her work at the Harvard Square Shelter were not lost on the homeless men and women staying there. Likewise, Mooney felt like she was gaining enormously from the experience as well. In response to a question about how she would feel when the shelter closed for the season in April, Mooney responded, "Devastated. I will feel absolutely devastated. I can't even think about it. But thank God I have another year. I can't even handle that thought." Similar to Rusty Sadow a decade before her, Mooney's addiction to the shelter seemed to be full-blown. And like Sadow, Mooney's addiction came about, in part, because she was utilizing the shelter as a tool for resolving the adolescent identity crisis that Erikson characterized as centered upon the questions, "Who am I?" and "What role will I play in the world?"[37]

While Mooney's addiction was full-blown, two Harvard freshmen showed signs of a *burgeoning* addiction to the Harvard Square Shelter. In September 2008, Ashwin Ganguli arrived at Harvard for his freshman year from Bangalore, India. A computer science major, he also wrote poetry and drew. Similar to his American peers, Ganguli's involvement with the Harvard Square Shelter began as a result of his shock at the homeless men and women congregated in Harvard Square:

> "The first night I was in college, I went to buy something at CVS [Pharmacy], and I went out there around 11 p.m. I was working on a drawing — a sketch — and I needed a ruler. I saw someone else, and we were just hanging out, walking around, and then I saw someone lying on the ground, and it wasn't so cold then, but it was getting colder, and where do they go? I felt angry, and at first I felt really sad. I felt super sad about it."

Here, Ganguli offered what Clary and Snyder describe as a value-expressive explanation for his commitment to the shelter, or what Brewer, Selden and Facer characterize as a "Samaritan" response.[38] Of course, Ganguli had witnessed homelessness in his native India, but he saw the situations as different. Ganguli explained that "Very few people die because they're homeless in India." Bangalore's tropical climate means that no one risks freezing to death by sleeping outside, and, according to Ganguli, in India, "If someone doesn't have a home, you go to the roadside and build like a hut. Or you get a huge piece of pipe, like the really big ones, and you find some sheets to cover the front up, and you live inside." Perhaps surprisingly, this teenager from a developing country was shocked and dismayed by the poverty he witnessed in Cambridge, Massachusetts.

Ganguli's decision to volunteer at the Harvard Square Shelter also emerged from his desire to do something "real." In his words, as a college student, "There's so much work, but none of it is really significant in the real sense. So I definitely felt like I needed a place where I could really help make a difference." In search of such a place, Ganguli signed up for a Friday overnight shift at the Harvard Square Shelter.

In a follow-up interview with Ganguli in March, his deepening passion for the shelter was evident. Though only responsible for a weekly overnight shift on Friday nights, Ganguli admitted that he had taken to stopping by the shelter several times during the week. In his words, "If I had enough sleep and enough time to get work done, I would probably go back in every day." He offered as an example an evening earlier in the week in which he had stopped by the shelter after dinner:

"One of directors was going out for Street Team, and he was going out alone. I had never done that before, so I just joined him. We got back at 11 p.m. I was doing some dishes, and all of a sudden it was the overnight shift. So I decided to stay back from 12 midnight to 3 a.m. because they were short one volunteer."

When adding these types of drop-ins to his regular overnight shift, Ganguli estimated that he spends 30 hours a week at the shelter: "Regardless of which shift I'm doing, or who I'm going to be working with, or what shift I'm working, [I know] it's going to be really exciting, really fun." Further evidence of Ganguli's passion for his work at the shelter was his certainty that "I'm going to be [volunteering] at the shelter for the next three years for sure." Midway through his freshman year, he applied to become a shelter supervisor and was undoubtedly on his way towards becoming one of the shelter's student-directors.

Another freshman volunteer, Nancy Mellor, also showed signs of her passion for the shelter developing into a full-blown addiction. Mellor was born and raised in a rural Ohio community that she described as "completely White, completely Catholic, and we're all of German heritage." In explaining her motivation to work at the shelter, Mellor offered the following description of the community:

"It's diehard Republican. They don't believe in any type of welfare programs. They just think that people should get up and go to McDonald's and get a job. And I don't agree with that. And I don't know exactly where I stand on the issues, and I think this will be a better opportunity for me to kind of make out why people are homeless. And what are the most effective ways to help them. That's kind of what I want to get out of it."

Here, Mellor expressed doubts about the most prevalent perspectives on homelessness in her hometown, but she by no means characterized herself as the town's liberal outcast. She appreciated the values her hometown has instilled in her, considered herself a devout Catholic, and served as a leader for Harvard's campus pro-life movement. After much deliberation, she voted for the Republican John McCain over Barack Obama in the 2008 presidential elections.

Yet Mellor had chosen to see her time at Harvard as an opportunity to learn about aspects of the world from which she was sheltered in rural Ohio. She considered volunteering at the Harvard Square Shelter an opportunity to learn more about poverty and inequality in America. In this way, Mellor characterized herself as motivated by what Clary and Snyder describe as a knowledge function — a desire to deepen her understanding of a particular aspect of the world.[39] In fact, Mellor said as much when she explained that her goals for her time at Harvard "go back to understanding. Understanding people, understanding the homeless . . . I don't know what I'm going to do with that, but I'm going to know stuff." Similar to several of the other students, Mellor utilized the Harvard Square Shelter as a means of pondering the "big questions" on her mind.[40]

In pursuit of this goal, Mellor signed up for an overnight shift at the shelter. She considered that she chose an overnight shift because "they said that was when the kids had the most interaction, as far as sitting down and being able to talk or watch a movie with the guests." Midway through her freshman year, Mellor added a second weekly shift to her schedule by signing up to staff the shelter's Resource Advocacy table from 7 to 11 p.m. on Tuesday nights. Mellor said of this decision:

> "I wanted to make it a little bit more real, I guess, like helping them to get back on their feet. I like it a lot. It's awesome! It's terrifying because it is their lives, and I don't want to mess up. There are so many resources out there. It is just a matter of finding them and maneuvering through the paperwork. . . . I'm nervous, but it's really good."

In these words, Mellor's enthusiasm for her work at the shelter is evident. And at the conclusion of her freshman year, she displayed all the signs of a burgeoning addiction: "I think every time I go to the shelter, I am always excited to go there. [It's] not a relief because it's work to be there, but enjoyable work." Mellor continued:

> "I know this is something I want to keep doing. I want to do it for all four years, and for the summer I want to work at the St. James Homeless Shelter in Boston. I just feel like, for the most part, these people just need a step; they just need one boost to know that these resources are out there for them and they can get back on their feet."

Mellor was already certain she would continue working at the Harvard Square Shelter for the remainder of her college career and admitted that she could envision herself becoming a supervisor or director at the shelter in the years ahead. Like junior Amanda Mooney, freshman Ashwin Ganguli and alumnus Rusty Sadow, Nancy Mellor found her work at the Harvard Square Shelter to be among the most rewarding and exciting ways she could spend her time. For her as well, this excitement was generated, in large part, by the role that the shelter played in helping her to move beyond the parochial view of the world offered by her hometown and develop her own understanding of how the world works and her role in it.

DIVING IN HEADLONG

What impact did all of this youthful enthusiasm have upon the homeless men and women staying at the Harvard Square Homeless Shelter? Harvard junior Larry Yoon believed that the volunteers' fresh energy is what makes the shelter such a great place for homeless men and women to stay. According to Yoon:

> "People are idealistic because they're not there every day, because they haven't been doing this for years. They're not jaded. They're not cynical about this. They're open to talking. They're willing to put in extra effort. . . . I think that's kind of more important than the warm bed, that sense of caring and compassion that seems to be a lot more apparent at the Harvard Square Shelter than at any other shelter."

Yoon's perspective was shared by several of the shelter's alumni. Rusty Sadow, the community organizer described earlier in this chapter, observed that the shelter's student-run structure meant that "our folks were inexperienced, [and] institutional knowledge was lost, but I think the truth is that the volunteers coming at it fresh meant there was very little burn-out."[41] As an example of the freshness with which volunteers approached their work at the shelter, Sadow recalled his "long, drawn-out relationship with Ashoke."

Ashoke was a homeless man from Bangladesh who claimed to come from a wealthy family. Rendering this claim believable was his excellent, formal English that sounded like it came straight out of a British private school. Ashoke appeared at the Harvard Square Shelter during Sadow's undergraduate days, and the two became close. As Sadow noted, "In a different circumstance, if we hadn't met at the shelter, he might be someone I would be friends with." The other homeless men and women staying at the shelter detested Ashoke, but Sadow chalked up their dislike to Ashoke's obvious preference for talking to the shelter's volunteers over the other homeless men and women staying at the shelter.

After several months at the shelter, Ashoke was arrested for what he claimed was a minor crime and sent to a displaced persons camp in Louisiana. During his several years of incarceration, Sadow exchanged a number of letters with Ashoke and, from time to time, included some money for prison-related purchases. Ashoke returned to Boston after several years of incarceration, got a job working in a car-rental agency, and then unfortunately suffered a massive brain hemorrhage. Sadow visited him at Massachusetts General Hospital while Ashoke was recovering from surgery.

A few months later, Ashoke asked Sadow to accompany him to court for what he described as a standard immigration hearing. There, Sadow learned that, over the past several months, Ashoke had been stalking and harassing a woman who had broken up with him after a few dates. Sadow also learned that the charge for which Ashoke had been sent to Louisiana involved molesting a 16-year-old girl. "In retrospect," Sadow admitted, "he was very good at manipulating me, and I was open to that." The hearing that Ashoke had described as a mere formality turned out to be a deportation hearing, and, at its conclusion, Sadow recalled that immigration officials "locked him up and took him away, and that was the last I heard of Ashoke."

Looking back on his dealings with Ashoke, Sadow acknowledged that Ashoke "was a chronic liar and I believed too many of them." However, Sadow offered this tale from his college days to make a point about the open-hearted nature of the Harvard Square Shelter's volunteers:

> "I talk now about Ashoke manipulating me, and you know I kind of approach it with that kind of cynicism, which is what anybody would do who is a professional social services worker. But none of us approached it that way. We took people at face value and treated them as humans. And I think that's what made it a decent place to be."

Here, Sadow suggested that the openness with which the Harvard students at the shelter approach their interactions with the homeless is an attitude truly unavailable to professional service workers.[42] The vast majority of professionals have heard too many stories already, been manipulated too many times, and had their heartstrings pulled in too many different directions to sit down with a homeless man or woman and listen to their stories without skepticism or judgment. This guardedness is by no means a character flaw, but rather the protective measure that, as Sadow noted, any professional would take to keep doing the good work that they do day after day.[43] Helen Van Anglen, a shelter volunteer in the early 1990s who went on to found a homeless shelter for victims of domestic violence, agreed that "Most people who work in shelters end up at this point where they end up disbelieving anything that a homeless person tells you about their past."

Sadow, having worked as a community organizer for the past decade, recognized that guardedness within himself:

"I'm much more conservative and risk-averse now than I was then. In many ways, I'm wiser and understand more about people. And that would have hampered me from doing the kind of work that I did back then. You know, I just dove right into it unabashedly without any reservations. And I wouldn't do that now. And I've absolutely no regrets about doing that, and I'm grateful that I did it back then. So anything that I've learned since then, it would have ruined my experience."

In short, Sadow asserted that the passion and idealism with which he approached his interactions with the Harvard Square Shelter's homeless guests are traits unique to that period of his life. Believing wholeheartedly in the homeless men and women he encountered required the optimism, idealism and naivety that are characteristic of emerging adulthood and which begin to fade away shortly thereafter.[44] Evidence for this perspective can be found in research by numerous scholars that younger volunteers report closer relationships with their clients than do middle-aged or older volunteers.[45]

How does this unrestrained passion and idealism play out each night inside the shelter? Harvard senior Lissette McDonald described an overnight shift from the winter of 2008 when a homeless woman confided in her about having been abused by her ex-boyfriend. When the woman began to cry, McDonald broke one of the shelter's policies and asked if she would like a hug. The woman nodded. As McDonald recalled:

> "I remember just sitting there with her in my arms, leaning her head on my shoulder. And here she is, probably this woman in her thirties. I didn't know exactly what to say. I just sat there and listened to her for a long time, and I don't think it helped anything, but I think it helped that night. And another director came down, and we talked to her, and I remember her thanking me for the hug, and that that meant a lot to her. But that was a tough situation because I'm not in any way trained, and I don't even begin to know where you would help someone. But listening is something that I can do, and that's something I learned quickly."

Here, McDonald described herself as becoming emotionally caught up in the struggles of a homeless woman staying at the shelter. The Harvard Square Shelter, like any shelter, has policies about physical contact with the guests, but McDonald — an untrained young adult — offered the human connection that this particular woman may have needed at that moment more than anything else.

In suggesting here that McDonald acted differently than most professional social services workers would have in that particular situation, I do not intend to hold up one as right and the other as wrong. Rather, I am suggesting that — as an emerging adult — McDonald was able to act in a way that an older professional simply could not. If that hug was precisely what the homeless woman needed at that particular moment, the developmental moment in which McDonald was doing this work allowed her to offer a type of interaction that cannot be found in other, more professionally run homeless shelters.

Harvard senior Robert Vozar described a different type of emotional connection with a homeless man staying at the shelter. Lee, a homeless man with whom he had grown close, tested positive for drugs one evening. The Harvard Square Shelter policy calls for an automatic two-week bar in those circumstances, and it was left to Vozar to break the bad news to Lee. What was worse, because the shelter was closing for the season in less than two weeks, Lee's ban effectively meant a ban until the following November when the shelter re-opened.

"It was one of those moments when it's clear what your responsibility is, but it's just upsetting to do it," Vozar recalled. Lee stormed out of the shelter in anger when he heard the news, leaving all of his belongings behind in his locker. Knowing that Lee would have to come back to the shelter to collect his belongings, Vozar wrote him a long note that he tucked into the pocket of Lee's backpack. According to Vozar, the note read something to the effect of, "Lee, I've really enjoyed hanging out with you. I'm really sorry to do this. I'm really sorry about the way things ended this season, but I have no choice." The two didn't cross paths again until the following November when the shelter re-opened for the winter. In regards to the note, Vozar related that Lee "never mentioned it to me this fall, but this fall he greeted me really warmly, and we shot the shit for like two hours the first night he was back. Which was great."

You would be hard-pressed to find any professional literature suggesting that social service workers write letters of apology to clients they have had to discipline, and it seems likely that most professional service workers would react to such an unpleasant task with emotional distance — if only out of the knowledge that this will not be the last homeless person with whom they have an unpleasant encounter.[46] For Vozar, however, a non-professional, his intuitive response was to treat Lee like a friend or family member with whom he was fighting rather than a client being disciplined. In so doing, he managed to preserve some semblance of Lee's dignity.

In describing what is so special about the Harvard Square Homeless Shelter, a formerly homeless woman, Lucy Draper, described the shelter and its student-volunteers as conveying "a non-professional family atmosphere." She added that "I think that the difference between some place like this and a professional shelter is that everyone there is open to believing the greatest possibilities for people rather than seeing their limitations."

Not every example of these young adults opening their hearts to the shelter's homeless guests is so emotionally fraught. Amanda Mooney, the Harvard junior profiled earlier in the chapter, described a homeless man with whom she had grown close asking her out of the blue if she had ever been in love. According to Mooney, her initial reaction was "Oh my God!" but she quickly ascertained he "wasn't trying to pick me up" or "wheedle information out of me." Mooney confessed that she *did* know what it felt like to be in love, and then proceeded to listen:

> "He just wanted to talk about himself. And so I just listened to what was going on with him and his girlfriend. And how their

relationship was going to play out you know, thinking about parole and thinking about where he was going and trying to rebuild his life. And you have conversations like that a lot. But just for someone to start it off so frank, it showed a lot of trust and vulnerability. And, it really meant something to me to be able to be that person to somebody."

It is likely that the majority of professionals working in homeless shelters would have cut off such a conversation at the first question. Out of a need to protect their own identity, or as a result of too many prior clients who *were* making a pass at them, the typical social services worker simply cannot make him or herself available for such conversations. But Mooney, in contrast, was genuinely moved by the vulnerability with which she was entrusted. Her genuine willingness (and even enthusiasm) to play the role of listener in this particular man's life was no doubt recognized and appreciated.

DOWNSIDES

In this chapter, I have sought to depict the passionate idealism of the Harvard students operating the Harvard Square Shelter as a tremendous asset in their ability to support the homeless men and women who stay at the shelter. However, this passion for supporting the men and women at their shelter is not without its downsides. Kathryn Tobin, a Harvard senior and student-director, described a negative interaction from 2008 between herself and one of the homeless men, Philip, in the shelter's Work Contract program. Philip, a recovering alcoholic, was working two jobs simultaneously in an effort to get his life back on track. He worked a daily shift at a local Wal-Mart from 5 a.m.–5 p.m., and then went to the dockyards in Quincy, Massachusetts where he had an under-the-table position unloading freight until nearly midnight.

As a result of his employment, Philip was granted an extended, ten-week stay at the shelter and assigned to work with Tobin to work towards securing permanent housing. Because he was working so late each night, Tobin gave Philip her cell phone number in case he needed to let her know he would be late for the shelter's midnight curfew or if he had to miss a scheduled meeting due to work at the dockyards. Unfortunately, Philip's alcoholism meant that once every few weeks he would go to a bar and drink himself into oblivion. One night, Philip called Tobin's cell phone intoxicated and upset. She recalled:

> "The professional thing for me to do at that point would have been to hang up the phone. But for some reason I didn't make that decision, and I kept trying to calm him down and trying to reason with him. And he launched into this story. He'd been in the first Gulf War, and he described the rape of a local woman to me, ostensibly I guess by people in his unit. And it was incredibly traumatizing, and that was pretty formative in terms of realizing that number one I had made this huge error in not hanging up the phone, and that maybe professionalism does come first, and secondly that perhaps this is a signal that I cared so much about his success that it was impacting my ability to make professional decisions."

In this situation, Tobin's unchecked emotional investment in working with Philip allowed a situation to unfold that was in neither of their best interests. The next morning, Philip called the Harvard Square Shelter and left an extensive apology for Tobin on the shelter voicemail, but, after that, she chose to include another, male student in all of her meetings with Philip. Here, perhaps, was a situation where the emotional and physical boundaries established by a professional social worker might have been best for all involved.

AH, YOUTH

In describing a few of the accomplishments of the Harvard students operating the Harvard Square Shelter and the varied ways in which they forged deep and genuine connections with the homeless men and women they are serving, I by no means intend to suggest that these Harvard students are in some way more talented or gifted than the dedicated professionals serving the homeless and other marginalized groups in a myriad of capacities. Rather, I am suggesting that these college-aged volunteers — at the crossroads between adolescence and emerging adulthood — are doing this work within a unique developmental period that allows them some advantages simply not available to more veteran service providers. Specifically, their optimism, idealism and relative freedom from "adult" responsibilities allow these young adults to throw themselves wholeheartedly into endeavors such as the Street Team or Lex Obain's college admissions process.[47] Moreover, because the shelter's college-aged volunteers regard these endeavors as opportunities to consider the big questions central to their own development, they approach these endeavors, not only whole-heartedly, but with energy, enthusiasm, and passion. As a result, the homeless men and women who are on the receiving end of this energy and enthusiasm do not have to feel as if they are anyone's burden or charity case. They know that the young adults they encounter at the shelter are not getting paid for their time, and thus can be assured that the energy and enthusiasm conveyed by these young adults is genuine.[48]

What is inevitable, however, is that many of these Harvard students — the ones who go on to work professionally on behalf of marginalized communities — will also go on themselves to develop thicker skins and a greater commitment to professional distance. Even by the end of their college careers, one can hear the rumblings of this thicker skin emerging. Rusty Sadow, the 2000 Harvard graduate who characterized himself as addicted to the shelter, offered the following description of his very last shift at the Harvard Square Homeless Shelter:

> "It was spring break of my senior year, and I was sticking around to help. Everyone had left, so it was a skeleton staff. There was this [homeless] woman, Michelle . . . [who] would not leave. And everyone was gone, and she was just taking her time packing her stuff in bags, repacking her stuff in bags. I said, 'Michelle, you have to go.' And then she accused me of harassing her, spit in my face, and called the police on me. And I thought, 'I've had enough of this.' That was actually my last shift at the shelter."

A community organizer for the past decade, Sadow has continued to work tirelessly for a world in which resources are distributed more equitably. By his own admission, however, there is a clear difference between his 30-year-old self and his 19-year-old self who "just dove right into it unabashedly without any reservations."

Several of the Harvard seniors involved with the shelter during the 2008–09 academic year described similar feelings of burn-out. For example, senior Robert Vozar described his discouragement as a sophomore when a homeless man lost his shelter bed for turning up drunk to the shelter but that "Now I've seen more people go through, and you get more used to different things happening to different people." Senior Kathryn Tobin admitted in April of 2009 that "I think I feel burnt out in general." She noted that a homeless man, Terence, who had secured permanent housing the previous year was right back in the shelter this year and that "To see him come back this year after losing his housing that he had gotten last year, I was really quite disillusioned at that point with how difficult it is to transition people out of homelessness." Junior Nathan Small, who had been working at the shelter since his sophomore year of high school, admitted that he sometimes felt a "sort of cynicism that I try to banish away a lot." As these students progressed towards graduation and the real world beyond that, the optimism and idealism that are a staple of this developmental moment were already starting to fade. Fortunately, just as Pastor Fred Reisz had envisioned nearly 30 years earlier, a whole reservoir of fresh-faced shelter volunteers were waiting to take their places.

Several years after graduating, alumnus Rusty Sadow returned to the Harvard Square Shelter to help out over Harvard's winter break What he discovered horrified him:

> "I agreed to volunteer an overnight shift. And I went, and I was horrified that this place was being run by such a young group of people who knew nothing about anything. The two women in charge were just so young, and everything about their demeanor, about the way they would give instructions, about their bearing, about their flippant attitudes, and I was like, 'Oh my God, I can't believe this was me!' I wasn't any older, and I don't think I was any more mature. And when adults came to the shelter, I wonder if they thought the same thing."

Like Sadow, several other alumni look back on their college-age selves with amazement at their audacity in believing they could operate a homeless shelter. Ward Welburn noted, laughing, that "Harvard is full of people who have incredibly high opinions of their self-worth. So I was quite clear that I was more than capable of the job." Amelia Ginsberg admitted: "Maybe it was a little bit Harvardian in thinking we could offer transitional services and really keep out folks who are on heroin or some of those things. But that's also just kind of youth." Likewise, Dr. Aaron Dutka expressed astonishment now at his role in running the Harvard Square Shelter: "I'm surprised we had the ambition to think we could even do that." Activist and writer Jim Hightower once said, "Those who say it can't be done should not interrupt those who are doing it."[49] Fortunately, for the homeless men and women who pass through the Harvard Square Shelter each winter, the young adults they encounter there cannot be swayed by the older, more cautious future versions of themselves. Instead, the homeless men and women staying at the shelter encounter passionate Harvard students who possess the optimism and idealism to believe they can play a role in combating homelessness. And, while there are many misfires, there are also successes each year as impressive as those of Lex and Francine.

Chapter 4

Seeking Connections

For a week every March, the CASPAR Homeless Shelter, a large "wet" homeless shelter on the other side of Cambridge, hosts a group of students from the University of Wisconsin who come to Boston over their spring break to visit the city and volunteer at CASPAR. Meghan Goughan, CASPAR's Assistant Director, noted that many of her clients enjoy the opportunity to converse with these Wisconsin students. As Goughan explained, "They can tell their story that maybe we all on staff have heard a hundred times. They can tell it for the hundred and first time without people being like, 'I gotta go run and do something.'" Goughan added:

> "Who doesn't love it when people ask them questions? When they feel comfortable, and when they feel like it's not being asked for some kind of game, being entered into a data system. It's because the kids are genuinely curious and want to know and take an interest in this person, if only for the hour they're sitting with them. I think a lot of people enjoy that."

This scenario that Goughan described plays out seven nights a week all winter long at the Harvard Square Shelter. Moreover, with nearly 100 different students working dinner, overnight, and breakfast shifts, the homeless men and women at the shelter have the opportunity to tell their stories over and over again. Shelter alumna Helen Van Anglen noted that this aspect of the Harvard Square Shelter is no small benefit. According to Van Anglen,

> "People don't usually get to tell their stories. And it's not unique to homeless people. Very, very few of us get to really tell our story about how we got to where we are and to tell it again and again, and rewrite it, and figure out, and connect the dots differently, or maybe go deeper and reveal something that we didn't reveal last time."

The Harvard Square Shelter offers precisely this opportunity to the homeless men and women who stay there.

One could see this opportunity play out in a conversation this past winter between Wellesley College sophomore Charlotte Wu and a homeless man named Nat. According to Wu:

> "There's a guest at the shelter whose name is Nat. He's one of the guests that I am particularly close to just because he's extra friendly to all of the staff members there. And I just remember one day he and I were just sitting down talking and he was just telling me about his day, the way he always does. And he was telling me that he went to the doctor's office today to see them. And I was like, 'Oh, are you okay? How are you feeling?' And he was like . . . 'Oh, I have HIV; I'm HIV positive.' And . . . he was telling me about how it affects his life especially as a homeless person. But it was more along the lines of how having HIV has affected his family life because now he's divorced from his wife, and he doesn't see his son that often. And how that one test escalated into this bigger problem. And it was a huge reality check for me."

In this conversation, Nat took advantage of an empathetic audience to reflect upon some of the substantial challenges in his life.

A second student's description of a conversation with Nat underscores Van Anglen's point about the value of telling one's story over and over again. Harvard senior Lissette McDonald also described a conversation from this past winter in which Nat "felt comfortable enough to tell me his story, that he had AIDS and his story about that. It was very sad, but it was nice that I had got to the point where he felt comfortable enough to confide in me." As a result of the nearly 100 different students necessary to keep the shelter running, homeless men like Nat have the opportunity to continually find fresh ears for the complex problems with which they are struggling.

EXTRAORDINARY LISTENING

Shelter alumna Anusha Ghosh recalled that the "unspoken rule" at the Harvard Square Shelter was that a volunteer's top priority should be "sitting down and listening to someone and what their story was." She noted that a number of her most meaningful shelter memories were of "late night conversations with people as they were coming in or people who couldn't sleep, or wanted to have that company." And, in fact, Ghosh — now an immigrant rights attorney in New York City — credited her experiences at the shelter with helping her to see "the kind of difference in a person's life you can make by just listening."

Similar to Ghosh, Harvard junior Nathan Small noted that "Rarely will we have any answers, or be able to relate to the specific experiences that these individuals have had. But it's just sort of about listening and being able to create conversation, and that's the best part of someone's day." Likewise, Junior Amanda Mooney acknowledged that "I would say a lot of the conversations are less a conversation than listening, to tell you the truth. A lot of the time you get talked at, and I think that's just as important." Mooney offered as an example a homeless man who had spent 45 minutes a few days earlier taking her all of the way through his family tree. According to Mooney, "You know, he might be telling you about his family tree but also he'll slip in, 'Oh, I am a recovering alcoholic and I've been clean for ten days.'" In those types of conversations, Mooney explained that her primary goal was simply to demonstrate that "somebody cares enough to sit down for 45 minutes and look them in the eye. Even if it's just smiling or nodding and saying, 'I'm sorry,' I hope it's cathartic in some small way."

A number of Harvard students explicitly recognized that their youth and inexperience offered them some advantages as listeners. Junior Jerry Chen said, "We offer drinks, food, stuff like that, but that's not anything that these guests can't get elsewhere. But still they decide to come here because we are student-based and we all have this, I guess, what other programs call 'youthful enthusiasm,' and we're willing to just sit down and have one-on-one conversations and many times just get really deep with the guests."

As evidence of this willingness, Harvard freshman Ashwin Ganguli talked about fighting through sleepiness on his overnight shifts to engage with the shelter's night owls at two in the morning. Ganguli admitted that sometimes "I wish I could stop having this conversation right now and go back to sleep. But I just try to keep in mind that there are a lot of people who wouldn't want to sit down and talk to them. I just try to listen to them." Junior Jerry Chen described a similar situation from the previous winter as he was closing up the shelter at the tail-end of an overnight shift:

> "I remember last year, a guest came in to claim stuff and this was at 8:30 in the morning. I went up to the vestibule and I started talking to her and she just had a lot of things to talk about, and she just kept talking. At first I was like, 'Okay, I'm sorry what can I do for you? Is there anything I could help with?' But after an hour and a half, it was 10 o'clock and I was going to be late for class. I just wanted to kick her out, but I felt [like] really what's the right thing to do here? And it was an internal conflict in that situation in being patient, and that's the kind of thing I struggle with all the time. I ended up waiting for her. I was a little late to class, but it was fine."

In these descriptions, both Ganguli and Chen chose to prioritize the role of listener over their own needs to go to sleep and class.

The students' willingness to serve as extraordinary listeners is not lost on the homeless men and women who stay at the Harvard Square Shelter. Joe Presley, who stayed at the shelter during two years of homelessness in the early 1990s, recalled:

> "When I was in rehab, I was having a difficult time finding housing and stuff like that. And there were times when I just wanted to give up. And they would sit there, and they'd talk to me. You know, I've seen them up with people till three in the morning just talking to them, and it's really very nice."

Nineteen-year-old Mike Andretti noted that "They're cool. Like they talk to you, so you don't feel lonely." He added that when a problem comes up that he wants to talk about, "If they don't have time, they'll make time." Other Harvard Square Shelter volunteers described additional ways in which they served as extraordinary listeners. Sophomore Antonia

Garcia-Brown explained that "I also go out of my way to sort of project non-judgmentalism." Perhaps as a result of this attitude, Garcia-Brown described a 21-year-old homeless woman who confided in her about a recent miscarriage. Garcia-Brown said, "Usually when I'm having a conversation with someone I just try to be a really good listener and be supportive. Focusing on what I'm trying to do usually gives me a weird sort of distance from what's going on."

Senior Hope Franklin described active listening combined with some perseverance and determination:

> There was one guest . . . [who] can come off as very rude, very terse. He's a little antisocial, I don't remember if he sat with other guests or not. I have this thing where I like to try to break through to people, and connect with them. It's like this personal challenge, and I find it satisfying . . . He was always walking around the shelter in a bike helmet. One day I asked him, 'So do you bike?' It was raining. 'How do you deal with this rain?' I questioned him a little bit, and he kind of warmed up to me. At the end, he came over as he was leaving and said, 'Have a good day and stay dry.' It was very short but very nice."

Here, Franklin described the Harvard Square Shelter at its best. More than just being willing listeners, the students who kept the shelter running were actively in search of these types of connections and genuinely thrilled when they occur. Looking back on her own volunteer days at the shelter, alumna Helen Van Anglen described the experience of being a confidante to several homeless men and women as "a gift in many ways." The fact that so many of the Harvard Square Shelter's volunteers look upon these interactions as a gift rather than a burden is, in large part, what makes it the "Cadillac of homeless shelters" in the eyes of so many of the homeless men and women who stay there.

EXTRAORDINARY LISTENING AND ADOLESCENCE

In describing the enthusiasm with which many of the Harvard shelter volunteers sought out connections and conversations with the homeless men and women staying there, I do not mean to suggest that these students were in any way more gifted, intelligent, or empathetic than the professional service workers staffing other homeless shelters and soup kitchens. Rather, it is the particular developmental phase in which these college-aged volunteers are situated — on the border between adolescence and emerging adulthood — that makes them uniquely suited to play the roles of listener and confidante.[1]

When sophomore Antonia Garcia-Brown noted that she "project[s] an air of non-judgmentalism" to the homeless men and women she meets at the shelter, Garcia-Brown was not merely describing a personal character trait but also a more general quality of her developmental phase. In Chapter 3, I noted that psychologist Erik Erikson characterized adolescence as a developmental period in which individuals are seeking to inform their understanding of the world and their role in it.[2] Psychologist James Marcia built upon Erikson's work by describing this identity development process as entailing four stages: diffusion, foreclosure, moratorium and achievement.[3] *Diffusion* describes the stage in which an individual has not yet made any choices about his or her role in the world while *foreclosure* entails simply adopting the beliefs and values of one's parents and other mentors. *Moratorium* is the stage in which an individual is actively exploring different perspectives on the world to inform his or her own worldview, and *achievement* occurs when individuals make firm commitments to a particular worldview and self-concept.

The majority of the college-aged volunteers at the Harvard Square Homeless Shelter might be characterized as in the moratorium stage of identity development. In fact, a central motivation for their volunteer work was to gain more experiences and perspectives through which to interpret the world. As a result, many of these volunteers were not only eager to hear the stories and perspectives of the shelter's homeless guests, but they did so with an air of "non-judgmentalism" due, in large part, to having not yet established firm conclusions about how the world works. Certainly, college students are capable of being judgmental about the choices made by others; however, these young adults were able to listen more openly to the perspectives of the shelter's homeless guests than are older professionals who have long since moved past their adolescent identity crises and possess firm convictions about how the world works.

A second reason the college students volunteering at the shelter were able to be extraordinary listeners is because, for these young adults, there was also a heightened social draw to their conversations with homeless men and women. A number of scholars have found that younger volunteers report greater relationship motivation than older volunteers.[4] In other words, younger volunteers are more drawn to volunteer work by the possibility of establishing social relationships with the clients they are serving. One could hear this motivation, for example, in junior Amanda Mooney's explanation that "It feels good when a guest approaches you to talk, just as much as they feel good when they can talk to someone. And it is kind of a little bit of an affirmation that what you're doing is mattering to someone." Likewise, alumna Helen Van Anglen recalled that part of the draw of the shelter "was that there were people who were interested in me. Who was I? Why did I want to be down there?" Clary and Snyder would likely characterize these young adults as motivated to volunteer, at least in part, by a social-adjustive function; in other words, as a means of expanding their social networks.[5]

THE GIFT OF WISDOM

CASPAR's Meghan Goughan offered a third way in which the developmental phase of the Harvard Square Shelter's college-aged volunteers allowed them to be extraordinary listeners. According to Goughan, a crucial ingredient in the shelter's success is that "people want to share their stories and might feel more comfortable sharing their stories with someone who is 20 [rather] than someone who is 40." She described the imparting of wisdom as "societally something that older people share with younger people" and that such a dynamic is tremendously empowering. As Goughan noted, "If people don't feel like they can tell you anything, or that you have anything to learn from them, I think that makes it just a little harder to move folks along." A formerly homeless man, Fred Slomiak, made a nearly identical point:

> "My main beef with a lot of the more structured places, okay, [is] they are always talking *to you*. You can learn in two ways. I can force you to learn my knowledge, or I can cultivate an exchange of ideas, and that's what I think fundamentally the Harvard Square Shelter offers."

As noted in Chapter 2, the juxtaposition of homeless people and Harvard students *could* have been an unmitigated disaster. Many of the students at Harvard come from affluent and insular families, and most are in the process of acquiring the social capital to go on to positions of power, privilege, and prestige. However, the Harvard students operating the shelter are nonetheless still college students — adolescents — and, as a result, their youth and inexperience offers the homeless men and women staying at the Harvard Square Shelter the opportunity to impart advice and offer wisdom.

In reflecting upon some of the advice she has received from homeless men and women at the shelter this past winter, Harvard senior Hope Franklin observed:

"I guess because they are older and I am genuinely curious about how they ended up where they are, where they've been along the way, and maybe they felt some element of that, so felt compelled to share parts of their lives with me as sort of this young adult, still a little unformed, figuring out her way in the world. I guess they felt they could offer their counsel. And also I think they have stories that they want to share."

Here, Franklin described a happy convergence where she was genuinely interested to learn more about the life trajectories of the men and women staying in the Harvard Square Shelter, and, in return, many of these men and women welcomed the opportunity to share the wisdom they had accumulated along the way. Shelter alumna Helen Van Anglen described such a dynamic as "really, really important, and it's something we have systematically stripped from human services. We tend to tell people, work on yourself, fix yourself, and then you can have a positive impact on other people. Which is nuts, and not what motivates people." In other words, Van Anglen sees giving homeless men and women the opportunity to contribute to the well-being of others as a crucial step in moving beyond their own challenges.

Van Anglen's perspective is supported by a robust body of scholarship on self-efficacy. Psychologist Albert Bandura defined self-efficacy as a belief in one's ability to accomplish a particular goal or set of goals.[6] Importantly, Bandura found that people's perceptions of their own efficacy largely determine how much effort they will exert to accomplish a particular goal and how long they will persevere in the face of challenges and obstacles.[7] For individuals contending with homelessness, then, a high sense of self-efficacy is a factor crucial to maintaining the focus and willpower necessary to secure permanent housing. One clear mechanism for strengthening an individual's sense of efficacy is by giving that individual an opportunity to positively influence others.

In Chapter 2, for example, Fred Slomiak described teaching a college student at the Harvard Square Shelter how to play chess. According to Slomiak, that opportunity to be a teacher instilled in him a sense of contributing, and he characterized that simple experience as "the definitive moment" in his ascent out of homelessness. Of course, Slomiak could have taught an older adult how to play chess as easily as a college student, but, as CASPAR Assistant Director Meghan Goughan noted, a more natural dynamic within American culture entails older people offering advice and wisdom to younger people. Moreover, as volunteers, the college students working at the Harvard Square Shelter may simply have more time and interest in sitting down to learn the rules of chess or listening to an hour-long explanation of a particular individual's experiences with AIDS.

So what did this imparting of advice and wisdom look like? This past March, Harvard senior Lissette McDonald accepted a job starting September of 2009 doing breast cancer research at the University of San Francisco. Originally from Vermont, McDonald knew little about the city that would be her new home. When she mentioned her new position to a homeless man at the shelter — an African American man in his mid-fifties — he launched into the role of advice-giver. As McDonald recalls:

> "When I told him that I was going to San Francisco, he was really excited and we talked for a long time, and he was just reminiscing about also living in Seattle for a while. I have family up there, and he was telling me about how you can take the hippie bus up to Seattle and all these great things. Then I was asking him stuff specifically like, 'Where do you recommend living? What neighborhoods?' That's a great conversation and it was really nice. It was sort of [like] he was advising me. It was a great dynamic to have in the shelter."

Here, McDonald described a conversation that was mutually beneficial. The homeless man with whom she was speaking had the opportunity to talk a little about himself and his past experiences as well as to offer McDonald some genuinely useful tips about her soon-to-be home. It was likely this symbiosis that led McDonald to describe the encounter as a "neat conversation" and "a conversation that you could have had in a coffee shop" rather than in a homeless shelter.

Former volunteer Helen Van Anglen and former guest Fred Slomiak would both say that giving homeless men and women the opportunity to be teachers is one of the most important gifts that the shelter volunteers can offer. In her interview at the close of the winter, freshman Nancy Mellor explained that "A lot of the guests love to talk about class conflict and the powers that be — the forces that push down the lower class and hold them in their places." Mellor described a particular homeless woman with whom she spoke often during the winter of 2009 who believed that "the whole economic recession was all orchestrated by the Bush administration." While Mellor had her doubts about such conspiracy theories, she admitted that the homeless men and women she met at the shelter "challenge my views, and when they do that, it is very empowering to know that you're affecting someone. So that's a reason a lot of the volunteers work there. And in return, the guests are people, too, and they want that, too. They want to try to affect us." Here, Mellor expressed her recognition that both the Harvard students and the homeless men and women at the Harvard Square Shelter are interested in affecting one another. As a result, Mellor actively strove "to give them that respect as a person of intelligence, of authority. If I can just be a student and give them the power to be my teacher, then maybe that means something to them."

Not all of the proffered advice was quite so serious. Junior Amanda Mooney noted that she has had hour-long conversations with one particular homeless man about "how to get a guy's attention" as well as "beauty advice which I've sometimes followed and have regretted." She also described examples of "don't eat this, it has this and this in it, from guests who are very into holistic medicine."

Quite a number of the men and women staying at the Harvard Square Shelter tried to help the students there become savvier. Wendy Burrell, the Divinity School student working with the volunteers on reflection, noted that she had overheard homeless men and women saying to the students: "You've got to pay attention to so-and-so; he's trying to pull the wool over your eyes. You guys don't know enough because you're too inexperienced and naive." From Burrell's perspective, those types of conversations between students and the homeless "affirm that we all have something to learn from each other."

Interestingly, several of the men and women staying at the Harvard Square Shelter used the term 'sheltered' to describe the Harvard students as impervious to the world's harsh realities. As a homeless man from this past winter, Frank Green, explained,

"These kids, with no experience in the real world, living sheltered lives . . . think that everybody that walks through the door that they can trust, that they're nice people. Welcome to the real world. You're talking about street people. Some of these people are nasty people. I've been out there, and I know the good ones and the bad ones."

Harvard junior Jerry Chen expressed a similar sentiment when he noted, "These guests are often times just years and years wiser than we are. First of all, they're a whole lot more street smart than we are. I feel so sheltered all the time, for lack of a better word." Junior Amanda Mooney described a homeless man staying at the Harvard Square Shelter who warned her that "The world is an ocean and that there were sharks and stingrays and moray eels out there to get me." In short, a number of the men and women staying at the Harvard Square Shelter saw it as their role to try to enlighten the college students they meet there about the harsh nature of the real world.

Other homeless men and women tried to look out for the student-volunteers in other ways. Senior Kathryn Tobin described a homeless man staying at the shelter who was working two different jobs in order to save money for an apartment. According to Tobin:

"We were talking about his situation, and he's like, 'You work so hard, you look so tired.' And I did look exhausted. I was probably sleeping five hours a night in the spring. But I just thought, this is ridiculous, right? This man worked harder than I will ever work in my entire life, and he felt bad that I was working too hard."

Likewise, Wellesley College sophomore Charlotte Wu commented that, at the conclusion of an overnight shift, numerous men and women would remind her to "get some sleep" or "you look tired." From Wu's perspective, "It's great that they also look out for me" in the same way she tried to look out for them.

Senior Kelly Parker, the shelter's supplies director, is barely over five feet tall, but she was responsible during the 2008–09 academic year for keeping the shelter stocked with groceries. She noted that, when carrying groceries into the shelter, men and women staying in the shelter

"would be like, 'Oh my God, that's so much stuff you're bringing in.'
And they'd always say, 'You're so small, how do you carry all this? You
should have someone help you with that.'" Of course, it is possible that
the homeless men and women at any shelter would express the same
concerns about adult workers exhibiting similar looks of fatigue or
carrying too many groceries. The fact that all of the Harvard Square
Shelter's workers are adolescents, however, seemed to create a comfortable opportunity for the homeless men and women staying there to
express their care and concern. It is no coincidence that students used
phrases like "grandfatherly," "paternal," "elderly," "like a father," and
"trying to give you life advice" to describe the tone and feel of these
types of conversations.

As full-fledged adults, there were also times when the homeless
men and women at the shelter possessed skill-sets that the Harvard
students had not yet mastered. Dr. Aaron Dutka recalled that, during
his volunteering days in the early 1990s, "There was one guy who had
been a chef at the Ritz . . . and when I was a supervisor, he would cook
breakfast in the morning." According to Dr. Dutka, "It started that he
would advise me on how to cook the meals because nobody [had ever]
taught me how to cook for 30 people." While state and shelter policies
prevent assistance in quite so hands-on a fashion today, Harvard junior
Jerry Chen noted similarly that one homeless man from the winter
of 2009 "was this excellent chef" and "some of the tips he gave us are
really good." Likewise, Harvard Divinity School student Wendy Burrell
described working an overnight shift in which she "messed up" the
coffee the following morning. According to Burrell:

> "I had three guests telling me, 'How did you do it? Why did
> you do that?' It wasn't mean. Other people were upset the
> coffee wasn't made, but these people were like, this is how
> you do it. This is a skill you need to have even if you don't
> drink coffee."

While Burrell may have ruffled the feathers of a few people in need of
a morning caffeine jolt, the fact that she gave several other homeless
men the opportunity to serve as teachers was no small gift to them. And
such an opportunity is far less likely to occur in the typical homeless
shelter staffed by a small number of veteran service providers. Looking
back on his own volunteering days, Ward Welburn concurred that the
homeless men and women at the shelter "do in fact take care of us. Very

much so." Likewise, alumna Helen Van Anglen recalled that "I got a lot of wisdom from the people there, and life advice."

Junior Jerry Chen described an incident this past winter in which he sat down with a homeless man who had stayed at the Harvard Square Shelter for several weeks but was now moving into an apartment. The man thanked Chen vociferously for all of his help. According to Chen, he said, "You guys are really just awesome. You help us whenever you can. I can't believe you guys are all volunteers." As the conversation concluded, Chen said that "It was kind of corny, but he gave me a little piece of candy, a cough drop. That was the only thing he had on him, but it was definitely symbolic of something." Though appreciative of all the help he had received from the students, this homeless man intuitively sought to do something to return the favor. Such opportunities to "return the favor" are not readily available in the typical social service setting, but at the Harvard Square Shelter — as a result of the Harvard students' youth and inexperience — such opportunities occur nightly. Recall alumnus Rusty Sadow's observation that "Perhaps our unprofessionalism was what made us such a great place to be, comparatively speaking, if you're homeless." Sadow was referring primarily to the idealistic and open-hearted approach that the Harvard students bring to their interactions with the homeless. Equally important, however, may be the opportunity that the students' "unprofessionalism" provides for the men and women staying at the shelter to serve, in some small way, as teachers, mentors, advisers, and parent-figures.

A TOLERANCE FOR ECCENTRICITY

The long-time director of another Cambridge homeless shelter recently remarked that the Harvard students operating the Harvard Square Shelter "have a tolerance for eccentricity that we don't have. We've seen a lot eccentricity before." What this veteran shelter director was alluding to is that another way in which Harvard students serve as extraordinary listeners is in their willingness to offer tremendous respect, compassion, and patience to homeless men and women contending with mental illness. According to the National Coalition for the Homeless, approximately 16 percent of the adult homeless population suffers from severe mental illnesses such as schizophrenia, bipolar disorder, and post-traumatic stress disorder.[8] In large urban cities like New York and Boston, that figure may be closer to 35 percent.[9] According to sociologist Alisa Lincoln, "For many people with a serious mental illness, being housed has meant accepting being treated like a child."[10] In contrast, at the Harvard Square Shelter, Harvard senior Robert Vozar noted, "There are a bunch of [student] directors who, no matter how *not* with-it someone is, they'll sit with them and listen for hours." And numerous interviews with current volunteers revealed this to be the case.

Junior Larry Yoon explained that a homeless woman, Yolanda, who frequently stays at the shelter, will say things like, "Oh, all these people are stealing from me" or "That Macintosh ad is talking to me." However, Yoon added that "Even when she's not being reasonable, I still want to nod my head and say, what can we do for you? How can I fix that?" Freshman Ashwin Ganguli admitted that "with a lot of guests when I talk to them, it's hard to maintain an entire cohesive conversation because they tend to go on a tangent." Nonetheless, Ganguli credited one homeless man whom he acknowledged was probably "neurologically disconnected" with having "a lot of impressive things to say with respect to biology, and there are a lot of conversations I've had on biology with him." Regarding another homeless man, Ganguli described a rambling conversation about "the concept of time, [and] what time is" but added, "That was really interesting because I never thought about it that way before." If only due to overflowing caseloads, it is difficult to imagine a professional social worker having the time to offer this level of engagement to mentally ill homeless men or so genuinely pondering the points these individuals offer.

Other Harvard students also described themselves as actively seeking to learn from homeless men and women they recognize to be mentally ill. Sophomore Antonia Garcia-Brown described a homeless man approaching her and several other volunteers to warn them that "Just remember, you don't know. You guys came here so you already kind of know that you don't know, but you have to know that you don't really know." Reflecting on the warning, Garcia-Brown described the admonition as "pretty legit advice" and the homeless man who offered it as "kind of crazy, but in a charming way." Likewise, Harvard freshman Nancy Mellor explained that she consciously sought in her interactions with a mentally ill homeless woman "to open myself up to whatever she's saying" so as not to let stereotypes about the homeless or the mentally ill prevent her from really hearing what the woman had to say. Such demonstrations of respect for the homeless mentally ill are particularly important when one considers the finding from a 2007 study that a significant obstacle to connecting the homeless mentally ill with appropriate supports are their previous bad experiences with shelters and other programs.[11]

Perhaps the volunteer who most articulately conveyed these students' success in working with the homeless mentally ill was junior Louis Landau. Landau described the following conversation between himself and a homeless man named Charles suffering from schizophrenia:

> "He comes up to me and says, can I talk to you privately for a bit? And so we step aside and he says, 'So, I'm a paranoid schizophrenic, and I'm also being followed.' And I'm like, okay. So he asked me if I think he has any legal recourse against the people who were following him. And I'm like, 'I'm probably the wrong person to ask.' And so he talks a little bit about how he's being followed, and it's not at all logically inconsistent that someone who is paranoid could also be followed. And then eventually it turns out that he doesn't really mind being followed except in so far as it makes it very hard for him to get over his schizophrenia . . . I basically acknowledged everything he said. He seemed perfectly happy with the conversation."

Here, Landau described a conversation in which he treated a homeless man's paranoid concerns with utter seriousness. An older, professional service worker might have been less willing or able to engage in such a conversation, and in fact Landau observed that the few times "real adults" volunteered on his shift, things didn't go as smoothly. In fact, Landau observed, "In all three cases that have happened, there were almost shouting matches between guests and adults." He surmised that his and the other students' youth "makes us a little less willing to try to impose our wills on the guests whereas if you're the same age as them, you might be much more willing to direct them."

To illustrate his point, Landau described one of the shelter's few "adult" volunteers who got into a yelling match with a homeless woman in the middle of the night over whether or not the door to the women's bathroom could be closed. By shelter policy, the bathroom doors are propped open at night to discourage covert smokers. Leah, a homeless woman staying in the shelter, wanted to close the bathroom door for greater privacy, and the adult volunteer stopped her from doing so. By the time Landau arrived on the scene, the two women were in a yelling match and beginning to wake up the entire shelter. To the frustration of the adult volunteer, Landau immediately suggested that Leah go ahead and close the bathroom door. From his perspective, "Even if she started to smoke in the bathroom, which is pretty unlikely, it's not worth having to shout when 25 people are trying to sleep." The next morning, the adult volunteer angrily confronted Landau for "undermining her authority" and told him she would be praying for him.

Reflecting on that confrontation, Landau suggested: "The adult volunteers are less willing to accommodate seemingly unreasonable demands or to try to calm people down." He described, as a contrast, the other Harvard students on his shift who would make three different grilled cheese sandwiches in three slightly different ways because "there's no real reason *not* to meet such a demand." As Landau noted, "You're up all night. What else are you going to do, right?" As volunteers whose sole goal is to support the homeless men and women staying at the shelter, Landau and his peers could think of no reason *not* to accommodate peculiar preferences for grilled cheese sandwiches or to bend the rules for a particular woman using the bathroom late at night. Whether or not these accommodations were the right decisions, Landau and his peers' tolerance for eccentricity seems to represent a divergence from the rigidity of many other social service settings and perhaps contributes to the sense of many homeless men and women that the Harvard Square Shelter is a place where they are treated respectfully and humanely.

FUELING IDENTITY DEVELOPMENT

The connections and conversations forged inside the Harvard Square Homeless Shelter yield important benefits for the Harvard students as well. As noted earlier, psychologist Erik Erikson characterized adolescence as the developmental period in which individuals develop a deeper conception of the world and of their role in it by seeking out perspectives and points of view beyond their immediate families.[12] Psychologist James Youniss has long argued that community service has an important role to play in this maturation process.[13] As Youniss and colleague Miranda Yates have noted, "Community service experiences can be understood as encouraging youth to grapple with social, moral and political issues, and to reflect on their own role in society."[14] More specifically, Metz, McLellan, and Youniss commented:

Social cause types of service at least provide adolescents with challenging experiences by exposing them to unfamiliar people and compelling social problems. It may also put them in direct contact with adults and organizations that espouse moral political philosophies about social justice. In all of these senses, one can see the fundamental elements that Erikson described as essential for supporting adolescents as they construct their youthful identities.[15]

As described here by James Youniss and colleagues, a community service opportunity such as the Harvard Square Homeless Shelter can provide young adults with a fertile ground for considering the questions that constitute the central preoccupations of adolescence: Who am I? And how do I fit into the wider world?[16] One of the most effective ways for the shelter's college-aged volunteers to ponder these questions is by *listening* to the shelter's homeless guests. Here, under one roof, are 30 adults who can describe experiences and offer perspectives on the world and its challenges that are likely very different from those offered by the volunteers' parents, relatives, teachers, and classmates. The eagerness and enthusiasm with which the Harvard students listened to the stories of the shelter's residents, then, was not simply a product of kindness or sympathy. Rather, these young adults were soaking up important information to add to their growing understanding of how the world works and what role they would like to play in it.[17]

A number of the Harvard Square Shelter's volunteers explicitly recognized how much they have to gain at the shelter through listening and conversation. Wellesley College sophomore Charlotte Wu explained at the beginning of the winter that "I think I'm going to do an overnight shift . . . I really want to be able to talk to the people who come to the homeless shelter, and that seems to be the best shift for that." As for *why* she aspired to engage in such conversations, Wu expressed a desire to "walk away with kind of a deeper understanding of homelessness and poverty . . . and put more of a human-like face and attachment to the idea of homelessness." Harvard freshman Nancy Mellor explained that she too signed up for an overnight shift because of the greater opportunities for conversation: "I mean, the most basic necessity is food and shelter and clothing, and that is what the shelter gives people, but I want to be able to talk to them and realize how they came to be there." Likewise, Harvard junior Louis Landau explained that "I'd like to have an opportunity to interact with guests" in order to supplement a "fairly academic" understanding of homelessness with some "personal experience." Scholars Clary and Snyder would likely characterize all of these volunteers as motivated by a knowledge function — a desire to learn more about some aspect of the world, in this case, homelessness.[18]

Hope Franklin, a Harvard senior volunteering at the shelter for the first time, said in November of 2008 as the shelter was opening for the winter: "I don't think of homeless people as individuals. I sort of think of them as an aggregate . . . So I think there's some level of anonymity, facelessness to homelessness which I think will change." Interviewed again at the end of the winter, Franklin acknowledged that her interactions with the homeless had been the most meaningful part of the volunteer experience: "I've really enjoyed meeting the guests. Having a chance to interact with them, albeit a little superficially, but even serving breakfast, they come and joke with you. They are generally sort of interesting, funny people who are willing to share aspects of their lives."

Lester Pearsons and Liam Murphy put a different twist on their quests for conversation. Pearsons, a Harvard junior who grew up in England, offered the following explanation for his decision to volunteer at the shelter:

> "Being a middle class White person who pretty much has had a very privileged education and what not, you only see one demographic really. It's quite a varied demographic in many ways, like racially, socially, whatever, but the people here [at Harvard] have had similar types of experiences. And I'm very intent on broadening the range of people I come into contact with because you can never really expand as a person unless you expose yourself to [different people]. And I can't really imagine someone who's had more of a different life than me than someone who's living on the streets."

Here, Pearsons expressed a desire to broaden the community of people with whom he interacts and converses. Later in that initial interview, he acknowledged that "I don't really know how I think about homelessness" in large part because, "I've never really talked to a homeless person." He chose to sign up for an evening shift with the goal of changing that.

Sophomore Liam Murphy offered an explanation for his involvement

with the Harvard Square Shelter that overlapped with Pearsons'.
According to Murphy:

> "Well, there's a really great article that came out recently called
> 'The Disadvantages of an Elite Education.' I don't want to be
> that guy. I don't want to be the guy who can only interact with
> people of a similar level of college education. I want to be able
> to go talk to whoever it is, relate to them, understand that they
> are a person, that just because I have a degree doesn't mean
> anything in the grand scheme of things, that we are the same
> person, and therefore be able to talk."

In this explanation, Murphy referred to a 2008 article published in the
American Scholar in which Yale Professor William Deresiewicz argued
that a disadvantage of attending an elite university such as Harvard or
Yale "is that it makes you incapable of talking to people who aren't like
you."[19] Murphy was determined not to turn into such an individual and
saw the opportunity to converse with the homeless men and women at
the Harvard Square Shelter as one mechanism for avoiding such a fate.
Interestingly, in his book on young adults entitled *The First Year Out*,
scholar Tim Clydesdale explicitly noted that middle-class and affluent
young adults typically have very little contact with Americans from
other social classes. According to Clydesdale:

> While working-class teens often work at jobs that require
> them to serve middle and upper-middle-class Americans, the
> inverse rarely holds true. This gives working-class teens first-
> hand knowledge of affluent consumers, while reinforcing the
> insularity of middle and upper-middle-class teen experiences.[20]

For students like Pearsons and Murphy, the shelter served as an antidote
to the insularity Clydesdale describes. Particularly noteworthy was the
consciousness with which these two young men recognized the insular
nature of their lives and took steps to ameliorate it.

PLAYING THE GURU

In several of the comments of the Harvard Square Shelter's first-time
volunteers, one can hear a note (or sometimes more than a note) of

voyeurism — a sense of the homeless men and women these students met at the shelter as an exotic "other."[21] Such voyeurism may seem off-putting, but a number of former volunteers actually described this attitude as contributing to the Harvard Square Shelter's unique atmosphere. As former volunteer Amelia Ginsberg recalled:

> "Definitely I think the guests preferred our shelter, at least some of the guests, not only because it was small, but because it was less institutional, you know, was staffed by kids who were in this weird way kind of excited to be interacting with homeless people. Let's not deny that there's a kind of bizarre dynamic to the whole thing, but my sense was that guests enjoyed that aspect. They were treated with some level of respect and interest that they wouldn't have been down at some of the shelters in Boston."

Here, Ginsberg acknowledged the voyeuristic impulses of some of the shelter's volunteers but simultaneously recognized that this enthusiasm for interacting with an oft-ignored group of individuals had its benefits as well. Harvard Professor Julie Wilson agreed with Ginsberg's perspective, explaining that "I think one of the worst parts about being homeless is being invisible, and you are not invisible at the Harvard Square Shelter."

Looking back on his own volunteer days as an undergraduate in the late 1980s, Ward Welburn offered a similar perspective about the benefits that such voyeurism bestows upon the homeless men and women staying at the shelter:

> "And I also think for some of them, they like being the guru, and sitting there and having some kid for whatever reason in rapt attention sort of listen to them, you know, hold court and stay up till two in the morning talking about whatever wisdom they have, and this person sort of lapping it up."

A textbook case of the dynamic described by Ginsberg and Welburn was offered by Harvard sophomore Antonia Garcia-Brown. Garcia-Brown began working an overnight shift at the Harvard Square Shelter in November 2008 and then added a weekly shift at the Resource Advocacy table as well. In describing her interactions with the men and women she met at the shelter, Garcia-Brown offered the following anecdote from a conversation with an older woman named Leah:

"This one woman came to the Resource Advocacy table to ask for a subway pass and I started talking to her for about an hour about this time when she was 21 and went down to Chile to do volunteer work. This was at the time of the Pinochet dictatorship, [and] she just gave us this insane story about how she literally almost got shot to death for being an American. She couldn't find the place she was supposed to go to, some family that she was staying with. After a couple of days she realized that she was endangering them by being American and staying with them. That was a really intense conversation. My co-resource advocate and I were like, 'Whoa!'"

In this story, one can easily envision this homeless woman, Leah, enjoying the opportunity to hold Garcia-Brown and her peer in the "rapt attention" that Welburn remembered from his own shelter days. The value of this opportunity for an audience and conversation cannot be overemphasized.

Harvard senior Robert Vozar grew close enough with this same homeless woman, Leah, that he invited her to his family's home for Passover Seder in the spring of 2009. Vozar noted:

"I've once or twice tried to make overtures that I'd be happy to help with the material side of things, about looking for housing. And I don't think that that's what Leah's looking for. That's not that she doesn't want to have a house, but I don't think she thinks that I'm going to help her get a house. What she's interested in is someone to talk to and, you know, have a normal relationship with."

Similar to Garcia-Brown, Vozar recounted conversations he had engaged in with Leah about her work in Chile as well as her perspective on philosophers he had studied in class such as Augustine, Plato, and Aristotle. As Harvard Professor Julie Wilson noted, "I think that there are a lot of people who are generally lonely who are living on the streets out there, and this is a conversation. And they have some wisdom to impart to the students."

This is not to say that every homeless person is interested in such conversations. As alumnus Ward Welburn qualified, the Harvard Square Shelter draws to it a particular segment of Boston and Cambridge's homeless community, and there are certainly homeless people who "wouldn't be able to put up with these idealistic students wanting to talk to them for two hours." Likewise, former guest Joe Presley noted that the Harvard Square Shelter "is not for everybody. You have to be prepared for students to sit down with you, and it's a shock. I know a woman that was there recently, and she was totally shocked by and put off by the students showing that much interest in her. She left." There are very few aspects of life for which one size fits all, but a particular segment of the homeless community seems to relish and benefit from the opportunity to hold court with a replenishing reservoir of idealistic young adults.[22]

CONVERSATION PIECES

The homeless men and women staying at the Harvard Square Shelter may also find the Harvard students they meet there easier to talk to than the adults they encounter at other shelters. After all, these young adults hail from all different parts of the United States and world, and are deeply engaged in the process of taking classes, reading books, and mulling over ideas. Several formerly homeless men and women noted how much they enjoyed the opportunity the shelter provided to interact with young adults in such a formative phase of their life. For example, Fred Slomiak talked about how the shelter allowed for "a cultural exchange" because "people don't realize how well read homeless people are, or how much they study art and culture, or are involved in politics." He added:

> "Fundamentally, what the Harvard Square Shelter offers is so important because I know the people on the street, they love to talk to the college kids and learn from them, and they may be talking about a book they had read, or how they feel about government or politics or whatever."

During her two years of homelessness, Lucy Draper described as "really special" the experience of simply talking with the Harvard Square Shelter volunteers "about food, cooking, salvaging, and then it went kind of from there to stuff like books." Likewise, Ralph McGann described his enjoyment at getting to talk to young people "coming from all over the country, all over the world." As he recalled:

"I met a kid in 2002 from Borneo. That's in Malaysia. I studied geography and animals very well, so we were talking about Mount Kinabalu, a mountain in Indonesia, and a lot of people wouldn't expect me to know something like that. I have access to the Comparative Zoology library at Harvard. I've been going there since I was 16 because I have a personal interest in zoology."

In short, McGann relished the opportunity to meet and talk with young people who were excited about ideas. As he commented, "There are people out there that are very well educated that are homeless." This claim was underscored by a *Boston Globe* article in July 2009 about a weekly book club that has sprung up composed of corporate lawyers and homeless men and women. When one of the lawyers offered to bring lunch each week for the book club, the homeless participants turned him down. According to *Globe* reporter, Jenna Russell, "They had enough free meals, they said, they wanted something else — camaraderie and stimulating talk."[23] Both of those elements are available nightly at the Harvard Square Shelter.

Freshman Anna Robinson, who worked an overnight shift during the winter of 2008–09, noted that sitting in the shelter's dining area with one of her textbooks created an easy entrée for homeless men and women interested in starting a conversation. According to Robinson, "A lot of people were just like, 'Oh, what are you reading? Are you interested in that?" Particularly in regards to a course she was taking on the American Revolutionary War, Robinson found that "Some people definitely had a lot of knowledge about it."

Other volunteers reported similar types of conversations. Sophomore Lester Pearsons noted that many of the men and women he met at the Harvard Square Shelter "will ask you personal questions, not too personal, [like] 'what are you studying?'" Senior Hope Franklin described a homeless man who would "always seek me out [to ask], 'How's your environmental studies? What are you talking about this week?'" Likewise, junior Amanda Mooney noted that "Most of the conversations I have that touch on my student life are interested, thoughtful questions about what do you study? What do you want to be? Is it okay living so far from your family? Just stuff like that."

Other Harvard students described deeper conversations with homeless men and women about their classes and readings. Harvard senior Kathryn Tobin recalled her conversations with a homeless man,

Marcus, about her American intellectual history course. According to Tobin, "We were reading DuBois and the speeches of Martin Luther King and Malcolm X, etc., and Marcus is black, and we were talking about the different trajectories of the civil rights movement and what was effective." Tobin described those conversations about her coursework as among her favorite because "even if I'm a Harvard student and he's contending with homelessness . . . we can have a good conversation about it and reflect on what it means to be an American together even though we're very different."

Tobin cited another homeless man, Ray Diaz, in the acknowledgments section of her senior thesis. An economics major, Tobin wrote her senior thesis on poverty rights and land distribution in the American West from 1830 to 1910. She ended up discussing several of her ideas with Diaz, a homeless man in his late sixties who had spent time in the American West. She brought him a copy of the completed thesis the night before the shelter closed for the season in April of 2009.

Junior Melissa Sanguinetti recalled a long conversation with an older homeless man during her freshman year of college after she had just declared herself a religion major. According to Sanguinetti:

> "We had this very intense discussion about religion and its role in government and its role in people's worldviews. And how it shapes society. And it was just kind of a topic that is so deep that it's the kind of thing you talk about in class. And here I was having this really intense conversation with this guy. Intense enough that he remembers it this year, and it was sort of this conversation that you don't have with a lot of people, so it was just really meaningful to have it with this stranger and have it be equally beneficial."

Sanguinetti went on to describe how this particular homeless man remembered the names and backgrounds of a number of the shelter's volunteers. She explained that his interest in what students were studying and learning came across as "very grandfatherly."

And, of course, the student-volunteers and homeless adults covered subjects other than classes as well. Wellesley College sophomore Charlotte Wu noted, "When the [2008 Presidential] election was going on, we'd talk about politics . . . We would butt heads on different candidates, and they'd be like, 'Oh, well, I like Obama's healthcare plan. And I'd be like, 'Well, actually Hillary [Clinton]'s plan was like this.'" Wu also described playing Scrabble with other volunteers and homeless guests. A Wellesley College student, Wu admitted that "Even I sometimes find it intimidating to play speed Scrabble with Harvard students cause there's this image of them. But the fact that the guests would play with us and have a good time was awesome." On a similar note, University Lutheran congregation member Julie Wilson recalled a time from the late 1980s when her ten-year-old son and a friend were volunteering at the shelter. According to Wilson, "Willy, my son's friend, was a nationally ranked chess player in elementary school, and he was engaged in a chess tournament with a homeless guy. And the guy said, 'You can't take him away because we're tied one to one, and this is the playoffs,' and I called his mother who was upset because I said I couldn't take them away."

Similar to ten-year-old Willy, the Harvard students operating the Harvard Square Shelter often sought to share their interests and passions with the homeless men and women staying at the shelter. As noted earlier, Harvard senior Robert Vozar's conversations about philosophy and religion with a homeless woman, Leah, led him to invite her home for his family's Passover Seder. According to Vozar, "I don't think I can have every shelter guest over my house for dinner . . . but I do think that it's the kind of thing where there's sometimes moments which can be at least for me and hopefully for someone else, very uplifting." Likewise, Harvard senior Kathryn Tobin invited homeless men and women from the shelter to attend one of her intramural boxing matches, and junior Amanda Mooney provided interested shelter guests with tickets to one of her singing group's a cappella concerts. As Mooney said, "I think it was a very big display of shelter spirit when ten guests came to my a cappella concert. I made a sign-up list for free tickets and ten people came in addition to 15 students." Excited about various facets of their life outside of the shelter, the Harvard students volunteering there made an effort to share these interests and hobbies with the homeless men and women at the Harvard Square Shelter.

TABOO TOPICS

A question posed to all of the current and former shelter volunteers was whether there were particular topics of conversation they deliberately steered away from out of recognition of the different worlds inhabited by Harvard students and the homeless. Several students explained that they believed they had better relations with the homeless when they were honest about the privileges they enjoyed and stresses they encountered. For example, Ward Welburn recalled:

> "The example that I've used for years is people would come back from vacation, and they'd have a tan, and they'd be very evasive with a guest who'd ask, 'What'd you do?' and so forth. Whereas I would be honest: I went to Florida. My parents flew me down, and I had a great time, and it was great. What do you think of my tan? And people were much more able, I felt, to respect people who were able to talk to them like fellow human beings rather than talk like they were somehow other or distant."

Here, Welburn described his philosophy of being upfront about the privileges he enjoyed as the son of a wealthy Massachusetts family. Likewise, sophomore Antonia Garcia-Brown related how she initially tried to keep her own problems to herself, but ended up discarding this approach: "At first, sometimes I would feel bad complaining about having a pretty big test tomorrow because they are homeless. Their lives suck more than mine. After a while, I realized that most people just want conversation." Along similar lines, senior Robert Vozar offered the following description of being consoled during the 2009 winter by a homeless man, Lee, when Vozar's application for a prestigious fellowship was rejected:

> "I had a moment a couple weeks ago when I'd had an interview, and I didn't get something that I was really hoping to get. Lee, a guest, had a good line. He said, 'Rome wasn't built in a day, and you know lives are big projects...' Even though I was interviewing for a fancy fellowship and didn't get it, and Lee was homeless, he was totally happy to actually empathize with me and say, 'Wow that sucks, I'm really sorry for you.'"

Lee's attempt to assuage Vozar's disappointment points to the genuine mutuality of the connections that form between the shelter's Harvard volunteers and homeless guests. Aborigine Lila Watson once famously told missionaries who had come to Australia that "If you have come to help me, you are wasting your time. But if you have come because your liberation is bound up with mine, then let us walk together."[24]

What makes the Harvard Square Shelter unique is that the Harvard students volunteering at the shelter and the homeless men and women staying there are truly walking together. Both groups benefit from the influence of the other.

CONCLUSION

In explaining what makes the Harvard Square Homeless Shelter such a special community, Pastor Donald Larsen likes to tell the following story about a former shelter "regular" named Ralph:

> "Ralph has been a shelter guest on or off for about 15 years. He is a heavy-set guy. He is in his mid-sixties now. He is an alcoholic. He has a studio apartment and has had one for some years. But even though he has his own place now, he still came [to the shelter] and the students for about a year really struggled with the idea. He wanted to come sleep here, but he had his own place. Why? Because this was Ralph's community, and the students recognized that and finally after a lot of anguish, finally said to Ralph, 'No you really can't do that.' But what they did do was to invite him to keep coming for meals."

In this anecdote, Pastor Larsen sought to convey the extent to which the Harvard Square Shelter provides many homeless men and women with far more than "three hots and a cot."

Certainly, the vast majority of the men and women passing through the shelter would trade in their bed at the shelter for a studio apartment any day of the week; however, McGann is by no means the only individual who experiences the Harvard Square Shelter as a valued community. Former volunteer Kristin Sommers described a homeless man, Carl, who depended on the shelter to serve as his surrogate family. As she described it, "I remember talking to Carl a lot, and when Carl was in the hospital, he would call us a lot . . . I think the shelter was his family." Sommers recalled that, during his frequent hospital stays, Carl would call up the shelter's main number just to talk to whichever Harvard students happened to be volunteering that night. The shelter's college-aged volunteers had become like his children.

There are many ways in which the Harvard students running the shelter foster a strong sense of community between themselves and the homeless men and women who stay there, but perhaps the most important is their ability to be extraordinary listeners. What makes such listening possible is that these Harvard students have something to gain from listening to the stories and experiences of the shelter's homeless guests. Their own identity exploration demands exposure to additional perspectives on how the world works, and this demand is satisfied, in part, by the stories and points of view these homeless men and women can offer.[25] It is this symbiosis that gives conversations between the shelter's guests and volunteers a different flavor than those between the homeless and professional social workers. This is not to privilege one type of conversation over the other, but rather to suggest that the Harvard students volunteering at the shelter are able to offer the homeless men and women who stay there a form of active, appreciative listening that literally only adolescents can provide. They are not merely *willing* to listen to the experiences of the shelter's homeless guests; they are *eager* to listen. They express not only *sympathy* for the circumstances in which the shelter's homeless guests find themselves, but *fascination* about how these men and women arrived in those circumstances. They are not merely *patient* recipients of the advice that the shelter's homeless guests have to offer, but *grateful* for these alternative points of view. The community that results from this mutuality is an extraordinary one.

Chapter 5

Outside the Box

Anyone who has spent time in Boston is likely familiar with *Spare Change News*, a newspaper founded, written, and sold by homeless men and women all over the city. This bi-weekly newspaper with a circulation of more than 10,000 bills itself as "covering news, opinion, arts, homelessness issues and social justice."[1] Also notable about *Spare Change News* is its two-fold mission. As stated on the newspaper's website:

> By focusing on homelessness issues within the pages, we strive to educate our readers on the myths surrounding homelessness while encouraging them to join the fight against homelessness; additionally, we exist to help homeless, formerly homeless and low-income individuals earn a living by becoming vendors of *Spare Change News*.[2]

Specifically, each vendor purchases the paper for $0.25 per issue but sells the paper for $1.00 per issue, making a $0.75 profit on each sale. While many Bostonians have seen or even purchased *Spare Change News*, few know that the newspaper originated in 1992 in the Harvard Square Homeless Shelter.

According to Joe Presley, one of the newspaper's founders:

> "All 11 founding members at one time or another were in the Harvard Square Shelter. We were all there together when the

whole project really took off. We talked about it more, communicated more, the students were encouraging us . . . There was a general feeling that we should do this."

Presley says he and the other founding members "wanted to find a way to make money and to stop relying on the system which didn't seem to be doing us any good at all." Several of *Spare Change*'s founding members had seen copies of *Street News* in New York, a publication that had begun in the late 1980s and was sold by New York's homeless. Where *Spare Change* differed from *Street News*, however, was that Presley and the ten other founders wanted "homeless people to run it, own it and make the decisions." Nearly 20 years later, *Spare Change News* is still working hard on both facets of its mission.

This chapter focuses on the unique ability of the college students at the Harvard Square Homeless Shelter to practice outside-the-box thinking and respond nimbly to change. With regard to *Spare Change News*, perhaps the Harvard Square Shelter can take credit for little beyond providing a roof over the heads of the newspapers' founders. It seems possible, however, that the creative thinking demonstrated by the Harvard students at the shelter also led them to encourage the innovative spirit that generated *Spare Change News* right under their roof.

Harvard Square Shelter co-founder Fred Reisz discovered early on that "Students were able to go with the flow, so to speak. [They] weren't as professionally defined, so they had a little more flexibility and could roll with the punches." Former homeless czar Philip Mangano suggested that one of the Harvard Square Shelter's greatest strengths is its "youthful idealism, which has a nimbleness, because it's not entrenched bureaucracy. It's a constant infusion of new ideas and new people." Mangano added that many long-term social services workers become so entrenched in a particular way of thinking that they grow resistant to innovation whereas the young adults operating the Harvard Square Shelter have no qualms about "putting into place the innovative ideas" they believe can provide additional support to the men and women they are serving. Harvard alumnus and former state senator Joshua Villanueva suggested that the youth and inexperience of the shelter's volunteers "leads them to be fearless" in trying out new strategies and approaches to combating homelessness as well as "more able and willing because of their fearlessness to take on some of those core problems in direct service and public policy endeavors."

Former guest Lucy Draper offered a somewhat different take on the "nimbleness" of the shelter's college-aged volunteers. According to Draper, one of the tremendous strengths of the Harvard Square Shelter is that its leaders are "a whole group of very energized, very bright kids who are perceiving things. They are in an academic environment. They are used to seeing things and writing." In short, Draper suggested that the Harvard students operating the shelter are in a period of life where they are constantly being asked by their professors to think, reflect, analyze, and evaluate. Draper believes these students bring this same analytic lens to the policies and procedures at their shelter. And because they are not professionals, they exhibit far less reluctance to admit failure and try something entirely new. As Draper noted, "There is a level of intellectual confidence in these students so that they can be open to all sorts of possibilities." This openness to possibilities is perhaps best exemplified by the many adaptations to the shelter's Work Contract Program.

THE WORK CONTRACT PROGRAM

When Pastor Fred Reisz and Stewart Guernsey founded the Harvard Square Shelter in 1983, they assumed that the shelter would only exist for a few years as an emergency stop-gap measure. When homelessness showed no signs of abating, however, Pastor Reisz realized that a shelter that had been established as a temporary band-aid functioned like a band-aid. Relying on a reservoir of idealistic but unprofessional college students, the shelter did an excellent job of providing "three hots and a cot," but did little in the way of connecting homeless men and women with the services they needed to get off the streets. As Pastor Reisz noted, "That more professional level of moving people into the housing system, the job system, we struggled with in the early years. It's better now, but it's not something easy for students to do; it's something for people who are connected with those systems, [and] know how they work." This challenge of connecting homeless men and women to key support services arguably remains the Achilles' heel of a homeless shelter whose workers turn over every few years. As current volunteer Deanna Galante explained, "There are these really important connections with community leaders, but because we're so transient as a staff, it takes longer than it should [to form them]."

All that said, the nimbleness of the Harvard Square Shelter volunteers led to their establishment in 1991 of a Transitional Housing program to try to move away from exclusively "band-aid care." According to Harvard Professor Julie Wilson, one of her graduate students wrote a master's thesis en route to his degree from the John F. Kennedy School of Government in which he proposed that the Harvard Square Shelter dedicate six to ten of its beds to "longer term tenants." Dr. Aaron Dutka was one of the student-directors involved in implementing this plan. According to Dr. Dutka:

> "A couple of directors were peeled off to focus on that. So we had ten beds that we reserved for the transitional program, and we instituted that as a new model while I was there. So that was a big challenge because you would allow people to stay in those ten beds for months; I think it was 90 days or something."

By Dr. Dutka's recollection, the creation of the Transitional Housing program immediately led to a series of new challenges for the shelter. One challenge was that many of the homeless men and women in the transitional program "became entitled" and regarded the shelter as more theirs than the homeless people staying only for a week at a time. According to Dr. Dutka, this attitude "infringed upon the ability of other people to be comfortable in the shelter." Dr. Dutka also described the tension between having two programs under the same roof with very different goals: "one was band-aid care, and the other trying for longitudinal, chronic care."

Looking back, Dr. Dutka described the program as "not working badly" but also expressed surprise that "We had the ambition to even think that we could do that." In this comment, he echoed the observation at the outset of this chapter by former volunteer and state senator Joshua Villanueva that youth and inexperience allows the shelter's volunteers "to be fearless" in trying out new strategies and approaches to combating homelessness. Without doubt, fearlessness was required in this endeavor. As Dr. Dutka pointed out, "I'd never submitted my resume anywhere, but we were going to help [homeless people] find jobs and transitional housing." Amelia Ginsberg, who led the transitional program in the late 1990s, recalled:

> "I remember having a lot of guilt around feeling like I wasn't doing enough for the transitional clients the year that I was in charge of that service. . . . I felt this chronic sense of, I should

know more, I'm not doing enough to help them access the services that we told them that we would help them access."

Despite these doubts, the Transitional Housing program unequivocally had its share of successes. For example, Fred Slomiak credited the transitional program with giving him the stability to begin his rise out of homelessness after three years on the streets in the mid-1990s. By the start of the new millennium, however, alumnus Rusty Sadow believed that the likelihood of homeless men and women transitioning out of homelessness had changed. Specifically, during Sadow's undergraduate years from 1996 to 2000, the housing prices in Boston nearly doubled. According to Sadow:

"In 1996, a guy could come in the shelter, and whatever had happened in his life previously, we could help him find a job, get him in the transitional program, work with him over several months to save up money, do a housing search, and then move guys out into their own apartments. And I can remember carrying suitcases into a new place. You could find a new place for $300, $400, even $500 a month that they could afford with the job that they had. That was 1996. By 1999, I don't remember anybody moving out. If they did, it was because they'd gotten on a list for subsidized housing seven years earlier, and it finally came through. So the job in my mind kind of changed during that period from helping people who could be helped to managing people in a miserable situation without being able to change that situation."

Harvard alumna Anusha Ghosh, who volunteered at the Harvard Square Shelter shortly after Sadow, expressed a similar frustration "that I could not produce a concrete change for anyone there."

Sadow and Ghosh's perspectives on housing and homelessness are reinforced by recent economic analyses which have demonstrated that the higher the rent in a particular community, the greater the incidence of homelessness.[3] As David Lyons, the President of the Public Policy Institute of California, has explained, increased rental and housing prices have "literally forced the lowest-income renters into the streets."[4] While frustration with this state of affairs ultimately led Sadow into community organizing and Ghosh into public interest law, the Harvard Square Shelter's Transitional Housing program had to adjust to these new challenges. In the early 2000s, the program's name changed from "Transitional Housing program" to the "Work Contract program" out of a sober recognition that fewer people were genuinely positioned to transition out of homelessness in just a 10–12 week span. The number of available beds for the program dropped from ten to five.

As noted by Sadow, transitioning out of homelessness was no longer simply a matter of helping homeless men and women find jobs and then set up a bank account and a savings plan. With the surge in housing prices, homeless people "could hold a job, they could work 40 hours a week, but that wasn't going to [be able to] pay the rent." Now, transitioning out of homelessness meant qualifying for subsidized housing or being accepted into a long-term transitional housing situation.[5] To connect homeless men and women with those kinds of resources required professional connections beyond the students' abilities, and so, in the mid-2000s, the Resource Advocacy program was created to supplement the much-reduced Work Contract program.

According to Deanna Galante, one of the shelter's Resource Advocacy directors during the 2008–09 school year, the Resource Advocacy program is made up of about 15 volunteers who participate in a multi-day training and then take turns staffing an information table inside the shelter from 7:30–10:30 p.m. each night. The goal of the program is to help interested men and women connect with professional services. As Harvard sophomore and Resource Advocacy volunteer Antonia Garcia-Brown said, "We have a big list of various programs that they can go to. We fill out various verification forms with them that they might need, like verification of homelessness, things like that." Garcia-Brown added that the Resource Advocates can also give out subway passes to homeless men and women who need the fare for various types of appointments and job interviews. Another sophomore, Liam Murphy, remarked:

> "We would talk with the guest and say, 'Hey, how's it going? Blah blah. Do you have this? Do you have Section 8? Have you heard about Mass Health?' And just kind of seeing them and figuring out what their needs were and seeing how we could bridge their needs with services."

Murphy added that, during the winter of 2009, he helped shelter guests apply for food stamps, make appointments with subsidized housing agencies, put together resumes, and "sometimes we would fill out recommendations because all they needed was a well-written recommendation." Murphy also helped interested men and women to connect to programs for smaller needs such as free eye care and eyeglasses.

Mike Andretti, who stayed at the Harvard Square Shelter in 2009, said that the resource advocates helped him to get a new ID card, apply for food stamps, and sign up for classes at a local community college. Frank Green credited the resource advocates with helping him to update his resume.

Sophomore Liam Murphy described two homeless guests with whom he felt like he made real progress during the winter of 2009. One guest, an elderly homeless woman named Nina, first needed help attaining an ID, and then working through a snafu with her social security disability checks. Next, Murphy helped her to attain a post office box, and finally worked with her on applying for Mass Health — Massachusetts' version of universal healthcare.[6] Another homeless man with whom Murphy worked, Luis, actually qualified for Section 8 housing, a program that provides low-income individuals with a voucher that they can apply towards a rented apartment. In Luis's case, the voucher was for $1,200 a month — enough to find a reasonable apartment. Murphy worked with Luis on Craigslist to find potential apartments; he recalled that on the day Luis closed on an apartment, he sent Murphy and the other students an email saying, "Thank you so much guys. I really appreciate it. You helped me out a lot." Murphy said, "I remember I was walking into the [Harvard] Science Center, and I got the email on my phone, and it just put me in a great mood!"

Freshman Nancy Mellor also volunteered as a Resource Advocate during the 2008–09 winter. According to Mellor, she became involved with the program because "I wanted to make it a little more real, I guess, like helping them to get back on their feet. There are so many resources out there. It is just a matter of finding them and maneuvering through the paperwork." Mellor described a young homeless woman with whom she worked with this past winter who had just finished bartending school and needed work to support her one-year-old daughter. Mellor helped her put together a resume and also to enroll in a General Educational Development (GED) program. According to Mellor, the young woman was excited to get started on her GED and "very sincere about trying to get back on her feet."

Through the Resource Advocacy program, the Harvard students operating the shelter have continued to demonstrate a nimbleness in making the changes necessary to best serve the homeless. As homeless czar Philip Mangano noted:

> "The Harvard Square Shelter, thankfully, has evolved from simply that social service frame to more of a solution-oriented frame. They may not use the nomenclature of a business approach but, nonetheless, when you treat a person as a consumer, you ask them what they want, then you go create that product, that's the basics of American business."

From Mangano's perspective, the ability of the Harvard Square Shelter to make adjustments based on its guests' needs represents a business-oriented approach that he wishes more homeless shelters could adopt. Rather than explicitly trying to draw upon business principles, however, it would seem that the shelter's flexibility comes from having a set of managers — college students — who simply turn over too quickly to become wedded to a particular way of doing things. When it no longer seemed reasonable to devote ten beds to the Transitional Housing program, the students dropped the number of beds to five. When the moniker "Transitional Housing program" no longer seemed to fit, the students changed the program's name to the Work Contract program. When the Work Contract program no longer seemed to be filling a more general need within the shelter, the Resource Advocacy program was born.

All of these modifications seem reasonable, and yet there are few organizations that can adapt so quickly to changing times and circumstances. As noted in earlier chapters, I by no means intend to imply that the college students running the Harvard Square Shelter are more intelligent than professional service workers or have a better feel for combating homelessness. Rather, the developmental moment in which these young adults are situated — on the border between adolescence and emerging adulthood — leads them to approach change with a fearlessness that their older colleagues cannot match. And, as noted in previous chapters, even Harvard alumni tend to look back with astonishment at their own exploits as leaders of the Harvard Square Homeless Shelter. Like any set of professionals, these Harvard alumni have grown wiser and more expert with time, but less nimble as well.

ENDOWING THE SHELTER

If the Work Contract and Resource Advocacy programs represent the Harvard Square Shelter's ability to adapt to the changing needs of the homeless, perhaps the greatest examples of outside-the-box thinking over the past two years are the shelter's Street Team and endowment campaign. The Street Team — described in detail in Chapter 3 — represented the Harvard students' attempt this past winter to bring the shelter's resources out into Harvard Square. On Sunday through Friday nights, teams made up of three students donned purple and blue backpacks and circulated around Harvard Square giving out sandwiches, engaging in conversation, offering referrals to the Harvard Square Shelter and connecting homeless individuals to the efforts of the Resource Advocacy program.

After the shelter closed for the season, the Street Team directors — Larry Yoon and Jerry Chen — began to draft a handbook for operating Street Team with the goal of making the program a sustainable one. In other words, recognizing that their time as college students would soon be coming to an end, Yoon and Chen sought "to make sure the program is as easy to run as possible." While the Harvard students who come after Yoon and Chen will undoubtedly move Street Team in the direction that seems most appropriate to them, this proposed handbook will certainly give them a useful foundation from which to start.

Equally indicative of the Harvard students' innovative thinking was the Harvard Square Shelter's endowment campaign that began in 2007 and concluded in 2008. Every year the Harvard Square Shelter receives $31,000 from the Massachusetts Housing and Shelter Alliance for expenses that include paying rent to the University Lutheran Church; electricity, gas, and water bills; food and supplies; and wages for a nightly security guard. All told, the Harvard Square Shelter's yearly expenses typically hover around $45,000 — leaving the shelter's development and administrative directors responsible for fundraising for the difference.

In 2007, one of the shelter's new administrative directors, Nathan Vozar, had a roommate on Harvard's chess team, and Vozar learned from his roommate that all student groups at Harvard have the right to buy into Harvard's $30 billion endowment as long as they can make a minimum investment of $25,000. According to the shelter's other administrative director, Leo LaSala, "You just dump in as much money as you want. You lose your principal, but you get 4.5 percent every year."

You can never recover the principal, and then any excess that the fund earns get reinvested in the principal. So the principal keeps growing, but the 4.5 percent payout remains the same."

From Vozar's perspective, "If the chess club has an endowment, the shelter should have an endowment." That way, rather than having to scramble each year to cover a $15,000 budget gap, the shelter would have a annual guaranteed payout in addition to their funding from the Massachusetts Housing and Shelter Alliance. There were only two problems: the students running the shelter had no experience running a capital campaign, and the leadership of the University Lutheran Church wasn't thrilled by the plan. As Harvard professor and University Lutheran congregant Julie Wilson commented:

> "We just agonized over this setting up [of] an endowment because we didn't want to be endowing homelessness. And we worked with the students on the writing of how this endowment was going to be managed because while we might personally think that we are not going to eradicate homelessness anytime soon, that is not what we want the mission to be."

Likewise, Pastor Don Larsen explained:

> "Within the Uni-Lu community, there was a lot of division of opinion about the endowment because the doors of the shelter opened in part with a commitment to working towards a day when the shelter would no longer be needed, and there are a substantial number of us in the community who don't buy the idea that widespread homelessness must always be. We recognize that there have been big ups and downs in homelessness in the history of the United States, and there are ways of combating that and bringing that number down. Some of us were concerned that endowing the shelter somehow implied its permanence."

In short, when Pastor Reisz, Stewart Guernsey, and the University Lutheran congregation decided to turn their basement into a homeless shelter, they imagined this state of affairs lasting one or two winters at the most. Now, 25 years later, the Harvard students operating the shelter wanted to raise an endowment to fund the shelter into perpetuity.

Such a plan gave the congregation pause for thought before ultimately giving its blessing to the plan and offering the students a seed grant of $20,000 for their endeavor.

With little experience in fundraising, student-director Leo LaSala described himself and his peers as "dipping our hands into as many buckets as we could think of." They raised a few thousand dollars by asking every shelter volunteer to request a donation from his or her family. They did a mailing campaign to all of the Harvard alumni who had ever volunteered at the shelter as well as another mailing campaign to Cambridge residents. They hosted an a cappella concert and several other fundraising events on campus. They asked prominent shelter alumni and Harvard faculty members to generate lists of friends and colleagues who might be willing to contribute, and then contacted these friends and colleagues through jointly authored letters. As LaSala noted, "We pulled out all the stops and did whatever we could think of."

At times, the campaign became incredibly stressful. Senior Kathryn Tobin described the endowment campaign as dominating her entire junior year of college and that "Me and Robert [Vozar] were on email 20 hours a day trying to raise this amount of money." Tobin described one moment in the fall where the pressure to raise money overwhelmed her. Each year, students at the Harvard Business School raise a substantial amount of money to donate to charity and then invite different philanthropic organizations to compete for the money by doing a presentation about the reach of their various organizations. As Tobin recalled:

"We had found out the day before we were presenting that they wanted a PowerPoint, so we didn't have anything, and I had just pulled an all-nighter to finish a paper, but I knew that this other director, who was the only one who was also available to do it, had a paper due the next day. So I offered to do the presentation if he would be able to present it with me that day. And so I finished the presentation at 5 a.m. I went to bed, [and] I overslept. The alarm didn't go off until 11 a.m. It was super, super, super close. I got there two minutes before, and the PowerPoint presentation for some reason didn't work. They didn't recognize the flash drive or something like that, so it was a logistical thing that probably was my fault. If we had gotten there earlier, we could have figured out a way to make it work."

Whether or not the technological glitch was to blame, the Harvard Square Shelter did not win the sought-after funding from Harvard Business School. The other student with whom Tobin had been presenting — who was also frustrated and exhausted — vented his anger at Tobin. Sadly, both students described the loss of their friendship as a casualty of the endowment campaign.

The young adults embarking on this endowment campaign had so little experience with fundraising that they weren't even sure of the dollar amount to set as the campaign's goal. According to Leo LaSala, "Some of us really thought we were going to make it to $100,000, and others were like, 'We really want to make the $25,000 so we can invest in the endowment in the first place, and anything on top of that is gravy.'" In the end, in just nine months, the students raised an astounding $130,000. It turned out that one of the shelter's alumni had gone on to become the chairman of a Russian investment bank, and his $20,000 donation was the one that broke the $100,000 mark.

The CASPAR Shelter's Meghan Goughan described herself as "blown away" by the success of the endowment campaign and noted that the students had actually managed to raise more money than several of the larger Cambridge shelters who employ a full-time development officer. Ironically — and unfortunately — Harvard's endowment dropped 30 percent in the economic downturn of 2009, so there was no payout at all in the Harvard Square Shelter's first-year as a part of Harvard's endowment.[7] That is certain to turn around in future years, of course, and the extraordinary success of the shelter's college-aged volunteers in endowing the shelter is indicative of their ability to fearlessly carry out a challenging endeavor.

THE LOTTERY

The endowment campaign represented a clear example of the ability of the Harvard Square Shelter volunteers to work towards a substantial goal. The nimbleness with which these Harvard students can make a "mid-course correction," however, was best exemplified by their switch to a bed lottery midway through the 2008–09 winter.

Since its inception in 1983, the Harvard Square Shelter has given out beds to homeless men and women on a first-come, first-served basis. In its first years of operation, homeless men and women literally lined up single file outside the shelter's front door. The first 30 people were invited inside for the night. In subsequent years, homeless men and women could telephone the shelter at 7:30 a.m., and if there were four shelter beds coming open that day, the first four people who called were assigned those beds for the week. If someone didn't show up that evening to claim the bed, the first person to call in after 9:00 p.m. was awarded the bed for the night. In the early 2000s, the students decided to give out beds for two-week periods rather than one-week periods, but the first-come, first-served philosophy remained intact. However, in 2009, the growing number of homeless men and women with cell phones began to cause problems.

As junior Larry Yoon revealed, a group of about six homeless men figured out how to game the system. If one of the six men needed a bed, all six would meet up at 7:25 a.m. and use their six cell phones to flood the system on behalf of the one individual in need of a bed. Whoever got through first at 7:30 a.m. would simply reserve the bed on behalf of the friend in need. According to Larry Yoon, "It wasn't against the rules [but] . . . I think we all kind of felt it was unfair to all of the people who need an emergency shelter." Or as freshman Nancy Mellor noted, "It was a manipulation of the system." Likely exacerbating the situation was that these six men boasted loudly to the other guests and students about what they were doing.

In March 2009, senior Robert Vozar raised concerns about this manipulation at the weekly director's meeting, and a week later the student-directors made the switch to a lottery system for giving out beds. Under the new system, anyone could call in between 7:30 and 8 a.m., and then all of those names were fed into a computer program written by student-director Jerry Chen that randomly selected the recipients of the beds. At a community meeting about the change in the bed assignment system, a number of homeless men and women expressed their unhappiness with the change. Several people expressed their opinion that "the computer thing was not fair because people could hack into the system." According to Harvard freshman Nancy Mellor who was present at the meeting, "One of the comments the guests made was, 'We are a lot more intelligent than you think we are.'"

Another homeless man told Mellor that a lottery system could bring more dangerous characters into the shelter. According to this man, "You know us, you trust us, but you open up the lottery, well, all the bad ones are going to come in here." Frank Green concurred. According to Green:

"You're going to have it so there's a bunch of thieves in here. I said, people aren't going to want to come here any more. You're going to ruin what you have, and I said your parents aren't going to want you volunteering here when they find out the characters that are in this place. I said, basically you have a nice little place, and you're going to ruin it. . . . You're trying to open it up to the whole world, and you can't save everybody."

Despite Green's concerns, the Harvard students went ahead with the switch to a lottery system and, according to Harvard senior Leo LaSala, it "worked really, really well" and "makes the process a lot fairer." Few organizations — much less homeless shelters — could have adapted so quickly to a problem, but the shelter's college-aged volunteers saw no reason not to immediately change a procedure that had stopped working the way it was intended to. The fact that the shelter had been utilizing a particular system for the past 20 years did not deter them in the least from making changes as circumstances required.

HEARING CHANGE

Philip Mangano attributed the Harvard students' propensity for change to "youthful idealism" and Lucy Draper credited their "intellectual confidence." Both of these explanations fit within the framework for understanding adolescence and emerging adulthood described in earlier chapters. As noted earlier, psychologist Jeffrey Arnett characterizes emerging adulthood as "the age of possibilities, when optimism is high and people have an unparalleled opportunity to transform their lives."[8] Arnett also describes emerging adulthood as "the age of instability."[9] In these descriptions of emerging adulthood as a period filled with substantial changes, Arnett is primarily referring to the opportunity for particular individuals to explore new pathways and directions in regards to their own lives. As they enter a developmental period so characterized by change, however, the Harvard students running the Harvard Square Shelter are far less intimidated or wary of change than their senior colleagues directing other homeless shelters in Massachusetts and across the country.

Adult development scholar Robert Evans has noted that, in many cases, young adults and adults in mid-life literally hear the word "change" differently.[10] While young adults associate the word change with growth, development, and enhancement, older adults associate change with risk, loss, and a challenge to their competence. As Evans explains, "Our construction of meaning is cumulative and grows more fixed over time. The longer we live, the more events and experiences we incorporate into our structure. The larger the structure, the more difficult it is to revise"[11] According to Evans, it is largely due to this hardening of our structures of meaning that "change is less welcome to the old than to the young."[12]

An expert in adult development, Evans notes that, although there are many advantages to mid-life, "they do not stimulate innovation or increase one's appetite or readiness for change."[13] In mid-life, individuals are typically beginning to acknowledge their own mortality, watching their children grow up and move out, and contending with the decline and ultimately death of their own parents. Evans says that, in the face of all of these changes, many adults in mid-life "look to their work as the one constant that *won't* change."[14] In contrast, young adults like the college students running the shelter typically look upon the impending changes in their own lives with optimism and enthusiasm.

Evans' comparison of older versus younger adults can also be situated in Erikson and Marcia's identity development frameworks.[15] In Chapter 4 it was noted that Marcia expanded upon Erikson's work by dividing the identity development process into four stages: diffusion, foreclosure, moratorium, and achievement. The majority of the college students running the Harvard Square Shelter might be described as in a state of moratorium; they are actively seeking out new perspectives and ideologies to inform their understanding of the world. Older adults are more likely to be in a state of achievement, having already made firm commitments to a particular worldview and self-concept. Within this identity development framework, then, one can see how the Harvard Square Shelter's college-aged volunteers might make adaptations and changes with greater "nimbleness" than their older colleagues. Still in a state of moratorium, the majority of these young people have not yet fixed upon a particular philosophy or approach to either management or social service. Their older colleagues at other homeless shelters, in contrast, are likely to hold a more fixed perspective on how one goes about operating a homeless shelter and combating homelessness. As a result, the Harvard students operating the shelter approach change and decisions with a fearlessness that many of their older colleagues have simply outgrown.

Evidence of this fearlessness can be seen in the Harvard students' willingness to consider feedback from the homeless men and women who stay at the shelter. During the 2008–09 academic year, the Harvard students held community meetings in the shelter every few weeks in order to solicit feedback from the shelter's homeless clientele about how the shelter could better meet their needs. Senior Leo LaSala praised a particular homeless man for being "very good at pointing out when our rules don't work as well or when they feel arbitrary to people." Likewise, Harvard senior Robert Vozar characterized the numerous critiques of another homeless woman, Leah, as genuinely helpful:

> "There's a guest who I ended up talking to more in the spring named Leah who [had] . . . a lot of very thoughtful criticisms about policies. You know she's very concerned about this rule that we had to keep the bathroom doors open. She said it was a violation of privacy. And not just that, but it was an environment where people were more vulnerable to sexual assault if this door is open. And, I think there were some good points to what she said. We didn't change the rule substantially. We changed it so the doors are only open now 11:30 p.m. to 7 a.m. instead of being opened from then until 8 a.m. But I think that she made some good points.

In this explanation, Vozar made it clear that he and other shelter directors gave serious consideration to Leah's criticisms and made adjustments to their policies accordingly.

Along these lines, Harvard junior Nathan Small explained that, as he became a more experienced volunteer, he grew increasingly willing to think critically about which of the shelter's policies do and do not make sense. According to Small:

> "As I have gotten a more holistic sense of what we do, I think that I've been encouraged to think more critically about our rules, and about what rules are there for good reason and what rules are just sort of there, and we enforce them, but maybe they're more of a hindrance than a help to people."

Probably every organization in every sector has policies on its books that have outlived their usefulness or never were particularly useful to begin with, but the Harvard students running the shelter were unusually committed to reflecting upon, refining, and adapting the shelter's policies to meet the changing needs of the homeless.

BELOW FREEZING

A second mid-course correction from the winter of 2008–09 offered a clearer look at the debate that accompanies change at the Harvard Square Homeless Shelter. For the past 15 years, the maximum number of people allowed into the shelter had been set at 25, and there were precisely 25 beds. However, when the temperature dropped below 15 degrees Fahrenheit, the policy had been to set up four more cots around the perimeter of the shelter's dining area and to invite in an additional four people. As Harvard senior Kelly Parker said:

> "Basically, we had this discussion about why did we choose 15 degrees — it's sort of arbitrary . . . Should we change the temperature? Should it be a higher temperature because what's the difference between 15 degrees and 16 degrees? And say at 9.30 p.m. It's 17 degrees? Can you give out beds even though it will probably go down to 15 degrees by the end of the night?"

The shelter directors considered these questions and, by a large consensus, agreed to raise the "temperature threshold" for setting up additional cots to 32 degrees Fahrenheit. In other words, whenever the nightly temperature dips below freezing, an additional four people would be allowed into the shelter. As Kelly Parker noted, with the Boston climate, "That means we're having an extra four beds almost every night."

A more vigorous debate broke out about the appropriate number of additional cots to set up on those cold nights. One director suggested that the perimeter of the dining area could accommodate as many as nine additional cots. As Harvard junior Nathan Small observed:

> "There are tradeoffs in this decision. Bringing more people into the space means we're serving more people, but maybe it means we're serving the people in the space not quite so well. So these are the tradeoffs. And I think it's an interesting question, and related to how we see our mission, and related

to whether we see it as serving as many people as possible, or trying to serve a more concentrated population."

The student-directors turned out to be quite divided over this issue. Sophomore Christopher Kitts said:

"When it comes to cots, I was on the side that we should allow more. I was okay with the fact that people would be less comfortable and more crowded as long as people were off the streets. I suppose I'm a little less concerned with the idea that the shelter is the Hilton of homeless shelters and more concerned with the idea that people have more food and are warm."

In contrast, senior Lissette McDonald remarked:

"Safety is a big concern: safety of yourself, safety of the volunteers, and safety for the other guests that are there . . . I'm also torn because the core part of me still likes to side with people's needs, but the part of me that has grown up in the shelter and has learned what can happen and that things can go wrong is sort of the conservative side of me. I definitely have concerns about letting more people in."

After substantial debate, the student-directors arrived at a consensus whereby they would let more people in if an additional director could come in to the shelter to keep the homeless-to-student ratio in check.

Looking back on the debates from his own volunteer days, Dr. Aaron Dutka described the shelter as genuinely "ruled by committee" and admitted that he still "idealized that sort of team environment where everyone has a say, and everyone sort of counts equally and brings their own expertise." Dr. Dutka acknowledged he has never seen such an egalitarian leadership structure since his shelter days but also believed it was necessary for a student-run homeless shelter. As he noted, "The judgment of any one 20 or 21 year old is probably not up to the challenge of running an organization like that. But the collective judgment of that group, I think, really did make that possible."

Over the course of just four weeks in 2009, then, the Harvard students operating the shelter made several fundamental changes to their organization. They decided to increase the number of homeless

that makes it feel a little more like a regular shelter." She also regretted policies that — for health code reasons — now prohibited homeless men and women from helping to prepare the shelter's meals or even entering the shelter's kitchen.

Harvard Square Shelter co-founder Stewart Guernsey acknowledged all of the ways in which the shelter circa 2009 has improved upon his own efforts back in 1983. At the same time, Guernsey noted:

It really is a much more establishment approach [today]. The approach I took was, here is a dire emergent problem that's got to be addressed today. I don't have time to set up a corporation, to get approval of the city of Cambridge, to get actual new beds and mattresses because people are freezing now. And while I certainly see the advantages of the social entrepreneurial approach, I also see the advantages of the jumping into the water approach and doing what you can where you can.

In the nostalgia of the Harvard Square Shelter's alumni, and their resistance to change, one can see the challenges that other organizations face in continually making adaptations. If Pastor Reisz, Ward Welburn, Stewart Guernsey, or Professor McGonagle were still directors at the shelter, it is far less likely that an endowment campaign would have been launched, a resource advocacy program developed, or the practice established of drug testing and breathalyzing potentially intoxicated guests. Were Pastor Fred Reisz still involved in the shelter's operation when this year's student-directors contemplated a shift to bed allocation via a lottery system, Pastor Reisz would have been there to explain why such a plan had already been considered and rejected in the mid-1980s. And perhaps one of the reasons the University Lutheran congregation expressed such hesitation about the endowment campaign was precisely because so many of the congregation's leaders *were* a part of the effort in 1983 to create a basement shelter and could recall the anti-establishment principles guiding the shelter in its early years. Raising funds to buy into the Harvard University endowment felt to these congregants like a far cry from Catholic Worker or creative non-violence sensibilities.

Of course, the differences between the college student-volunteers 25 years ago and today should not be exaggerated. Joshua Villanueva, who volunteered at the shelter from 1986 to 1988, chose to enter city and state politics upon graduating from Harvard — not a particularly anti-establishment endeavor. And current senior Kathryn Tobin characterized her high school mentor as the "last socialist in North Dakota" and referred to her own tendency to "idealize certain socialist texts." Clearly, the shelter volunteers of yesterday and today are not entirely separate species. Yet, there seems to be no question that the Harvard students operating the shelter in 2008–09 were far more influenced by a spirit of social enterprise than creative non-violence. As Harvard senior Robert Vozar said, "I think we can dramatically improve how much we actually help homeless people by applying the same standard to our social policies that we expect from our drugs and [that] we expect from our projects in the developing world." By "same standard," Vozar meant that there should be "randomized evaluation of programs [in which] we randomly assign some people to the program, assign some people not into the program, and actually see" what is being accomplished.

Vozar was not alone in his focus on evaluation. The students in charge of the Street Team kept meticulous records of the number of homeless individuals spoken to, food distributed, and referrals made. As described earlier in this chapter, they planned to utilize these data to inform their planning for the second year of Street Team and also in the creation of a handbook for the student-volunteers that succeed them. It is perhaps not surprising, then, that Philip Mangano, who seeks to bring traditional business strategies such as cost-benefit analysis into the field of combating homelessness, regards the current crop of Harvard students operating the Harvard Square Shelter as more innovative than their colleagues at traditional homeless shelters. Many of those colleagues are the contemporaries of Ward Welburn, Pastor Reisz, and Professor McGonagle whose commitment to this work was informed by a very different set of ideas and who, for all of the reasons described by psychologist Robert Evans, resist seeing the world through a different lens. In describing the adaptations and adjustments that the Harvard Square Shelter has undergone over the past 25 years, my intention is not to compare the merits of different generations of volunteers, but rather to note the "unusualness" of an organization that has been able to make such dramatic adaptations in such a relatively short period of time.

In describing the nimbleness with which the Harvard Square Shelter volunteers make changes and adaptations, I do not mean to imply that all of their changes and adaptations are always for the best. One could likely fill another chapter with ideas that never came to fruition or had to be quickly abandoned. However, in the examples offered in this chapter, I have sought to demonstrate ways in which the spirit of flexibility and innovation with which these young adults manage the shelter leads them to search continually for the most effective ways to support the homeless people staying there. And when these young adults misstep — as inevitably happens — their flexibility allows those missteps to be corrected quickly as well.

THE OLD GUARD

Having focused this chapter on the nimbleness of the young adults operating the Harvard Square Shelter to adapt to the needs of the homeless, I close with one final example of change-in-progress. Sophomore Christopher Kitts was an overnight supervisor during the 2008–09 winter and planned to take over in 2009–10 as one of the shelter's administrative directors. Like the hundreds of students who have come before him, Kitts was eager to place his own stamp on the policies, procedures, and principles governing the shelter. Kitts said, "I think there's a lot of inertia with people saying this is the way things are, they generally work, there's not a reason to necessarily change them." As his own turn as a director approached, Kitts was eager to implement numerous changes that included "allowing more people in at different times during the year," "increasing the number of beds we give out," and "expand[ing] who we distribute food to." For the past several years, after the security guard leaves at midnight, the shelter has not allowed anyone else to come inside the shelter under any circumstances. Kitts hoped to change this policy. From his perspective:

> "We should not have empty beds no matter what. . . . My broader philosophy is that we should dispense all our resources. We have them, we're lucky to have them, we need to use them, or they go bad. A bed that goes unused, in my mind it spoils. It's gone bad. The same thing with food. I'd like to see us move in that direction."

Whether or not these adaptations occur will depend on Kitt's ability to form a consensus with the other Harvard students stepping up to lead the shelter. In his plans, however, one cannot help but hear the passion, enthusiasm, and commitment to continuous improvement that are the marks of young adulthood and constitute several of the shelter's greatest strengths.

Chapter 6

Sheltered *from* the Ivory Tower

W hen he arrived at Harvard as a freshman in 1986, state senator Joshua Villanueva felt like a fish out of water. A Cuban-American raised in a working-class community in Florida, Villanueva looked around his freshman dormitory and saw only affluent prep school graduates "genetically entitled to go to Harvard." Coming to Harvard suddenly seemed like an enormous mistake.

Ward Welburn arrived at Harvard two years later as the insider of insiders. His grandfather had been a humanities professor at Harvard for over 40 years and was described in his obituary by the *New York Times* as "the embodiment of Harvard." Welburn had attended an elite preparatory boarding school, and so he arrived at Harvard already friends with dozens of classmates and upperclassmen. For both Villanueva and Welburn, however, the Harvard Square Homeless Shelter came to serve as a refuge — a shelter — from the elements of Harvard that did not quite work for them.

Everything about Harvard felt alien to Villanueva during his freshman year: his affluent classmates, the harsh Boston winters, skiing, prep schools, finals clubs, and the rigor of academic classes for which he felt unprepared. Villanueva coped with his feelings of alienation by throwing himself into his schoolwork and his volunteer work at the Harvard Square Shelter. As he recalled, "It was almost work to the point of eliminating any sort of real social life while I was at Harvard."

Towards this end, he signed up for a weekly Saturday overnight shift at the shelter. As Villanueva explained, "By choosing Saturday night, it made my social life much easier at Harvard. Because one of my two nights was spoken for." In this way, the shelter served for Villanueva as a sort of "pressure valve." In his words, "It allowed me to escape some of the stuff I didn't necessarily want to be around, and which I didn't necessarily like or respect."

The Harvard Square Shelter also helped to turn Harvard into a more welcoming place for Villanueva. The shelter became a niche where he felt comfortable, and the other students he befriended at the shelter made "the social waters a little easier to navigate."[1] Looking back on his freshman year conception of Harvard as a playground for wealthy prepsters, Villanueva noted: "That Harvard was clearly not mine, and I had to figure out what was my Harvard."

The playground for wealthy prepsters *was* Ward Welburn's Harvard, but that didn't mean he particularly wanted it. Though he joined one of Harvard's elite finals clubs, Welburn admitted that "There wasn't much going on in the evenings that I found terribly interesting. . . . Was I going to go to the Hasty Pudding Club and drink myself into a stupor or go watch a movie or something? Why? Why did I need to do that? It never seemed appealing to me." Instead, Welburn began spending *both* his Friday and Saturday nights at the Harvard Square Shelter. According to Welburn, rather than partaking in a social life that struck him as "pretty boring and a waste of time . . . I figured I could be in the shelter doing something that's really needed."

The Harvard Square Shelter also captured Welburn's interest and excitement in a way that his academic courses failed to. As he described it, "I think college for me was not terribly interesting. Academically, I tended to be motivated more by personal relationships than by the material." Welburn's academic success in high school had been motivated in large part by his respect for his teachers and his desire to win their respect. In the more impersonal university setting, he felt less motivated to spend his time "reading stuff I didn't want to read and writing the boring papers I didn't want to write."[2] Instead, Welburn directed his energy and passion towards his work at the Harvard Square Shelter: "It's where my friends were. It's where I spent a lot of my free time, and it became a community within [Harvard], and it was also a very rewarding thing to be a part of. So I really prioritized it in terms of the time I had in college." For Welburn, the Harvard Square Shelter injected a much needed sense of meaning and purpose into his college years: "Nothing else really felt like I was doing anything that sort of justified my existence on the planet."[3] A religious young man who would later be ordained as an Episcopal priest, Welburn saw his work at the shelter as representing "a combination of my faith and my belief in service."[4]

In very different ways, then, Senator Joshua Villanueva and Reverend Ward Welburn utilized the Harvard Square Homeless Shelter as a refuge from aspects of Harvard that felt alien to them and as a testing ground for work, relationships, and experiences that they could not find elsewhere on the Harvard campus. Over the past 25 years, the shelter has played these same roles for many of the Harvard students who volunteer there.[5]

The preceding three chapters focused on the ways in which the developmental stage of the Harvard students operating the shelter allows these young adults to approach their volunteer work with unique levels of passion, flexibility, and desire for connection. These qualities offer significant benefits to the homeless men and women who stay there. The succeeding three chapters shift their focus to the ways in which volunteering at the Harvard Square Shelter provides substantial benefits for young adults in the process of transitioning from adolescence to emerging adulthood. A number of these benefits can be seen in the experiences of Joshua Villanueva and Ward Welburn; however, they are only two of the hundreds of Harvard students who have utilized the shelter as an escape from the "Harvard bubble."

BURSTING THE HARVARD BUBBLE

In 2008, Yale Professor William Deresiewicz wrote an article for the *American Scholar* that made the rounds on Ivy League campuses.[6] Entitled "The Disadvantages of an Elite Education," Deresiewicz's article argued that elite universities such as Harvard provide insular educational experiences that leave their graduates unprepared for the real world. Specifically, Deresiewicz asserted that an elite education "makes you incapable of talking to people who aren't like you" and "believe that people who didn't go to an Ivy League or equivalent school weren't worth talking to."[7] He concluded that the unspoken mission of elite institutions is to prepare students for life in the upper echelons of society.

Interestingly, nearly all of the Harvard students volunteering at the shelter during 2008–09 characterized their volunteer work as helping them to break out of the Harvard bubble. And, in fact, nearly every student used that precise phrase — "the Harvard bubble."[8] Senior Leo LaSala explained that he began volunteering at the shelter because, "I liked the idea of something that would break the Harvard bubble, something that would work directly with poverty." LaSala added that, after his first few overnights at the shelter, he made the decision to stop bringing along his schoolwork. In his words, "I very much liked being in the space and liked separating myself from Harvard . . . And then I realized it didn't feel right bringing my Harvard stress into this space where people have real problems." Likewise, in reflecting on his first year of volunteer work at the shelter, sophomore Liam Murphy remarked that "This is an experience I definitely want to keep [doing] because it helps me break away from the bubble." Junior Larry Yoon related how his work at the shelter "sustains me, not like physically because it's actually exhausting, but spiritually, morally, emotionally, because I'm outside the Harvard bubble."[9]

As noted, Erikson characterized adolescence as the period in which individuals move beyond a strict adherence to the values and world-view of their family and community and begin to seek out additional perspectives and points of view.[10] Erikson referred to the bearers of these additional perspectives as the "guardians of a final identity."[11] For many adolescents, the college years represent an opportunity to live in a more diverse environment, to hear new points of view offered by classmates and professors, and to reflect upon alternative ideologies never previously discussed or considered.[12] The Harvard Square Shelter volunteers who expressed enthusiasm for breaking out of the Harvard bubble, however, were pushing their identity exploration even further. Perhaps they recognized an element of truth in Yale Professor Deresiewicz's claim that elite schools may be racially and ethnically diverse, but "with respect to class, these schools are largely — indeed increasingly — homogeneous."[13] Deresiewicz quips: "Visit any elite campus in our great nation and you can thrill to the heartwarming spectacle of the children of White businesspeople and professionals studying and playing alongside the children of black, Asian, and Latino businesspeople and professionals."[14] The trajectory of Joshua Villanueva and many other shelter volunteers belie Deresiewicz's generalization; nonetheless, a number of these volunteers consciously identified the Harvard Square Shelter as a mechanism for escaping an insular college campus and thereby adding a more diverse range of perspectives to their process of development.

Breaking out of the Harvard bubble meant different things to different students. Harvard junior Amanda Mooney noted that she benefited from watching the shelter's homeless guests contend bravely with their own, more significant, problems:

> "The little two-hour slices, even as a breakfast volunteer, it's a complete departure from what we always call the Harvard bubble. . . . I just had so many interactions with guests who cope with their problems in a very graceful and dignified way, and it's a breath of fresh air to know that a heroin addict who's barely five months clean is sitting here calm and chill and being like, 'I'm making the next step towards fixing my life.'"

Mooney added that these lessons in grace have been useful for her because, as an aspiring doctor, she felt the pressure of sitting in class each day with hundreds of highly competitive classmates. Mooney admitted:

> "In high school, I was just very anxious about academic success, and it's something that I still care about, but I feel that I'm not getting any gray hairs over it. And I don't know if that's just aging and maturing, but I think the shelter does play a part in that."[15]

Senior Hope Franklin added that she learned from the shelter's homeless men and women about the importance of finding happiness in small, everyday moments. As she observed of the guests she encountered at the shelter:

> "You also feel good about things because here [are] people who have it really hard, and they are happy. They are happy to be getting breakfast, they are happy to be having a short conversation with you, so who am I to complain about aspects of my life when they can be so satisfied in theirs?"

In making this point, Franklin echoed an observation by shelter alumnus Dr. Aaron Dutka that working at the Harvard Square Shelter taught him about homeless people's significant survivor skills:

"It's a tough existence, and people live through it. And they're not always in despair. They're not always miserable, you know. They find a way to scratch some joy out of a part of different days. And you know they can treat others with kindness that you don't understand where that comes from. So that I learned there."

Senior Drew McGinty added that volunteering at the Harvard Square Shelter influenced him even when he was outside the shelter's walls:

"It can be the shot of reality you need. I mean if you're walking outside in the winter and it is just too frigging cold, I don't think I would be as happy with myself if the question coming up in my mind was, 'Oh shoot, good thing I live in this big old dorm. I really want to get some free brain break.' When the question is actually, 'Damn, how do people sleep out here?' You know, I feel like it has made me into a more thoughtful person in many ways."

"Brain break" refers to the snack put out each night in the Harvard dormitories for students in need of sustenance to fuel their late-night studying.[16] In this reference, McGinty perfectly captured the ability of his work at the shelter to redirect his attention from problem-sets and mid-terms to some of the weighty issues occurring just a few blocks *off* the Harvard campus.

Finally, it was notable that the volunteers from other universities used identical language to describe the shelter's effect upon their worldviews. For example, Wellesley College sophomore Charlotte Wu remarked that the Harvard Square Shelter "helped me realize that there's a world outside college because it can be like a bubble some-times. And realize that while we're in school, talking in class about really theoretical things, there are real world problems out there." Wellesley College undoubtedly qualifies as an elite institution as well, but it seems likely that the insularity all of these students describe is more a function of living in a microcosm filled with other young adults than the "eliteness" of any particular institution.[17]

Looking back on their college experiences, the alumni from the Harvard Square Homeless Shelter also invoked the image of a bubble to describe the shelter's importance upon their lives. Dr. Kristin Sommers, who volunteered in the mid-1990s, recalled: "In some ways it was a fantasy those four years of college and your bubble and going to school and your great life and people you're sharing it with, but I think the shelter grounded me to another community and things that are bigger than just me." Amelia Ginsberg, who volunteered in the late 1990s, noted that she specifically sought out the shelter during her freshman year of college because "I was becoming increasingly eager to find some sort of life beyond Harvard Yard."[18]

On a similar note, alumnus Dr. Aaron Dutka recalled making a decision to volunteer at the shelter rather than to pledge (or "punch") one of Harvard's finals clubs. Finals clubs — Harvard's version of fraternities — count approximately 20 percent of Harvard's male undergraduates as their members.[19] As a varsity water polo player and graduate of the prestigious Phillips Andover prep school, Dr. Dutka was a prime candidate for membership in one of these clubs. Yet, as he commented:

> "It just didn't feel like the whole finals club thing was going to add something different to my [college] experience . . . I didn't come to Harvard to meet more people like me . . . I didn't have an extreme aversion to people like me, but I didn't want to be surrounded by people like me all the time in a bubble. So I think probably the shelter was the biggest thing I did to get out of that."

The finals clubs — many of which prohibit non-members from attending their parties and events — represent a significant social outlet on the Harvard campus. However, Dr. Dutka recognized the importance of breaking out of the Harvard bubble for many of the reasons described above by current shelter volunteers. In describing himself as *not* wanting to be surrounded at all times by people similar to himself, Dutka underscored the way in which the Harvard Square Shelter facilitates its volunteers' identity development by providing access to a more diverse set of individuals and points of view. As James Youniss and his colleagues have noted, in this exposure to diverse viewpoints, "Youth learn about society and the various orientations they may take toward it. They may seek to support, reject, or revise the traditions they find. But in order for identity to develop, youth need to have social substance on which to reflect and build."[20]

A question posed to all of the current volunteers and alumni was the image that comes to mind when they think of the Harvard Square Homeless Shelter. A number of the alumni cited the steep staircase that led down into the shelter prior to the 1999 renovation. In reference to this vivid recollection, Rusty Sadow noted that "We were entering some place completely different than the rest of our lives at Harvard, and walking down the stairs and into a different world." Clearly, many of the shelter's current and former volunteers recognized their weekly entrance into this different world as offering significant benefits in regards to their own growth and development.

FROM HUMBLE BEGINNINGS

While all Harvard students might be characterized as "privileged" by virtue of the education they are receiving, by no means do all of the students volunteering at the Harvard Square Shelter come from lives of privilege.[21] In 1986, Joshua Villanueva may have felt like the only freshman on campus from working class roots, but, in fact, as a result of a 2006 financial aid initiative in which families with incomes below $60,000 pay nothing towards their children's tuition, Harvard now receives applications from a significant number of high school seniors with excellent academic records but limited financial resources.[22]

A number of the young adults volunteering at the Harvard Square Shelter described their volunteer work as a means of proving to themselves and their home communities that they had not turned into the stereotype of an over-privileged Harvard student.[23] Perhaps the student for whom this motivation was the strongest was Harvard junior Melissa Sanguinetti. Sanguinetti grew up in rural South Dakota, the daughter of a single father who worked as a guidance counselor at the local high school. According to Sanguinetti, she never would have applied to colleges outside the Midwest if she had not contacted South Dakota Senator Tom Daschle's office during her junior year of high school about interning in his Pierre office. One of Daschle's staffers urged Sanguinetti to apply to the Congressional Page Program — a program in Washington DC that brings approximately 30 high school students a semester to Washington DC to assist members of the House of Representatives.[24] In part because South Dakota Senator Tom Daschle was then the Senate minority leader, Sanguinetti was chosen to participate in the program. There, one of her teachers convinced her to apply to a single Ivy League institution — Harvard. By Sanguinetti's account, even despite her father's work as a school counselor, she had never heard of the common application or the SAT II exams that Harvard required, and her teacher at Page School went to considerable effort to help her put together her application.

Sanguinetti was accepted by Harvard in December 2005, but her father urged her not to tell anyone about the acceptance until April. According to Sanguinetti:

> "He was concerned that the financial aid wasn't going to come through and that people would think differently of me or of him. I guess he was just really concerned too that I was leaving and that I would somehow come back a very different person and just have lost touch with this state. I mean, everyone else has stayed in state."

This fear of losing touch with South Dakota played heavily on Sanguinetti's mind as well. She explained that "There is sort of this tradition in South Dakota where anyone who leaves is sort of a traitor . . . And I was kind of concerned in terms of, if I leave this state, how am I going to prove to people that I'm still connected?"

Perhaps the person whose opinion Sanguinetti valued most was her uncle, a public defender who had been active in the civil rights movement as well as in the Vietnam War protests. Many years earlier, her uncle had been accepted to Harvard Law School but had chosen to attend the University of South Dakota Law School instead. As Sanguinetti contemplated her acceptance at Harvard, she said that "I think my biggest concern when I got into Harvard was, 'What is he going to think of this?' Because I knew his history, and I think he was a little bit reluctant or hesitant. He was concerned I'd come back a changed person and have lost touch."

Upon arriving at Harvard for her freshman year, Sanguinetti immediately saw the Harvard Square Shelter as a means of demonstrating a connection to her South Dakotan roots:

> "I think, in some ways, it felt like more of a continuation of what other family members had done. Both my mom and her brother do public interest law. My dad is a school counselor. My grandma is a school counselor, and my godparents worked with the local homeless population doing mental health and job stuff. And so I was like, I'm still connected to these people at home because I'm doing similar sort of work."

Working at the shelter also assuaged Sanguinetti's guilt about pursuing a liberal arts degree. "Even the idea of getting a liberal arts degree is pretty ridiculous among the people I grew up with. It just seems like, why would you go to school for a degree that isn't directly useful? So the shelter was kind of like me saying, 'Oh there is a higher purpose to all this.'"

In Sanguinetti's mind, her work at the shelter allowed her to go home to South Dakota each Christmas and over the summer and convince people that she hadn't lost touch with her roots.[25] As she noted of her uncle, "Every time I go back, I think he's kind of relieved to see that I'm still the same person." Moreover, Sanguinetti used the shelter to deflect questions about perceptions of East Coast snobbery:

> "When people at home will ask me about the sort of finals club types of things or you know polo shirts and golf courses, I'm sort of sheltered from that aspect of the university. I don't really see that very often. The shelter has really become what I think of when I think of Harvard."

Ironically, Sanguinetti used the term "sheltered" to describe the role that the Harvard Square Shelter played in preserving her distance from the stereotypical Harvard student.

Other students described the shelter as playing a similar role in their own relationships with their home communities. Junior Amanda Mooney grew up in an affluent Michigan suburb but nonetheless recalled that during her senior year of high school "beloved teachers who wrote my Harvard recommendation letters [would] come up to me and be like, 'Don't change, you know, we love you, we love you [the way you are].'" Like Sanguinetti, Mooney learned that her work at the shelter could assuage her mentors' concerns:

> "When I send them emails about how my life is going, and I mention the singing I do and I also talk about the shelter a lot, and they're like, 'We're so glad you haven't changed.' And I always took that kind of with a grain of salt because in a way it's like, did you think I would have? But at the same time I feel almost proud. I'm just very grateful that I found this avenue."

Also like Sanguinetti, Amanda Mooney described herself at Christmas and over summers as getting "kind of barraged with questions about how do you handle the snooty Harvard students?" She too relied upon her shelter work to characterize herself as sheltered from elitist, wealthy classmates.

Several other student-volunteers focused less on pressure from their respective hometowns and more on an internal desire to remain connected to a less privileged conception of themselves. Junior Lester Pearsons grew up outside London where his mother worked in a factory and his father as a gas station attendant. He was the first person in his family to go to college. As Pearsons described it, "I feel there's some sense of my roots that have perhaps made me more humble than your [typical] Harvard roots. So I think that's something that makes me want to step away from Harvard students now and then." Pearsons saw his evening shift at the shelter as one means of taking a step away. On a similar note, freshman Ashwin Ganguli grew up in India and described himself as coming from "pretty humble beginnings." In the fall of his freshman year at Harvard, he signed up for an overnight shift at the Harvard Square Shelter out of fear that he might become "carried away by this whole Harvard bubble."

Sophomore Liam Murphy grew up in rural Oklahoma, the son of an unemployed father and a mother who worked as an assistant at the local bank. He described himself as receiving the maximum amount of financial aid that Harvard offers and saw his weekly shift at the Harvard Square Shelter as a means of keeping "me grounded in a sense of who I am and who I want to be." He also noted that, though his family has never experienced homelessness, "There are times that my family needed help like this." Perhaps not surprisingly, Murphy was drawn to a position as one of the shelter's resource advocates — a position in which he worked to connect homeless men and women to resources that could improve their situations.[26]

Psychologist Erik Erikson has written that adolescents seek to piece together a coherent identity by melding the beliefs and values with which they were raised and the new perspectives and worldviews they are acquiring as young adults.[27] Susan Harter has added that, as part of this process, adolescents can become "morbidly preoccupied with what they appear to be in the eyes of others."[28] Shelter volunteers like Sanguinetti, Mooney, Pearsons, and Murphy were clearly concerned about what effect the privileged ambiance of Harvard might have upon the ways in which they were seen by others and also by the potential effects of this ambiance upon their childhood beliefs and values. They regarded their volunteer work at the shelter as a means of staying true to a particular set of beliefs and values they had brought with them to Harvard and wanted to hold on to.

Because of stereotypes of Harvard as a bastion of elitism, it may be surprising to hear just a few of the personal histories of young adults who arrived at this elite institution from more humble beginnings. However, Lucy Draper — a formerly homeless woman who now directs a non-profit organization that helps the homeless get back on their feet — noted that for many years she has come to talk during freshman week at Harvard to a group of students interested in community service and that "There is always one person who has been homeless in the group in one form or another." It would seem that many of the students coming from such humble beginnings gravitate to the Harvard Square Shelter out of a desire to help others in similar situations but also as a means of preserving their sense of connection to the communities from which they came.

A RESPITE

In describing what he liked about volunteering at the shelter, senior Robert Vozar said, "It's fast-paced on the dinner shifts, but I just felt very comfortable there talking to people, doing my work. It's kind of like a respite even though it's the real world. In some ways being in the real world is like a respite from the Harvard campus." For many of its current and former volunteers, the Harvard Square Shelter served as a respite from various facets of their college experience. For some students, this respite took the form of a break from their academic work. As senior Elyse Margolis commented:

> "If I'm not there, the rest of the time I spend in the library or in my room or in class, and so those are all places where I like to be thinking about my academics, especially with the thesis. And with the shelter, I'm just so constantly busy every second there isn't time to stop and think, and it sort of is a refuge, and it is just a happy time where I am with two of my friends, and we listen to pop music."

Several other seniors described the shelter as a useful respite from their theses as well. For example, senior Leo LaSala said:

> "I was one of the very few shelter directors that didn't miss a single one of my shifts because of my thesis . . . I was like,

I spend all day writing my thesis, this is my time to *not* think about it. And even other stressful stuff that's happened with family stuff, relationship stuff, getting in there is a good way to have it all off your back."

Junior Jerry Chen expressed a similar sentiment in describing the shelter as his "safe haven." According to Chen:

"You go there, and it's like you adopt a new life. You're just like, school doesn't matter right now. People outside the shelter don't matter. That party you wanted to go to, that doesn't matter. It's like oh this needs to be done, that needs to be done. How can I better improve this? Do I sit down and grab a meal with a guest? Do I have time to do that? Sure, let's go do it, and you kind of are thinking so much that everything else just becomes less important, and it's nice because, outside of the shelter, I'm kind of a really neurotic person."

Senior Kathryn Tobin described the challenge of spending 18 hours a day in front of her computer for the four weeks before her economics thesis was due. She explained that the experience had resulted "in this kind of deep burn-out, and I think going to the shelter for a couple of shifts during spring break really helped reorient me again, took me out of the more introverted space I was in." According to Tobin, introversion was impossible at the shelter. "You need to be engaged in your outside environment or things don't work."

Psychologist Mihaly Csikszentmihalyi defines "flow" as an experience characterized by a "deep spontaneous involvement with the task at hand."[29] Individuals experiencing flow are concentrating deeply on the goal to be accomplished and are too engaged by this goal to experience feelings of anxiety, boredom, or distraction. In their descriptions of their volunteer work at the Harvard Square Shelter, students like Tobin, Chen, and others seemed to characterize their work inside the shelter as providing them with a flow-like experience. Fully engaged in their interactions with the shelter's homeless guests and the tasks necessary to keep the shelter operating smoothly, they did not have time to worry about academic pressures, conflicts with friends or senior theses. They simply focused on the work at hand. Csikszentmihalyi characterizes activities that result in flow as the ideal mechanism for growth during adolescence. From his perspective, "Flow experiences *realize* a person's existence; they build a self that is conscious of its freedom and history."[30] In short, Csikszentmihalyi would likely cite the Harvard Square Homeless Shelter as an important testing ground for many Harvard students' growing understanding of who they are and who they want to become.

Other students described the shelter as a respite from the general intensity of the Harvard campus. As senior Kelly Parker noted, "You come to college and you just sort of hit the ground running, and you're supposed to differentiate yourself academically. . . . It's pretty intense, and people care a lot about their grades. I suppose it [the shelter] has been a refuge." Likewise, senior Hope Franklin acknowledged:

> "Harvard also can reinforce a hierarchy or make you feel bad about yourself if you did badly on a test, you did not get whatever internship . . . and here is just a place where you can feel like you are doing something great. You feel good about yourself for helping other people."

Senior Lissette McDonald — a pre-medical student — stated flatly that "The first thing that comes to mind [when I think of Harvard] is competition. . . . It's the sort of race to get to the top, and to have a direction. The definition of success is very specific." McDonald added: "I often don't enjoy this environment, and the shelter is a part of being here that I really do enjoy."

Harvard alumni recall the Harvard Square Shelter as offering a similar respite during their own student days. For example, Helen Van Anglen remembered:

> "[Harvard is] just incredibly competitive, which just makes it a nightmare because it's always about who's going to get the better grade on the test, who's going to whatever, whatever, and your sense of self gets wrapped up in that. And then there's this place where you're stewards of something, and the competition is to make it as good as you possibly can, collectively."

Professor Dennis McGonagle — a shelter alumnus from the late 1980s — expressed an identical sentiment when he described the shelter as providing a respite from feeling "like you're always having to perform. Because the academic context is more about what your individual performance is going to be. At the shelter, it was more like can we all have a positive meal together?" According to both Van Anglen and McGonagle, the Harvard Square Shelter presented an opportunity for collective — rather than competitive — action.

Another set of students characterized the shelter as a respite from purely cerebral work. At the conclusion of his first season volunteering at the shelter in April 2009, Harvard junior Louis Landau said, "It turns out I like manual labor. Washing dishes can be fun." He also added that the overnight shift had provided some time for more free-form thinking. According to Landau, "A lot of my free time I try to spend doing research and math, and I don't have a lot of free time, but it's nice having time in the middle of the night when not too many people are up to think about things." Senior Hope Franklin noted "how it's very satisfying to be doing dishes, accomplishing something very tangible, concrete. You can see it rather than writing a paper or pulling theories out of who knows where and trying to synthesize them into some argument." Harvard junior Lester Pearsons observed that it was difficult sometimes to pull himself away from his academic work to go to his weekly evening shift at the shelter, but that he typically came away having appreciated the opportunity to do "a nice brainless thing" like washing dishes or mopping the kitchen floor. As Pearsons noted, "I always feel better leaving than I do going to the shelter."[31]

Other students describe their weekly shelter shift as simply a lot of fun. Senior Robert Vozar said, "I guess I think that it's fun. It's a nice respite from the campus, and you can goof off in the kitchen. And on my last shift, we had an 'eat the grossest food possible' contest." Sophomore Antonia Garcia-Brown, who characterized herself as overwhelmed by Harvard's competitive environment, described the shelter as a place that "pretty reliably turns around my mood." Alumna Helen Van Anglen recalled: "I felt like I belonged at the Harvard Square Shelter . . . I liked the people there. There were sort of real conversations, and it was fun." In these comments, one can see support for scholarship by Omoto, Snyder, and Martino that young adults often look to community service as a mechanism for satisfying relational needs as well as a break from a college campus that can feel overwhelming.[32]

A REFUGE

At one of the shelter's Resource Advocacy meetings in 2009, the Harvard students played a game in which one student would read a statement, and then everyone would go to a corner of the room that indicated their agreement or disagreement with the statement. Sophomore Antonia Garcia-Brown recalled that "One of the statements was, 'I sometimes feel more comfortable in the shelter than I do in class,' and pretty much everyone went to 'Strongly Agree.'" Similar to Senator Joshua Villanueva, a number of Harvard students during 2008–09 utilized the shelter as a refuge from a campus in which they felt like they didn't quite fit in. Senior Drew McGinty said, "There's many aspects of a typical Harvard personality that I just don't jive with." From his perspective, "Harvard is about climbing and economic betterment, and it's just there are a lot of people here whose drives are very different than mine." He recalled arriving on campus as a freshman and realizing pretty quickly that he didn't "click with everyone friendwise." McGinty's sense of alienation from his classmates led him to move off campus for his senior year, yet he described the shelter as his "home away from home here" and that his experience at the shelter had made Harvard "better for me in so many ways."

Junior Melissa Sanguinetti — the student from South Dakota — commented that "Freshman and sophomore year were really a challenge for me here to try to figure out how I fit into this scene." She compared Harvard to a "stiff suit that just was never going to fit right." Perhaps as a result of her discomfort with Harvard's social scene, Sanguinetti volunteered to work the Friday night overnight shift. As she joked, "I was actually very happy with Friday nights, maybe because my social life isn't that exciting." Fortunately, the other students Sanguinetti met through her involvement at the shelter "fit" her better. While most came from very different hometowns and families, Sanguinetti described the other volunteers she met and befriended as "kind of going in the same direction" as herself and possessing "similar worldviews and similar priorities." As she moved into the latter half of her college career, Sanguinetti felt as if the shelter had helped her to find a pocket of Harvard in which she felt comfortable. In her words, "Maybe the institution as a whole is not exactly a reflection of me, but this little niche of it is." Similar to Senator Villanueva two decades earlier, Sanguinetti's work at the Harvard Square Shelter helped her to find *her* Harvard.

Perhaps because they were now several years removed from the college experience, several Harvard alumni echoed Senator Villanueva in characterizing their volunteer work at the shelter as a refuge from Harvard's social scene. Professor Dennis McGonagle recalled: "I always signed up [to volunteer] on the same night, which was Saturday night. That tells you something about my feelings about the undergraduate party life." He described the Harvard Square Shelter — along with the community he found at the Harvard Divinity School — as having made his undergraduate years "tolerable." According to McGonagle, "I didn't really like being with other 20 year olds. And having two places where I didn't have to be with them, yeah, that's what kept it [Harvard] from being completely alienating." Alumnus Rusty Sadow, who worked a weekend overnight shift for his first two years at Harvard, characterized himself as someone who wasn't "super social" and that he felt that "hanging out with the people at the shelter is just as good a way to spend a Friday night as anything else." He also acknowledged a certain relief at the time in not having "to worry about making plans" each weekend.

Harvard junior Nathan Small characterized the shelter as a refuge for him in a somewhat different manner. As described in Chapter 4, Small — who grew up just a few blocks from Harvard — began volunteering at the shelter on Friday nights as a high school student at Cambridge Rindge & Latin School. This past winter, Small spent three nights a week at the shelter, working a director's shift on Wednesday nights and supervising the current crop of Cambridge high schoolers on Friday and Sunday nights. Reflecting on what he got out of the experience, Small explained that the shelter "is my most important community, and I depend on it a lot, both my relationships with the guests and my relationships with the staff." Small also admitted that his connection to the shelter had been influenced by the instability in his family life:

> "A big part of the shelter's meaning for me and why it's been such a huge part of my life is just that it really has been the most constant thing in my life for the past six years in terms of what I do, my friends, even my family, where I live, where I spend my time. . . . My mom passed away the year before my freshman year. So this place has always been really important to me."

Sadly, a shelter alumna, Helen Van Anglen, described the shelter as offering a similar type of refuge for her when her father died three weeks into her freshman year at Harvard:

> "I wasn't functioning on all cylinders necessarily and was mixed up and confused and feeling shat upon. And Harvard,

you know, isn't a particularly empathetic place, and it felt really divorced from what I cared about. . . . But why do we feel like we fit in at certain places? Maybe it's just that there are people there we can talk to, or we find people like ourselves, so I think that working at the shelter, I found some [like-minded] volunteers there."

Both Small and Van Anglen turned to their volunteer work at the Harvard Square Shelter as a mechanism for coping with the painful loss of a parent. In so doing, they embodied what Csikszentmihalyi and Larson characterize as an "ultimate achievement" in the transition towards adulthood — "transforming a misfortune in one's life or in the wider social environment into a goal that gives direction and meaning."[33]

KEEPING IT REAL

In his 2008 book, *The Path to Purpose*, psychologist William Damon asserts that "The most pervasive problem of the day is a sense of emptiness that has ensnared many young people in long periods of drift during a time in their lives when they should be defining their aspirations and making progress toward their fulfillment."[34] In short, Damon argues that too few young people are developing in young adulthood a sense of purpose — an intention to accomplish something that is "meaningful to the self and at the same time consequential for the world beyond the self."[35] In making the argument for the importance of purpose, Damon cites scholarship by Paul Baltes and Dan McAdams that has found individuals who try to make a positive difference in the world to live healthier, happier lives.[36] He also quotes nineteenth-century thinker Thomas Carlyle: "A person without purpose is like a ship without a rudder."

Similar to Ward Welburn, many Harvard students have sought and found such a sense of purpose at the Harvard Square Shelter. For example, freshman Ashwin Ganguli, a computer science major, explained that "There's so much work [in college], but none of it is really significant in the real sense. So I definitely felt like I needed a place where I can help make a difference." Junior Louis Landau, a mathematics major, made a similar point even more starkly: "Most of what I do is completely useless. Enjoyable, but that gets old after a while. And I mean volunteerism seems to be one of the most obviously useful and valuable things that we have an opportunity to do." Landau, who enjoyed his mathematics coursework enough to be considering a career as a math professor, expressed a need to be involved in something more immediately applicable to the problems in the real world.

Sophomore Liam Murphy began the 2008–09 year as an evening volunteer and then added a weekly shift at the shelter's Resource Advocacy table. He offered the following explanation for why he was drawn to the Resource Advocacy position:

> "It contrasted with some other things I was doing in that there was real stuff being done. Like if I went to a meeting of the Undergraduate Council, I couldn't say that I helped put someone in housing, that I had found housing for someone. And if I went to class and did well on one of my mid-terms, that was great, and that's what I'm here for, but at the same time it was awesome to go there (the shelter) and do something real and substantial."

As a pre-medical student, the majority of Murphy's classes were science courses designed to prepare him for medical school. Likewise, as a member of Harvard's Undergraduate Council, he was involved in decisions that impacted Harvard's undergraduate community. Yet, Murphy still felt the Harvard Square Shelter could make his life as a college student feel more purposeful.

Students like Ganguli, Landau, and Murphy enjoyed their coursework but saw their volunteer work at the shelter as an important supplement to their academic lives. Other students enjoyed their coursework far less. For example, senior Lissette McDonald — also pre-med — described the shelter as something that she "sort of grasped onto as a volunteer freshman spring, and it just pulled me through." According to McDonald, "[In] classes you're learning for yourself and, like the shelter, I had these responsibilities, and I was getting things done that were allowing something to exist and run and provide a service." For McDonald, the opportunity to play a meaningful role in keeping the shelter operating was an important balance to the insularity of her academic classes.

Sophomore Antonia Garcia-Brown expressed this same perspective even more strongly. During her freshman year at Harvard, Garcia-Brown had experienced a bout of depression in which she ceased going to classes.

The only commitment she continued to keep was her weekly appointment to tutor an elementary school student in the Boston Public Schools. After taking a year off from Harvard, Garcia-Brown returned in 2008–09 in much better health, but continued to find her community service — this time, at the Harvard Square Shelter — the most meaningful part of her week. As a result, she said towards the end of the shelter season in April of 2009, "Next year, I'm just going to chill out about academics, and just do what I need to get by academically so that I can go and do things that actually matter to me." Particularly in Garcia-Brown's case, meaningful volunteer work was crucial to her being able to stay motivated enough on a day-to-day basis to remain a student at Harvard.

Other students described the importance of doing meaningful work in conjunction with their peers. Junior Lester Pearsons asserted, "My individual contribution doesn't make a big difference. It's just the fact that me and hundreds of other people are needed for this thing to work, and without these little cogs in the machinery, it wouldn't work." Here, Pearsons expressed his recognition that the two hours a week he volunteered at the shelter were part of a larger effort that allowed an important organization to thrive. On a related note, junior Jerry Chen commented that he appreciated the opportunity the shelter provided to work alongside classmates "who genuinely care about something." Here, Chen expressed his belief that he benefitted from collaborating with peers who were committed to a purposeful endeavor. Scholar Sharon Daloz Parks has described organizations like the Harvard Square Homeless Shelter as offering young adults "networks of belonging."[37] According to Parks, such networks provide young adults with a "sense of connection and security" that are crucial for their growth and development.

A number of shelter alumni also described the Harvard Square Shelter as giving them an opportunity to do something real as they made their way through their undergraduate years. Helen Van Anglen said of her shelter experience:

> "I liked being there. I think the authority was important to me, not the authority over people, but if you're a student, it's not that everything is chewed up for you, but I certainly felt like a lot of what I was learning at Harvard was divorced from what actually mattered to me."

At the Harvard Square Shelter, Van Anglen discovered a project connected to what actually mattered to her and an organization of which she was proud to be a part. As she noted, "I think that it's actually incredibly important for people to feel a part of something bigger than themselves." Dennis McGonagle echoed this sentiment with his explanation that the shelter offered him the opportunity "just to be part of something larger." Here, Van Anglen and McGonagle expressed a sentiment similar to current students Lester Pearsons and Jerry Chen, all of which underscore Erik Erikson's identity development framework.[38] Erikson asserted that a typical response to the adolescent identity crisis is for individuals to seek out organizations and groups with which they can align themselves. According to Erikson, affiliation with such groups allows adolescents to counteract their "newly won individual identity with some communal solidarity."[39] Likewise, in his classic book, *Freedom Summer*, about college students involved in the Civil Rights movement, scholar Doug McAdam observed that "The feeling of belonging or membership in something larger than themselves was stressed by many of the volunteers as the most important legacy of Freedom Summer."[40] Affiliation with such movements and organizations also offers adolescents an opportunity to "try on" different ideologies and understandings of the world.

The desire to do something purposeful expressed by so many Harvard Square Shelter volunteers represented another way in which the relationship between students and the homeless in the shelter was a deeply symbiotic one. As noted in Chapter 4, many of the homeless men and women staying at the Harvard Square Shelter relished the opportunity to serve as teachers and advice-givers to the younger, impressionable college students they met there. Simultaneously, the Harvard students regarded their volunteer work as a means of positively impacting the world in a way that their daily academic responsibilities did not. In short, both groups were buoyed by the opportunity to have an effect upon the other.[41]

A SPECIAL COMMUNITY

The Harvard Square Shelter also offers its volunteers an entrée into a *new* community. This is likely no small piece of what draws nearly 100 volunteers to the shelter year after year as scholars such as Constance Flanagan and Allen Omoto have found that a sense of camaraderie is an integral component of a meaningful service experience, particularly for young adults.[42] Likewise, Clary and Snyder have reported that, for many volunteers, community service plays a social-adjustive function — a means of expanding one's social circle.[43]

In keeping with these findings, a number of shelter volunteers and alumni also credited the Harvard Square Shelter with introducing them to a more diverse cross-section of the Harvard community than they would have encountered on their own. This is due, in part, to Harvard's House system. All Harvard freshmen are grouped together in Harvard Yard and then are randomly assigned to spend their next three years in a particular dormitory (or "House").[44] However, freshmen may choose up to eight friends with whom they will be assigned to this particular house. It is quite easy, as a result, for students on the lacrosse team, debate club, or in the computer science department to choose a half dozen friends from their particular niche and then spend the next three years living, eating, and competing with this small group of individuals. Intimate friendships form, but the result can also be a high level of insularity.

Alumnus Dr. Aaron Dutka credited the shelter with introducing him to "a group of people who I wouldn't have met otherwise at Harvard who were very different as far as their interests and activities." Dr. Dutka spent his sophomore, junior, and senior years at Harvard living with a large group of his teammates from the water polo team. In his words, volunteering at the shelter provided "an entrée into a different social circle, and those are really important and good friendships that I forged." Senior Lissette McDonald agreed that, through the shelter, "I've met a lot of people that I otherwise wouldn't have met at Harvard, just people studying different things, people involved in all sorts of other kinds of extracurricular activities, people going on to do a variety of things."

The shelter also provides opportunities to break down stereotypes. Sophomore Christopher Kitts — a student who cited Harvard Hillel as his primary on-campus community — described his surprise at getting to know another student on his shift who was "politically conservative, very East Coast preppy, like walked into the shelter with green pants and boat shoes." To Kitts' surprise, this classmate turned out to be entirely reliable in his commitment to the shelter and the first student to volunteer for unpleasant tasks like cleaning the shelter's bathrooms. Kitts admitted that the encounter had altered his impression of some of his Harvard classmates with whom he crossed paths least often.

A number of students remarked that friendships formed through the Harvard Square Shelter developed very quickly. Junior Deanna Galante explained:

"On the overnight shift, you basically are paired with someone in the middle of the night responsible for the entire shelter. As a freshman, that's a pretty big thing. There's just a bond with spending the night in the shelter with someone. Falling asleep, sleeping in bunk beds. It felt like a sleepover, and it was nice as a freshman to have that."

Current freshman Anna Robinson described a similar experience on her overnight shift during the 2008–09 winter. As she noted, "You're up at three o'clock in the morning, and it's kind of like a bonding experience." In reference to the friends she had made through her overnight shift at the shelter, Robinson added that "I know them in a different way than I know my roommates. . . . You get to know them a lot faster through just talking and what might not otherwise come out." What both Galante and Robinson described were the bonds that form as individuals work together in pursuit of a common mission. Junior Larry Yoon added that, at the shelter, he found "a special group of people where we can share our thoughts about what's wrong with the world and how it's going to get better." Perhaps as a result, alumnus Dr. Aaron Dutka recalled his friendships with other students at the shelter as "serious adult relationships." He said: "It was the work that brought us together, but we cared about each other."

Another sign of the maturity of the relationships formed at the Harvard Square Shelter was the admiration with which the volunteers described one another. Senior Leo LaSala noted that, at the shelter, "There's this sense of support you get from people that is really impressive and something that I haven't found much yet at Harvard." Junior Jerry Chen described his fellow volunteers as "some of the best people you will find on campus. Truly kind people, and people who care for not just the well-being of the people they're close to but the general well-being of everybody." Junior Amanda Mooney remarked, "Every time I talk to my mom, every phone conversation, I feel like I mention something that I saw a staff member do, and how cool is that? Isn't that a great person? And I really do aspire to be like them, and I hope it's working. I hope they're rubbing off on me."

In their book, *Making Good*, Wendy Fischman and colleagues asserted: "Especially in the United States, the influence of peers is substantial. Involvement with peers who adhere to a high standard is likely to influence a young person to assume an admirable moral stance."[45] Supporting this claim is scholarship by Linda Sax and colleagues which has found that the best predictor of a college student's engagement in social activism during college is the level of activism of the student body at that particular college.[46] In other words, the beliefs and values of a student's peers will have a significant impact on what a young person comes to value during college. The friendships that these young adults form, then, with peers at the Harvard Square Shelter play a role in reinforcing each other's commitment to service work and activism.

In his research on student activism in the 1960s, Doug McAdam reported that the experience of driving down to Mississippi to campaign for civil rights "did more than simply radicalize the volunteers." According to McAdam:

> It also put them in contact with any number of other like-minded young people. Thus, the volunteers left Mississippi not only more disposed toward activism, but in a better structural position, by virtue of their links to one another, to act on these inclinations.[47]

When McAdam interviewed these individuals 25 years after the fact, nearly half were still in contact with at least one person whom they had met during their summer of civil rights campaigning. One can imagine the current volunteers at the Harvard Square Shelter reporting a similar maintenance of ties 25 years down the road, and in fact many of the shelter alumni *did* report such ties. Helen Van Anglen counted three peers from the Harvard Square Homeless Shelter among the Board of Directors of her non-profit organization which provides support to homeless women. Alumna Lana Zielinski and her husband met at the shelter, and alumnus Dr. Aaron Dutka recently served as the best man at the wedding of a colleague he met at the shelter. When Massachusetts' legalization of same-sex marriage in 2004 allowed Ward Welburn to marry his long-time partner, their union was presided over by his colleague and friend, State Senator Joshua Villanueva. Clearly, the Harvard Square Homeless Shelter has fostered dozens of important personal and professional relationships and, in so doing, reinforced the commitment to service work and activism of many shelter volunteers as they moved forward into adulthood.

It must also be acknowledged that several current Harvard students also described the strain that their commitment to the shelter placed upon external friendships. Junior Deanna Galante said, "My roommates really don't understand why I work at the shelter, so they're not extremely supportive of it, which can be kind of hard." According to Galante, her roommates resented the fact that her commitment to the shelter meant they saw her less often than they liked. Junior Amanda Mooney described a nearly identical experience with her own roommate. As she explained of her work at the shelter, "It's the love of my life, and you know she's not a part of it. . . . And that's something that causes jealousy or resentment." Senior Kathryn Tobin offered the following description of the tension the shelter caused with her best friend at Harvard:

> "When I supervised the Friday night overnight [shift] and also subbed frequently on Saturday night overnights, that really was difficult for both of us. . . . She wanted to see me more than she was. She was angry at me, she was angry at the shelter. . . . And she didn't want to go to the shelter, and she hasn't been to the shelter, and this is my roommate of four years and best friend at Harvard."

At the end of the winter of 2009, Tobin expressed disappointment that her roommate had declined her invitation to visit the shelter just once to see the organization that Tobin had committed herself to so devotedly during their four years of college. In these descriptions, one can see that, in connecting Harvard students to an organization and peer group from which they derive significant support and meaning, the Harvard Square Shelter also causes some stresses for these students' friendships outside of the shelter.

CONNECTIONS TO OLDER STUDENTS

While the Harvard students at the shelter admired the peers with whom they were volunteering, they expressed even greater admiration for the upperclassmen with whom they came in contact through the shelter. A number of volunteers described their initial involvement with the shelter as *motivated* by the urging of an older student. Senior Robert Vozar said, "There was a girl named Libby Passante. She went to high school with me, and she was a senior when I was a freshman. We were good friends in high school . . . and she said, 'Robert, you're signing up to be a volunteer.'" Sophomore Christopher Kitts commented, "I had a friend that had volunteered at the shelter before and said that he really enjoyed it. This was the beginning of my freshman year, fall. He was a senior at the time." Alumna Helen Van Anglen recalled:

> "My closest friend at boarding school preceded me at Harvard by a year, and he started volunteering at the shelter, and I got a call very early my freshman year from him one evening saying the guy who was supposed to volunteer didn't show up tonight, can you come down?"

In these anecdotes, the young people volunteering at the Harvard Square Homeless Shelter confirmed previous research that has found a significant factor influencing whether or not one becomes involved in community service is simply whether or not one is *asked* to participate.[48]

Other volunteers described themselves as inspired by the upperclassmen who served as supervisors and directors on their shifts. Freshman Ashwin Ganguli commented that his supervisor during the fall semester "carried herself with so much dignity, it's incredible. She made all the right decisions, and she could be so casual, so modest." Senior Drew McGinty recalled that, watching his supervisors as a freshman, "They were just most happy to be there, and I loved that they knew what they were doing. And I saw something in them that I wanted to have in me." Likewise, freshman Nancy Mellor noted: "Watching the way the supervisors interact with the guests, that is what I try to model. They are so respectful, but they don't let themselves be walked all over by the guests. They show respect and sincerity in everything they do." Junior Amanda Mooney recalled: "The staff members were totally role models, you know, as a freshman coming in, wondering who's doing something right around here." Psychologist Albert Bandura has written that "Identity development takes place in part through identification with admired others."[49] Likewise, Ann Colby and colleagues have found that "When students work closely with inspiring people, they can internalize new images of what they want to be like."[50] In the deep admiration that the Harvard Square Shelter volunteers expressed for the upperclassmen they work alongside, one can hear them gathering images and examples of the types of young adults they would like to become.

The admiration that these and other underclassmen expressed for the shelter's more veteran volunteers was particularly notable among a generation of young people who are reluctant to cite public figures they admire. Whereas previous generations of young adults tended to name individuals such as Jackie Robinson, Eleanor Roosevelt, Neil

Armstrong, and Rosa Parks as their heroes, numerous scholars have noted the reticence of today's young adults to do likewise.[51] These scholars have speculated that the intense scrutiny with which contemporary public figures now contend makes their foibles and imperfections all too evident to young people. Fischman and her colleagues have worried that "In the absence of examples that are in some sense larger than life, it may be difficult for young people to have high ethical aspirations."[52] The inability of so many young adults to cite larger-than-life heroes only increases the importance of the mentoring role that older students operating the Harvard Square Shelter play in the development of their younger peers.

CONCLUSION

This chapter has sought to demonstrate ways in which many of the Harvard students volunteering at the Harvard Square Homeless Shelter utilized the shelter as both a testing ground for identity exploration and also as a place to take shelter from some of the academic, social, and personal pressures that are a part of young adulthood. Different volunteers utilized the shelter in different ways. For some, the shelter represented an opportunity to escape from the Harvard bubble while others found work there that felt more purposeful than their academic studies. A number of students utilized the shelter as a mechanism for staying connected to an earlier version of themselves. Others sought to emulate the upperclassmen they met there. For virtually all volunteers, their work at the shelter offered exposure to a more diverse community of peers and adults, and a temporary respite from everyday pressures of all kinds.

The preceding three chapters focused on ways in which the passion, flexibility and desire for connection of the Harvard students who run the Harvard Square Shelter provide the homeless men and women who stay there with a unique atmosphere of dignity and respect. What seems to make this unique atmosphere possible is the symbiotic nature of the shelter — the fact that so many of its volunteers also utilize the space for a different type of shelter. Looking back on four years of work at the shelter, senior Leo LaSala admitted ruefully:

"I've definitely gotten more out of it than I've put in, and I think almost everybody realizes that. There's almost a little guilt about it because our mission is to help other people, but we come out thinking: I really learned a lot, grew a lot, and it's been a very formative part of my life."

LaSala and his peers should feel no guilt about their use of the shelter as a staging ground for their own development. The fact that the shelter exists for the benefit of not only the homeless who stay there but also its volunteers is precisely what disrupts the traditional provider–client dynamic, offers the homeless unique opportunities for transformation, and makes this student-run model worthy of replication in major cities across the United States.

Chapter 7

The Best Class
at Harvard

In 2006, during her freshman year at Harvard, senior Lissette McDonald had the type of conversation at the Harvard Square Homeless Shelter that she hopes every shelter volunteer gets to experience. As McDonald told it, a homeless man in his forties noticed she was wearing a Harvard Crew T-shirt and asked if she was on Harvard's crew team. In the conversation that ensued, the man mentioned that he had been on his high school ski team. As McDonald recalled:

> "I asked him where he went to school, and he said, 'Oh in Vermont,' and I'm from Vermont. And so I asked him where, and he said 'Montpelier,' which is where I'm from. And so we found out that we both went to Montpelier High School. And I was also on ski team in high school, the cross country ski team, and as soon as he found out the connection, he just got so excited. We stood in the laundry room and talked for over an hour, and it ended up being that his ski team coach was the principal when I was in high school. And we had had some of the same teachers. Montpelier is a small town, so we started talking about families in the town, and he actually knew the family of my best friend growing up. So all these connections. And I knew where he lived. And things like that . . . And he told me his story. I think he went to Emerson College, but he

165

dropped out. And I think he had issues with substance abuse, so it was very much like, wow, this man is coming from exactly the same place that I'm coming from. And that was really eye opening."

As McDonald noted, it would be difficult to walk away from such a conversation without recognizing that the men and women staying at the shelter are real people with "life stories [that] aren't necessarily all that different from my own." Even without such an intensely personal encounter, the majority of other Harvard students volunteering at the shelter for the first time in 2009 managed to learn a similar lesson as well.

Senior Hope Franklin described herself as shocked to discover through her weekly breakfast shift at the shelter that "if you'd passed these people on the street, you wouldn't know they were homeless or struggling." The clearest example of this discovery came from her conversation with a homeless man who worked each day as a driver and tour guide for Boston's Duck Boat tours. As Franklin explained, "I think about the tour bus driver, the surprise of finding out that he just has this regular employment. I could have interacted with him in everyday life and so now [I'm always] wondering if the sales clerk I'm buying whatever from, I wonder if they're homeless."

Junior Lester Pearsons — also a first-time volunteer in 2009 — expressed a similar level of surprise at the appearance of the homeless men and women he encountered at the Harvard Square Shelter: "I was surprised by how well a lot of them dressed. I felt like maybe certain aspects of their lives aren't going great, but they still have pride in their appearance." He described his astonishment at the sight of a homeless man in the shelter "taking ages to iron his jeans" and admitted sheepishly, "This is probably a little inappropriate, but there's one gal who's young, she's attractive. You just don't expect that."

Junior Louis Landau believed that spending the winter of 2009 volunteering at the shelter left him far more aware of the "ridiculous stereotypes people have about homeless people."[1] His mother, for example, was tremendously concerned about him catching tuberculosis or being stabbed during his weekly overnight shift and insisted on a phone call home the morning after each of his volunteer shifts. Landau also noted the uproar that followed First Lady Michelle Obama's 2009 trip to a homeless shelter in Washington DC:[2]

"A week ago there was a picture of Michelle Obama, speaking in a shelter. And a homeless person was taking a picture of her with his cell phone. And this picture sparked ridiculous outrage, because how could this homeless person have a cell phone? But it's really fairly common. And it makes sense, right?"

To Landau, it now made perfect sense that a homeless person might own a cell phone, but he admitted that, prior to volunteering at the shelter, "I probably would have said the same thing about the cell phone." He felt good about having eliminated some of the misconceptions in his own mind about what it does (and doesn't) mean to be homeless.

Wellesley College sophomore Charlotte Wu described how her weekly overnight shift at the Harvard Square Shelter led her to correct a classmate's misconceptions about homelessness in her constitutional law class:

"We were talking about the right to vote and citizenship and all of that. And someone in my class was saying that homeless people shouldn't have the right to vote because most of them are insane and . . . they don't have jobs and they shouldn't have the right to vote because they're not informed. And I remember getting really upset hearing that and rebuking everything that they had said because when he brings up homelessness, it immediately brings me back to working in the shelter and particular people that I know who do work very hard and who are very well informed, even more so than students such as me. I was like, 'No, that's not the case at all!'"

In all of these comments, one can see the role that the Harvard Square Shelter played for its weekly volunteers in humanizing men and women contending with homelessness. As senior, and shelter director, Leo LaSala said of his goal for his volunteers: "For me, the most important thing they can do is to lose the stigma about homelessness and to lose the stereotypes. Everything else can flow from that. Just learning that, hey, homelessness is an adjective that means 'I don't have a house.' It's not a defining characteristic of my personality." Homeless czar Philip Mangano described a similar aspiration for Harvard Square Shelter volunteers: "I think an important part of that volunteerism is breaking down some of the myths and stereotypes about homeless people and disadvantaged people, who they are, what their aspirations are. That's a very important understanding."

Psychologists describe fundamental attribution error as a tendency to over-emphasize the amount of control that individuals have over events in their lives.[3] As a result of fundamental attribution error, individuals tends to regard another person's situation as indicative of the "type" of person they are rather than the result of circumstances over which the individual may or may not have control.[4] For example, senior Hope Franklin was surprised to discover that a gainfully employed tour guide could be homeless because she did not imagine a tour guide as the "type" of person who could be homeless. Likewise, junior Lester Pearsons was surprised to find himself attracted to a homeless woman staying in the shelter because he did not imagine a homeless woman as the "type" of person he could be attracted to. In short, then, for the shelter's volunteers, their encounters and conversations at the shelter served to counteract some of their most ingrained stereotypes about the homeless.

Harvard junior and shelter supervisor Melissa Sanguinetti described a trajectory in thinking about homelessness that she watched her volunteers cycle through from the beginning of the shelter season to its conclusion:

"[The volunteers] would come in, wouldn't know what to expect, they had some preconceived ideas, but were kind of a blank sheet. Then they would have a really good conversation with a guest, maybe they would eat dinner with them, maybe a guest would open up to them, and it would just blow their minds. And they'd be like, 'Wow I love homeless people! This is great. What a Kodak moment that was!' And they run and tell all their friends that they had this really cool bonding experience and kind of romanticize it, and then something happens, like a bad incident, or something, and then all of a sudden you're just thrown this left hook and like oh, maybe it wasn't as simple as I thought. Maybe people do have deeper issues. Maybe this isn't the safe, happy place I thought it was. And so they swing the other way. And then by the end of the semester, they're like, 'Oh I get it! People aren't perfect, and they aren't horrible. They're human, they have good days, bad days, just like us, and you can't expect them to be perfectly happy and smiling all the time, and you can't expect them, or you hope, they're not angry and demanding and violent either. But there's this happy medium that makes them just like everybody else, and no longer do you glamorize it, and no longer do you have these really negative stereotypes. You just recognize that they're normal people that have had a different set of situations."[5]

Here, Sanguinetti offered a description of the trajectory that many of the shelter's new volunteers seem to follow. Lucy Draper, the former guest who now runs a non-profit organization committed to helping the homeless, noted that if the Harvard Square Shelter is capable of helping nearly 100 Harvard students each year arrive at a more personal understanding of homelessness, then the shelter has the potential to genuinely impact our wider society's response to homelessness. As Draper noted, "If you look at the multiplier factor of 70 or 80 kids really understanding homelessness and who people really are and what it takes to end it, you know that's a huge wealth of information and education and opportunity to change things." And, of course, as soon-to-be Harvard graduates, many of those young adults will likely carry that knowledge with them into positions of considerable influence.

Such influential advocates are crucial for a constituency — the homeless — who elicit reactions of disgust from the majority of American citizens. As noted in Chapter 1, Princeton psychologist Susan Fiske has found that showing photographs of the homeless to individuals attached to an fMRI scanner reveals a sequence of reactions in the brain "associated with feelings of disgust towards objects such as garbage and trash."[6] Fiske's conclusion from this research was that many Americans, when they think about homelessness, do not conceive of homeless men and women as real-life human beings. Imagine a town hall meeting or ballot initiative, then, where issues affecting the homeless are up for debate. In such settings, individuals who can speak to the humanity of the homeless and debunk misconceptions about homelessness are sorely needed.

The words of a number of new volunteers at the conclusion of the 2009 winter underscored Draper's optimism about the shelter's potential to impact society. Wellesley sophomore Charlotte Wu noted:

"Now when I think of homelessness, I think of more of a transition than a dead end. Because, before, homelessness seemed like this problem that couldn't be fixed or at least I didn't know

170 SHELTERSHELTER

how to fix it. And now I feel that I may not be able to do it on my own, but there are solutions to homelessness."

Harvard junior Lester Pearsons commented that "Now it seems a bit more that it's not just an affliction of the lowest classes; it seems also to just be an unfortunate thing that happens to people who are in precarious life situations. . . . Before it was kind of us versus them. There was this huge divide. Now it seems a little [like] the divide has closed." Junior Louis Landau — the mathematics major — observed that "I think I have a probably more positive view of homeless people than average. I probably rate the role of misfortune as the cause of homelessness more highly than personal characteristics. . . . I would say that's due to talking to the people there, discussing how they got there." In her interview, Charlotte Wu expressed an interest in pursuing public service law; Pearsons described an interest in international development; and Landau envisioned a career as a mathematics professor. Each described a different takeaway from a year of putting a face on homelessness, but each seemed positioned — in the diverse fields they will enter — to combat stereotypes and advocate for the just treatment of the men, women, and children Philip Mangano refers to as our "poorest neighbors."

HEAVY RESPONSIBILITY

A winter of volunteering at the Harvard Square Homeless Shelter seems capable of putting a "face" on homelessness.[7] For the Harvard students who assumed leadership positions within the shelter as supervisors and directors, however, the impact of the shelter reverberated even more deeply. Certainly, the supervisors and directors spent more time at the shelter than the volunteers they manage. Between working a shift, attending the weekly staff meeting, and responding to shelter email, most of the shelter's supervisors and directors spent somewhere between 15 and 20 hours a week at the shelter or working on shelter-related business. A volunteer, on the other hand, might spend as little as two hours a week there. The factor that seemed most responsible for the different experiences of these two groups, however, was the heavy responsibility which the supervisors and directors took on as the shelter's leaders.

What did this heavy responsibility look like? Shelter alumnus Dr. Aaron Dutka recalled:

"As an 18 year old, or 19 year old or 20 year old, I was determining whether someone was going to sleep inside or not. So
that was a responsibility. You had a basically limited resource
which there was a high demand for, and you had to kind of
figure out the best way to distribute it."

Along similar lines, Harvard senior Leo LaSala acknowledged that staff
members never forget "the first time you have to tell someone they
can't stay, for whatever reason. . . . They come to the door drunk, or
not even drunk but above the limit, but you just have to tell them they
can't stay." LaSala recalled:

> "The first time I had to give a drug test to someone . . . I'm the
> one who stands there to watch them pee, make sure they're
> not tampering with it, and then read it off. And he tested
> positive for weed, which is what it looked like. And he was
> very adamant that he hadn't been smoking that day — he'd
> just come out of rehab for it, so it was in his system still,
> but he wasn't high. And I was like, 'There's nothing I can do
> about it. I have to assume otherwise because this test is here.'
> But you know personally I believed him. He didn't smell. He
> didn't look particularly out of it, he wasn't acting particularly
> strange, but I didn't really have a choice."

There are very few young adults expected to contend with so weighty
a responsibility as determining who can and cannot have shelter for a
given night, yet this is a daily part of the experience of being a supervisor or director at the Harvard Square Shelter. For this reason, CASPAR's
Meghan Goughan admitted that "I do worry about those kids because
putting someone out on a 20-degree night is such a hard thing, and
it's always such a gray area about right and wrong. And that's the kind
of stuff that weighs on your mind two hours later, 12 hours later, two
days later." Even for professionals like Goughan, such responsibility can
be difficult to take on. In taking on this responsibility, however, these
Harvard students see, not only that the men and women staying at the
shelter are human, but also the significant challenges with which they
are contending as they seek to put their lives back on track.

Other Harvard students and alumni described particular encounters
to convey the responsibility that accompanies a leadership role at the
Harvard Square Shelter. For example, sophomore Christopher Kitts

described a situation from the winter of 2009 in which he had to assist a guest who had defecated on himself:

> "A guy woke up in the middle of the night, had gone to the bathroom on himself, and was very embarrassed. It was about the time where people would start waking up in the morning. He needed a new pair of underwear and at that point I realized how difficult it would be to be so dependent on other people for basic needs. I felt bad and maybe a little uncomfortable with how humiliated he must have felt and the fact that I've never had to experience something so basic and so fundamental like not having underwear to put on in the morning."

Here, Kitts described a scenario that may strike a chord with adults who have ever had the challenging and often sad experience of caring for elderly parents.[8] However, it seems likely that, on that given winter night, Kitts was the only student on the Harvard campus voluntarily taking on such an adult responsibility. And, in his words, one could hear Kitts going beyond the experience of putting a face on homelessness to genuinely considering the ways in which the experience of being homeless strips men and women of their dignity.

Junior Amanda Mooney described the experience this past winter of having to remove a homeless man, Nat, from the shelter's Work Contract program. The program allows guests earning more than $250 a week to stay in the shelter for ten consecutive weeks while they make progress towards securing permanent housing. One of the requirements of the program is that guests set up a savings account and bank a significant percentage of their weekly paycheck. Nat was a few weeks into his stay at the Harvard Square Shelter and had put away several hundred dollars when his ex-wife — who has custody of their two children — experienced a financial crisis of her own. As Mooney related:

> "The ex-wife emailed and said quote, unquote, 'We're up shit's creek.' And he showed me the email. And, basically, he gave her all the money he'd saved. And, I believe him, too. He and I were very, very close. And, you know I still talk to him all the time. And all his progress was wiped out. . . . And, he was like, 'Is there anything I can do [to stay in the program]? I'm like, 'No, Nat. I'm sorry.' And he was like, 'I want to change my decision.' I'm like, 'I know you want to.' It was tough. It was

tough in a lot of ways because I wanted to see him succeed. And I really felt that if I was there to help him, it could happen."

Though Mooney cared deeply about Nat's success and admired his decision, she nonetheless had the responsibility — as the shelter's Work Contract director — to enforce the consequences of Nat's decision to give up his savings. It was no surprise when Mooney commented at the end of the shelter season that her work at the Harvard Square Shelter had "made me grow up a lot." Her work at the shelter had offered her a window into the complexities and variables that an individual like Nat faces in trying to pull himself out of homelessness.

Alumni Amelia Ginsberg and Rusty Sadow remembered an experience from their own days as shelter directors that remained jarring even a decade later. As Sadow recalled:

"There was a guy who had recently come out of prison. A Puerto Rican guy, I believe. Very good looking, very charismatic, very friendly, very popular amongst the staff. And he had sort of pulled aside each of the staff individually and had let us know that he was HIV positive. And the way he told each of us was that we were the only one he had told, and he didn't want other people to know, but he wanted us to know in case anything happened. But it turned out he was having unprotected sex with a woman who was staying in the shelter, and he did not have the courtesy to tell her. But obviously a lot of people knew about it. And so I don't remember the name of the woman, but she was sitting in the shelter in the woman's room, hearing people on the other side of the divider talk about this guy being HIV positive. And she heard it."

Sadow described debates among the shelter's directors and supervisors about whether they should continue to allow such a person to stay in the shelter. As Sadow said, "I mean, they didn't have sex inside the shelter. It wasn't our responsibility. Who are we to judge? But he was a monster." Both the situation itself and the ensuing debate about whether the shelter had any right to turn this man away forced that winter's supervisors and directors to confront complex and tragic moral questions that — to use Sadow's phrase — offered them a "much deeper sense of the world." For her part, alumna Amelia Ginsberg recalled her interaction with the homeless woman victimized by that relationship:

"She told me one day — they must have broken up or something, and he wasn't coming around any more — and she told
me that he was HIV positive, and he had infected her and had
never told her that. And he had done it, and she wasn't the
only person he had done it to."

In reaction, Ginsberg recalled herself thinking, "That really happened?
People can really do that to other people?" Characterizing herself and
the other directors and supervisors as "so fucking sheltered with our
lives," she believed those types of experiences at the shelter had played
an important role in her development and understanding of the world.

Literally every one of the shelter's supervisors and directors — past
and present — could offer examples of encounters in which they
grappled with situations and responsibilities far beyond that of the
typical young adult. Junior Jerry Chen recalled a homeless man who
had confided in him that "I can't do this any more," and Chen suddenly
found himself in a conversation with an individual contemplating
suicide. Junior Nathan Small described a series of intense conversations with a homeless man diagnosed with a terminal illness and the
challenge of dealing with that individual as he lashed out emotionally
at everyone around him. Small described the burden of "trying to work
with him to say, look, this [behavior] is unacceptable, but also really
empathizing and realizing here he is dealing with this massive event
in his life, and so that was really tough." And alumna Lana Zielinski
described a night in which a pregnant woman and her boyfriend
claimed that she had miscarried in the shelter bathroom. According to
Zielinski, "I remember thinking, 'I have no idea what to do.' Because
they were this utterly dramatic couple, and I had no idea whether this
was true, not true, and I remember feeling like this is above and beyond
what you ever have in your mind to deal with." These shelter directors,
as well, were describing experiences that put far more than a "human
face" on homelessness; those experiences shined a spotlight on the
complexity of the challenges with which the men and women staying
at the Harvard Square Shelter are contending.

"COMPLEXIFYING" HOMELESSNESS

In his classic study of college students who participated in the 1964
Freedom Rides to desegregate America's Deep South, sociologist Doug

McAdam reported that "It wasn't anything as narrow as their attitudes that changed, as much as it was the way they saw and interpreted the world."[9] McAdam went on to describe the Freedom Rides as *the* transformational experience in the lives of many of these young activists. Many of the Harvard Square Homeless Shelter's student-leaders described the heavy responsibilities they have taken on at the shelter as having had a similar effect upon their own lives. Or as University Lutheran Deacon Selma Brooks is fond of telling students, "You go to Harvard to learn, you come to the shelter to grow up."

Shelter alumnus Joshua Villanueva explained that working as a supervisor at the Harvard Square Shelter served to "complexify my understanding of how homelessness connects to a spectrum of issues." Specifically, Villanueva described the shelter as having fueled his interest in housing policy: "On one hand, [combating] homelessness can come from home ownership opportunities and everything in between in terms of rental and housing subsidized programs, and supports that we've put in place to keep people in supportive and long-term housing and out of homelessness." Perhaps it is not surprising that, following his graduation from Harvard College, Villanueva went to work for a Boston City Councilor on affordable housing issues. According to Villanueva, "There were some clear connections between the people I saw at the shelter and some of the folks who were being gentrified out of their neighborhoods." For Villanueva, the "complexifying" that came out of his work at the Harvard Square Shelter occurred at the intersection of housing and homelessness — issues that he continued to focus on in both the state legislature and the non-profit world.

For alumnus Dr. Aaron Dutka, the "complexification" occurred at the intersection of homelessness and mental and physical health:

"So I think that people who are in a homeless shelter on the one hand, people who are homeless and stay homeless, the chronically homeless, that's not just bad luck. That happens for a reason, meaning people have multiple real challenges that they have to confront. So I'm talking about substance abuse, mental illness — those two specifically. So I think there are certainly people who had a fire in their house, came to the shelter temporarily, were there for a week, and then they were gone. They didn't stay homeless. But the chronically homeless, it's not an accident."

Working at the Harvard Square Shelter offered Dutka a look at the two tiers of homelessness — the majority of homeless men and women who experience homelessness as a short-term state and get back on their feet within a year or two, and then the smaller segment of the homeless population whose multiple, additional challenges render their home-lessness more intractable. Perhaps it is no surprise that Dutka — who went on to medical school after graduating from Harvard — chose to focus his professional efforts on treating substance abusers and men and women suffering from HIV/AIDS.

Liam Murphy offered a clear example of a current student experi-encing this 'complexification' during the winter of 2009. A Harvard sophomore, Murphy spent two nights a week at the shelter as a dinner-shift volunteer and then as one of the students manning the Resource Advocacy table. It was his work as a resource advocate that offered him a vantage point into the relationships between homelessness and public policy. Murphy described his surprise and frustration at discovering ways in which public policy can actually cause road blocks for men and women trying to pull themselves out of homelessness:

> "Take a guest who has social security or SSDI, and they are okay with that $700 a month, and while it lets him get by in a sense, at the same time it's a Catch-22 because they can't really better their situation, because they'll end up avoiding getting a job and getting more than that. Because if they had a job they would make $800–900, but they would have to work. But now they get $700 and don't have to do anything. So it's just kind of hard to see that kind of situation where the guest is perpetually stuck and can't get out of it."

Here, Murphy describes the Catch-22 of an individual receiving dis-ability payments who could only afford an apartment by supplementing these payments with a job; however, getting a job would mean forfeit-ing the disability payments that made the scenario possible in the first place. Another wrinkle Murphy encountered in his work as a resource advocate was that if individuals on SSDI (social security dis-ability insurance) saved more than $2,000, then they lost their monthly stipend. Such a policy creates a disincentive for saving, and nearly guarantees homelessness in a Massachusetts rental market that calls for prospective tenants to put down first month's rent, last month's rent and a security deposit. As Murphy declared, "The system is broken."

For Murphy, the "complexification" he experienced at the Harvard Square Shelter was a deeper awareness of the role that public policy can play in both supporting and, unfortunately, inhibiting the efforts of homeless men and women to pull themselves out of homelessness. For Murphy, this learning had clear implications in regards to his own plans of becoming a doctor:

> "I think it shows me that the people who have the more individual focus — for example, in my case, like when a doctor goes in every day and treats patients — need to try to inject their ideas and their opinions more on a policy level. Because, if not, you have the system as it is now, and it just doesn't work."

Similar to Senator Villanueva and Dr. Dutka before him, Murphy described an emerging recognition of the professional role he can play in addressing the issues that "complexify" homelessness. For all three individuals, one can characterize the Harvard Square Homeless Shelter as having exerted a significant influence upon the identity development process.

Erikson described the adolescent identity crisis as centered around two fundamental questions: How does the world work? And what is my role in it?[10] For Villanueva, Dutka and Murphy, their experiences at the Harvard Square Shelter cast a light upon some of the systemic challenges faced by individuals struggling with poverty and homelessness, and, in so doing, offered up issues that Villanueva and Dutka have chosen to address through their professional endeavors. Though only a college sophomore in 2009, Murphy seemed poised to do the same.

The Harvard Square Shelter also "complexified" students' understanding of the relationship between structural and personal factors that contribute to homelessness. Pastor Fred Reisz, co-founder of the Harvard Square Shelter, noted: "Those who tended to come to work at the shelter, particularly in the earlier years, were pretty idealistic, and had a lot of idealistic motives." A number of the shelter alumni credited the shelter with adding a more nuanced understanding of homelessness to their unfettered idealism. For example, alumnus Dennis McGonagle offered the following description of his worldview as he stepped into the Harvard Square Shelter for the first time:

> "I was all the way on the far extreme just from sheer adolescent rebellion and deductive reasoning before I ever met a

homeless person. I mean, certainly when I started working at the Harvard Square Shelter, I had the attitude that if I encountered a person experiencing homelessness, and I have a $20 bill in my pocket and he doesn't, then he has as much right to that $20 bill as I do, and it's completely paternalistic and inappropriate for me to presume that I would know better how to use it than he would. So that would have been my attitude at the beginning."

As is evident in this description, McGonagle began his work at the shelter with the fervent belief that homelessness is due entirely to structural causes: unemployment, low wages, racial discrimination, etc. Such fervency is not unusual among young adults. Erikson noted that, in the course of the identity development process, adolescents often adopt and grasp onto "simplistically over-defined ideologies."[11] Likewise, Sharon Daloz Parks has noted that adolescents' worldviews often take on a highly "ideological quality."[12] She explains: "This occurs because the new meaning that the young adult has the courage to compose and embrace is held with great tenacity, since the new meaning must ground an equally new and still fragile self."[13] In other words, adolescents reaching out for new worldviews and perspectives often feel compelled to grasp onto these perspectives with great ferocity.

According to McGonagle, however, working as a shelter director shifted his perspective "from a pure structural position to the kind of modified position that the roots of this are structural, but once people have been shaped by the culture of homelessness, you can't just do a purely structural thing and expect them to adapt back to mainstream society." In other words, McGonagle came to see the ways in which personal factors such as mental illness and alcoholism could interact with structural inequities to contribute to an individual's long-term homelessness. As a result, McGonagle admitted:

"I don't give money to people who panhandle. I carry Cliff bars sometimes to try and give them out, which is just terribly demoralizing because they're almost always refused. So now my belief would be that the person who's panhandling is struggling with an addiction, and I'm doing them no favors by giving them money."

Alumna Amelia Ginsberg described a similar shift in her worldview.

Ginsberg noted that her work as a shelter director "deepened my compassion for people who are less privileged and have been screwed by our system, and gave me a much better understanding of how our system screws people." Importantly, though, Ginsberg added that "My view of it all became less romantic, too." She explained that moving from a volunteer to a supervisor to a director at the Harvard Square Shelter facilitated her discovery that "righteous, idealistic arguments about how to solve problems are inevitably only part of the story, and like there is this incredibly complex reality of people like Ray Diaz who, like, there's no solution for." Certainly, that doesn't mean giving up on long-time homeless men like Ray Diaz who appear to be contending with severe mental illness. Ginsberg noted that "There's ways that we can do things better, there's ways that we can provide more care for people like him." However, her several years working with guests like Ray Diaz allowed her to see the genuine complexity of the problems facing at least a segment of the homeless population and not to "totally romanticize and have this condescending view" about how easily such problems can be solved.

Alumnus Rusty Sadow characterized the shift in thinking described by alumni McGonagle and Ginsberg as moving from an ideological perspective to a more pragmatic perspective on how to effect change. Erikson might simply describe these individuals as progressing towards a mature adult identity.[14] Without doubt, the Harvard Square Shelter played a leading role in this process. In fact, as Sadow commented:

> "I feel like working at the shelter, for all of us, made us wise beyond our years. To come out at age 22 with that set of experiences going onto our next career was just so invaluable. I mean, even just thinking about the stories and their impact on me, like the guy who spread AIDS around the shelter. Or I remember this other night, there was this guy who had basically come right out of prison, and this was his first night out of prison. He was a White guy in his mid-forties. And he had been in prison for 25 years for beating a Black kid to death during Boston's bus riots. It's hard to say how that affected me except to say that it gave me a much deeper sense of the world. I think it made all of us a lot more mature than we would otherwise be."

In these words, Sadow characterized his volunteer work at the shelter as

a significant catalyst in his development of a mature adult identity. In so
doing, he struck a chord similar to the majority of the Freedom Riders
who, even 25 years after their foray into the Deep South, McAdam
characterized as fundamentally shaped by the "conception of politics
and self formed in Mississippi."[15]

In the crop of Harvard students working as supervisors and directors during the winter of 2009, one could see this "deeper sense of the
world" in development. Harvard junior Melissa Sanguinetti became one
of the shelter's overnight supervisors in November 2008. In November,
Sanguinetti offered the following perspective on homelessness:

> "I'm from a very working class area, and saw a lot of very hard
> working people who just could never exist on minimum wage,
> just no matter how many piecemeal jobs you have, could never
> afford even just general cost of living, even in a place like South
> Dakota. So I'm very familiar with the idea of the working poor
> and just the way the system works, and the way that things are
> structured. You could be working extremely, extremely hard
> and still not be able to make it. . . . And so I think the argument
> that people are poor because they don't work hard enough is
> so offensive to me that I can't quite grasp it."

Here, Sanguinetti offered a clear-cut structural explanation for homelessness and poverty: poor people are poor because the minimum
wage is too low. Sharon Daloz Parks might characterize Sanguinetti
as having grasped onto this ideology with great tenacity. By virtue
of her new role as a shelter supervisor, however, Sanguinetti had the
opportunity to interact closely with homeless men and women, be
present for the staff's weekly policy meetings, and deal with several
crises as they arose.

Three of the most difficult moments Sanguinetti faced inside the
shelter over the winter of 2008–09 challenged her beliefs about the
purely structural nature of poverty. First, a homeless man staying at
the shelter with whom Sanguinetti had become close was discovered
to have been permanently barred from the shelter ten years earlier
for violent behavior inside the shelter. Then in December of 2008,
another homeless man showed up late to the shelter on Sanguinetti's
night only to discover that his bed had been given away. He pushed
his way into the shelter, declared Sanguinetti a racist, and became so
physically threatening that one of the other student volunteers called

911. Ultimately, the police had to escort the man out of the shelter. And finally, Sanguinetti participated in a policy discussion about whether or not the shelter should run criminal background checks on men and women who come to the shelter, with several student-directors arguing that, as students, they lacked the experience or training to be working with individuals with violent criminal histories. This proposal to start running criminal background checks was soundly rejected, a decision with which Sanguinetti agreed in principle but left her worried about the likelihood that she and her volunteers were interacting each night with men and women capable of tremendously unpredictable behavior.

In short, Sanguinetti's involvement in the shelter as a supervisor — one of the 28 students responsible for the management of the shelter — was a much more intense experience than her previous role as an overnight volunteer. Reflecting on this experience, Sanguinetti remarked:

> "I think that probably the most valuable thing is that I came in as one of those very starry-eyed idealists, and I refused to think anything negative about the homeless. I was kind of guilty of romanticizing the working class life and thinking back to, I don't know, my own experiences and stuff. And so it was good for me to see the really good times at the shelter and the not so good. And I think I have a firmer grasp of reality after that, and maybe more of a practical idea of what works and what doesn't work."

The experience by no means caused Sanguinetti to shed her passion for the work at the Harvard Square Shelter or her commitment to combating homelessness; however, one could hear in these words her growing recognition of the complexity of working with a traumatized community like the homeless and the beginnings of a shift from ideology to pragmatism. For her as well, the Harvard Square Homeless Shelter played an important role in her progress towards a mature, adult identity.

A PUSH TOWARDS SOCIAL ACTION

One might fear that a deepening recognition of the complexity of social problems such as homelessness would discourage young adults from directing their energy and talents towards addressing these problems; however, this did not seem to be the case with the majority of Harvard students operating the shelter. As senior Leo LaSala noted, "Probably something that's common across shelter directors is recognizing the world isn't fair but not giving up on it. If we were really giving up on it, we wouldn't have put in all that time trying to fix it." Emerging adulthood is the age of "possibilities" and a period of peak optimism in the life course. Perhaps, then, the college years are the optimal time period for individuals to be introduced to society's most vexing social ills in all of their complexity.

Alumnus Rusty Sadow attributed his work over the past decade as a community organizer to his discovery at the Harvard Square Shelter of the complex linkages between homelessness and affordable housing. As Sadow explained, when he started volunteering at the shelter in 1996, a homeless man or woman was capable of finding a job, saving money, and finding an apartment to live in, and in fact Sadow recalled helping numerous people move out of the shelter and into their own housing. By 1999, however, the rise of the housing market had changed everything. According to Sadow, rental prices in Massachusetts had risen to the point that homeless men and women "could hold a job, they could work 40 hours a week, but that wasn't going to pay the rent." There simply wasn't housing that workers earning minimum wage could afford. As Sadow said, "So the question became, how do we change that situation? Because we were all powerless in that situation. And that's what got me interested in organizing."

Sadow began working as a community organizer immediately after college and focused his efforts on affordable housing issues. Since then, he has worked on a number of different social issues including healthcare and voting rights, and he credited the understanding of the world he developed at the Harvard Square Shelter with leading him in this professional direction. As Sadow noted, "I would be a completely different person doing completely different things if it weren't for my experience at the shelter." In this way, he again credited the Harvard Square Shelter with having played a substantial role in his development of a mature adult identity.

The same can be said for former state senator Joshua Villanueva who credited his experiences at the shelter with inspiring "all my work on housing, my decision to go to law school and focus on affordable housing as a professional area, and then to make that a big part of my time in the [State] House."

Alumna Anusha Ghosh responded similarly to the challenges she observed at the Harvard Square Shelter. In her role as one of the shelter's directors, she came to recognize the complexity of the challenges facing the homeless and grew "frustrated with the idea that I could not produce a concrete change for anyone there." This frustration propelled Ghosh into law school: "Law School became appealing because [it entailed] learning a specific field that you could apply in different ways to help people do things that they want to do whether it's representing them in housing court and helping them keep their home or working to get someone benefits." In law school, Ghosh immediately found a mechanism for applying her developing legal skills to the issue of homelessness. She joined a program that sent law students into New York soup kitchens and homeless shelters to give legal advice. Ultimately, Ghosh's professional work came to focus more on immigrants' rights than on combating homelessness; however, she attributed her desire to become a lawyer to her recognition from working at the Harvard Square Shelter that the challenges facing the homeless require allies with concrete skill-sets rather than simply energy and idealism.

Just as one could observe the shelter's current supervisors and directors developing a more nuanced understanding of homelessness, their growing commitment to social action was apparent as well. Junior Nathan Small — who began volunteering at the Harvard Square Shelter as a high school student — described a mounting frustration in April 2009 reminiscent of that articulated by alumni like Sadow and Ghosh. As Small explained, "I've been here for six years. And a lot of the people I see here are people I've seen here for six years. Six years is a long time." The conclusion Small drew from this long-term homelessness was that the current strategies and policies for combating homelessness are insufficient:

> "I think that we do need changes in the way we think about homelessness, the way we attack homelessness in this country, but if we're serious about eliminating the root of the problem, it's going to come through education reform and healthcare reform, and so I think it's definitely directed me towards policy. . . . So I don't really have any idea how that's going to happen, but I think that working with educational policy would be really fascinating."

There are many levers with which to attack social problems such as homelessness. Rusty Sadow turned to community organizing while Anusha Ghosh turned to the legal system. Though only a junior in college, Nathan Small seemed to be moving towards work in the policy realm or perhaps education. In either case, he, too, seemed poised to become an alumnus who can credit the Harvard Square Homeless Shelter with having deeply influenced his professional trajectory.

Another shelter staff member, sophomore Christopher Kitts, was considering a career in politics similar to that of alumnus Joshua Villanueva. As Kitts proceeded through his first year as an overnight supervisor, he admitted that his new role in the shelter's operation was emotionally draining. According to Kitts, "The problem is so overwhelming [and] all encompassing. What we do is good work. At the same time, we're one of probably thousands of shelters across the country, yet this is still an epidemic across the country."

For Kitts, the frustration he experienced from his vantage point at the Harvard Square Shelter pushed him to consider the role of politics in effecting social change. In an interview in November 2008, having only just begun his role as an overnight supervisor, Kitts suggested vaguely that he could see himself pursuing "some type of public service work." Interviewed again at the end of the winter, however, his thinking about future professional pathways had grown more specific:

> "I'm much more likely to think about trying to go into public policy, maybe even elected office just because there are such tremendous structural problems, overarching problems. I mean, you think about the number of hours we put into the shelter collectively over the course of the year and then think about the time it takes the President to sign legislation for millions of dollars for homelessness. There's this larger structural problem that it seems like that's the place to have the greatest impact."

Perhaps Christopher Kitts will be the next Harvard Square Shelter alumnus to decide that the challenges and complexities he witnessed at the shelter can best be addressed through the political process.

Senior Robert Vozar saw academia as the means through which he could best address the limitations to combating homelessness he witnessed at the Harvard Square Shelter. An economics major, Vozar's perspective on homelessness resonated deeply with Philip Mangano's observation that "If good intentions, well meaning programs and humanitarian gestures could end homelessness, it would have been history decades ago, with all of the good intentions we have in Cambridge, Boston and around our country." Vozar appreciated the intangibles that the Harvard Square Shelter offers the homeless, but was perhaps the most focused of any of the student-directors on how, *specifically*, the shelter could contribute to a decline in homelessness. As another director explained of Vozar, the questions with which he was most concerned are: "How many people have we fed? How many people have slept with us? What percentage of the homeless population has asked for our services?"

In the future, Vozar envisioned himself working to apply the tools of economic analysis to social policy. He described several economists who have started doing randomized-assignment evaluations of programs in the developing world and in public education, and expressed his belief that such evaluations could be useful in evaluating policies designed to combat homelessness. As Vozar observed, "I think we can dramatically improve how much we actually help homeless people by applying this same standard to our social policies that we expect from our drugs and we expect from our projects in the developing world now. So, I think I'm interested in bringing randomization stuff to social policy." Having secured a position in Washington DC with the Council of Economic Advisers following his graduation from Harvard, Vozar seemed to have taken the first steps towards this objective.

Perhaps a decade or two down the road, then, Robert Vozar will be working to evaluate the public policies that Christopher Kitts as an elected representative or Nathan Small as a policy-maker have proposed to combat homelessness. All of these young adults described their work at the Harvard Square Shelter as having deepened their awareness of the challenges to combating homelessness, but all three — and many of their peers — felt driven, as a result, towards the fields in which they believed they could most effectively grapple with these challenges. Homeless czar Philip Mangano believes that "As long as you're directly involved with the people who are being oppressed in one way or another, you have a better sense of what to do when the possibility of ending that wrong is available to you." Students and alumni like Rusty Sadow, Anusha Ghosh, Joshua Villanueva, Nathan Small, Christopher Kitts, and Robert Vozar have and will continue to occupy important roles in many different professional spheres. Their experiences at the Harvard Square Shelter informed and motivated their ability to use these roles to push for more just and humane support of Americans contending with homelessness.

The interests of these and other students in politics and public policy were particularly notable because of recent scholarship about the lack of interest among today's adolescents and young adults in entering these professional realms. Over the past 45 years, the number of college students who express interest in political issues has declined from 60 percent to less than 30 percent.[16] Psychology professor William Damon adds that "Few young people today imagine that they might find purpose in the public sphere as politicians, civic leaders, or community organizers. There is very little public leadership aspiration among today's younger generation."[17]

The Harvard Square Homeless Shelter seems to counteract a generational lack of interest in the public sphere by introducing its participants in a very intimate way to a significant social problem and, for the shelter's directors and supervisors, by offering them a significant role in working to address this problem. From this responsibility and experience emerge a passion for continuing to address these problems and a deeper interest in the jobs within both the public and private sector that will allow these young people to do so.

Finally, it is important to note that the descriptions by all of these volunteers and former volunteers of the systemic changes necessary to combat homelessness represent an exceptional understanding of the world for young adults to possess. In a recent study of young adults, scholar Tim Clydesdale asked his subjects to name three things they would like to change about the world. According to Clydesdale:

> Teens offered answers that projected individual-level changes on a global scale. That is, *individuals* should not commit crime and not be violent, *individuals* should not hate, *individuals* should love each other more, "be nicer" or have more religious faith. Few teens described truly macro-level changes (such as laws to cut pollution). Rather, when the vast majority of teens talk about the macro-level, if they talk about it at all, they describe it as the sum of the individuals it comprises. The solution to world poverty and hunger, for example, is simply getting "everyone" to be "less greedy" and "share more." The language of individualism is not only these teens' first moral language, as sociologist Robert Bellah and his co-authors wrote in 1985, it is their only moral language.[18]

Clydesdale found that the majority of American adolescents and young adults do not possess a sufficient understanding of the world to describe systemic changes that would need to occur in order to alleviate various forms of inequity and injustice. While it would be an exaggeration to suggest that young adults like Robert Vozar and Nathan Small demonstrated a precise understanding of the systemic structures that will need to be changed in order to effectively combat homelessness, these young adults did exhibit a much deeper understanding than the majority of their peers about the interaction between homelessness and a whole spectrum of other social issues including affordable housing, education, and healthcare. Moreover, they had begun to hone in on which of these fields they would like to enter professionally in order to exert the greatest impact upon combating homelessness.

REFLECTING THE SHELTER

A number of scholars who focus on the effects of service and service-learning describe the importance of providing students with a context for their service through reflection and academic content.[19] One of the few regrets that Pastor Fred Reisz expressed about the early years of running the Harvard Square Shelter was that "We really needed to have a better program to work with students to have them be able to process their experience and to integrate it into their academic work. Most of it was left to them without a great deal of help." One surprise, then, was the resistance of the shelter's volunteers, supervisors, and directors to formal opportunities for reflection.

Each year, the University Lutheran Church hires a graduate student from the Harvard Divinity School to guide the undergraduates volunteering at the shelter in a series of organized reflections. The divinity student for the 2008–09 year, Wendy Burrell, attended all of the shelter's staff meetings, worked a weekly overnight shift, and hosted seven or eight reflection events a semester. As Burrell described it, her goal in these reflection sessions was to push the college students operating the Harvard Square Shelter to "start intensely asking these deeper questions of — Why does the shelter need to exist? How could we put ourselves out of business? How could we connect these experiences that volunteers are having to larger social questions?"

While all of the shelter volunteers expressed appreciation for Burrell as a person and for her commitment to the shelter, they were less positive about the reflection experience itself. Sophomore Christopher Kitts explained that "The Div School student will come in and read a passage, and I just don't get that much out of it . . . The way people understand homelessness is not by reading articles but by working with people who are homeless." Junior Nathan Small commented:

"There were some [reflection sessions] especially at the beginning of the year that I thought went really well. I think there are other times when some people are sort of like, 'I don't know whether I want to talk about this right now.' Or, 'I don't know whether I really want to talk about this at all.'"

Small added that, for the larger reflection events, "I think that the attendance has been pretty poor. It's tough. People are busy." Likewise, junior Larry Yoon said of the reflection sessions, "They are useful when I attend them, [but] I haven't gone to a lot of them. I feel like attendance isn't that strong." Junior Louis Landau noted that one of the aspects of the shelter he most appreciated was that the organization "makes an effort to make sure they're actually having an effect, not doing reflections about their mission statement."

It is surprising that the same college students who were so deeply invested in talking and listening to the homeless men and women at the shelter were generally disdainful of organized reflection opportunities. One possible explanation for this disdain is that a formal reflection session strikes participating students as too "staged" an experience to be authentic — in some ways, the opposite of the "real world" experience that led so many to volunteer at the shelter in the first place. Paradoxically, a sizable portion of these same students expressed appreciation for the opportunity, through this research study, to reflect upon the experience of volunteering at the Harvard Square Shelter. Perhaps the formality of a research study — in which students sat down one on one with a university professor and participated in an audio-recorded interview — struck them as more "real" than a typical reflection session.

CLASS CONNECTIONS

Shelter volunteers were more positive about academic courses that provided opportunities for thinking about their work at the shelter, though, by and large, they were forced to seek out these experiences on their own. While a number of universities have sought to provide explicit connections between students' academic courses and extracurricular opportunities, Harvard has lagged behind on this front.[20]

Junior Jerry Chen enrolled in a philosophy class in the fall of 2008 entitled "Justice" that was taught by renowned political philosopher Michael Sandel.[21] According to Chen, a number of the philosophical perspectives he studied in "Justice" would come into his head at the shelter's weekly policy meetings when he and the other directors debated the best course of action in regards to various issues. He noted:

> "Ethics is something that's really come to the forefront this year, and seeing different ways people consider what's right. Like Kant, like Rawls . . . Because I think a lot of what we do with the shelter is debate about that. Like, what do we think is right? And we're really just projecting these philosophers' points of view."

As Chen listened and participated in the policy debates that are described in the following chapter, he consciously considered the ways in which different students' perspectives connected to the philosophers he was studying. Personally, Chen explained that the "one philosopher that I always think to is John Rawls and his veil of ignorance." Philosopher John Rawls believed that a useful tool for resolving moral dilemmas was what he called the "veil of ignorance."[22] In other words, what would you believe to be just if you did not know your own position within the dilemma? Chen relied on this tool to arrive at his own understanding of the best resolution for debates about how many homeless people to allow into the shelter each night, whether or not to leave the shelter's bathroom doors open to discourage smokers, and whether the shelter should run criminal background checks on men and women staying in the shelter.

Junior Nathan Small described the impact of a sociology class upon his beliefs about the Housing First program — a strategy for combating homelessness that places homeless men and women in independent housing with appropriate supports:[23]

> "We didn't really talk about homelessness much directly, but one of the things we talked about was how people conceive of communities. You know this push for Housing First has been

like well, you give somebody a place, but, their social network was all out on the street. And so, how do you reintegrate them into a community? And, I think it's a really interesting question because community is so important for everyone regardless of where they are. If you want to make Housing First programs work, I think that providing people with a sense of community in the new places that they're living is important. And, how you do that for people who have been out on the street for five, six, seven years seems like a really interesting challenge."

Here, Small applied a sociological perspective to the Housing First campaign championed by a number of homeless policy advocates at the state and federal levels. It seems likely that, in this analysis, Small was thinking of people like Ralph McGann who, despite having acquired his own room at a suburban YMCA, continued to come to the Harvard Square Shelter because of his social connections with the people there. Individuals like Ralph McGann — for the very reasons Small described — represent an important segment of the homeless community for Housing First advocates to consider if they want the program to succeed.

Sophomore Antonia Garcia-Brown and freshman Nancy Mellor began their volunteer work at the shelter in 2008 just as they simultaneously began a literature course entitled "American Protest Literature" that included texts such as Upton Sinclair's *The Jungle* and John Steinbeck's *The Grapes of Wrath*. For both students, the combination of volunteering at the shelter and reading these literary works deepened their doubts about the veracity of the American dream. Garcia-Brown said that *The Grapes of Wrath*, in particular, reminded her that "For a lot of people, they can work really hard, and they're just not going to get anywhere." Likewise, Mellor noted that the combination of the class and her conversations with men and women at the shelter pushed her to see that "There are so many other factors that influence your life, and just working hard is not going to make you a successful person. You need to have other things, [like] time and opportunity." For Mellor — who described herself as coming from a "diehard Republican" community in rural Ohio — these doubts she expressed about the American dream were a sharp departure from the worldview she had been exposed to at home.

Sophomore Liam Murphy and junior Larry Yoon both enrolled in 2009 in Dr. Paul Farmer's anthropology course on global health and social justice.[24] According to Murphy, the thesis underlying the course was that effective global health programs require a deep understanding of the particular culture and community in which one is trying to work. Murphy described his primary takeaway from the course as a belief that "blanket policies don't work. Like [in] Kenya, there would be certain factors that contribute to the prevalence of AIDS, [and] those would be completely different from say Peru, and those need to be taken into account, and changed to different programs if you like want it to be effective and sustainable." Murphy — who staffed the shelter's Resource Advocacy table — also described his belief that policies intended to combat homelessness "need to be more localized and centric." This perspective came directly from his anthropology course on global health.

For junior Larry Yoon, this same anthropology course pushed him to think more about the work he wanted to do upon graduating from Harvard:

> "The class has made me kind of think about where to go from the idealism. Like the tangible steps you take. It's kind of like what keeps the shelter going, just idealistic young students coming together to want to contribute to the greater good. What are we going to do after that? How are we going to continue to let that manifest in good works bettering the world?"

In addition to these larger questions, Yoon noted that he chose to write his final paper for the course about homelessness and the way in which Americans often characterize homelessness as a disease that the homeless have brought upon themselves. In very different ways, both Murphy and Yoon were clearly working to connect their coursework with their experiences at the Harvard Square Shelter.

Several students described senior thesis projects that connected to their work at the shelter. Senior Elyse Margolis spent the spring of 2009 working on a Social Studies thesis about the volatility of low income housing policies over the past 60 years. For Margolis — a first-time volunteer as a college senior — she had chosen the thesis topic as a result of her interest in public policy and then decided that she should volunteer at the shelter as a means of gaining some real-world experience with the topic she would be spending the year researching. Junior Amanda Mooney described the reverse scenario. Having become a shelter director in the fall of 2008, Mooney spent time thinking about how the shelter could play a role in the thesis she would write during her senior year of college as a biology major. Ultimately, Mooney settled upon a project which entailed measuring the stress levels of shelter directors during their shifts at the shelter by taking saliva samples midway through the shift and measuring the cortisol levels in the saliva. Her research question was focused upon whether a director's compatibility with his or her co-director influenced feelings of stress while managing the shelter. Her research could have implications for all sorts of team-oriented work and activities.

In short, then, there were numerous ways in which academic classes informed volunteers' work at the Harvard Square Shelter. That said, these Harvard students were largely responsible for synthesizing these two experiences on their own. The professors of these students' courses had no particular knowledge of the shelter, and in none of these classes were more than a few shelter volunteers enrolled at any one time. It is easy to imagine the value of Harvard offering a course (or set of courses) on issues related to homelessness designed specifically for the nearly 100 volunteers affiliated with the Harvard Square Homeless Shelter. While it is possible that students would reject such a structure as artificial in the same way they rejected the formalized reflection sessions, a deeper integration of service, academic learning, and reflection would seem to be invaluable.

CONCLUSION

In his 2008 book *The First Year Out*, sociologist Tim Clydesdale reported that the majority of the young adults in his study were uninterested in "connect[ing] their lives to deeper values or larger purposes."[25] Such a characterization does *not* capture the young adults volunteering at the Harvard Square Shelter. This chapter has sought to highlight the powerful *but different* takeaways of the weekly volunteers at the Harvard Square Shelter and the students who took on leadership roles as supervisors and directors. Specifically, the weekly volunteers experienced the breaking down of their stereotypes about homelessness while the shelter's supervisors and directors came to recognize the complex and intertwined nature of the factors that contribute to homelessness.

A landmark service-learning study by James Youniss and Miranda Yates in the mid-1990s identified a similar division among its volunteers.

In *Community Service and Social Responsibility in Youth*, Youniss and Yates focused on a parochial high school in Washington DC that combined an academic class on social justice issues with weekly service at a local soup kitchen.[26] In analyzing the journal entries that participating students wrote about their experiences at the soup kitchen, Youniss and Yates' divided the participating students' learning into three tiers. The first tier included the teenagers who had come to recognize the falseness of the stereotypes they carried about the homeless; the second tier included the adolescents who recognized the similarities between their own lives and the homeless men and women they encountered at the soup kitchen; and the third tier included the participating teens who had begun to consider the underlying causes of homelessness and the steps that might be taken to address these causes. In short, Youniss and Yates might suggest that the Harvard Square Shelter's weekly volunteers fall somewhere inside tiers one and two while many of the shelter's supervisors and directors are firmly ensconced in tier three.

Because all of the high school students in Youniss and Yates' study had spent the same amount of time at the soup kitchen, these scholars did not speculate about *why* different students had different takeaways from their volunteer work at the soup kitchen. For the Harvard students volunteering at the shelter, however, the most important distinction between the weekly volunteers and student-leaders seemed to be the leadership role itself. In taking on the responsibility to bar an intoxicated homeless man from entering the shelter; to sit and console a homeless woman ill with HIV/AIDS; and to make difficult policy decisions about who is and is not eligible for the Work Contract program, the college students leading the Harvard Square Shelter developed a deeper understanding of homelessness, of the wider world, and of their own role within this world. Certainly, there was tremendous value in the learning about homelessness accomplished by both the shelter's weekly volunteers *and* student-leaders; however, the deep "complexification" of homelessness that accompanied the shelter's leadership roles is worthy of the attention of university leaders across the country interested in fostering the identity development and commitment to social responsibility of their own student populations. At last count, more than 3.3 million Americans between the ages of 18 and 24 were participating in some form of community service, and nearly seven out of ten college students characterized their university as offering community service opportunities.[27] The experiences of the student-leaders at the Harvard Square Homeless Shelter, however, suggest that the opportunities for leadership and responsibility afforded these young adults played a crucial role in making their volunteer experiences at the Harvard Square Shelter such powerful ones.

Chapter 8

Learning to Lead

The first tumultuous debate among the Harvard Square Shelter directors took place before the shelter had even opened for business. On November 13 2008 — two nights before the shelter opened for the winter — the shelter held its opening dinner and invited a formerly homeless woman, MaryAnne Higgins, to open the dinner with a brief talk about her experiences at the shelter. Higgins, a woman in her mid-fifties, had spent much of the previous winter at the shelter but was now back on her feet, working for the city of Cambridge and attending night school. Higgins was honored to come and speak about her experiences and noted that, as a Christian, she would appreciate the opportunity to lead the assembled group in a prayer over the meal they were about to share together.

Despite its location in a church basement, the Harvard Square Homeless Shelter has always been avowedly secular. Senior Kathryn Tobin explained that, from her perspective, "We want to make this a comfortable space for everyone, but some kind of collective activity like that sets the wrong tone." Another senior director, Robert Vozar, though Jewish, argued, "It would be very rude and disrespectful to tell this woman who we invited to speak about anything to say you can't talk about this." The shelter staff went back and forth over the best response to an awkward situation and ultimately rearranged the schedule for the Opening Dinner so that Higgins' speech closed, rather than opened, the event. While Higgins certainly thanked God "for introducing me to

these beautiful students," the shift in schedule precluded a more communal prayer. And, with one decision already under the staff's belts,
the 2008–09 shelter season began.

The debate described in Chapter 5 over the number of homeless men
and women to allow into the shelter each night was perhaps the most
substantive debate of the shelter season. The most emotional debate
focused on the appropriate level of training for the shelter's security
guards following a night in which an angry homeless man had barged
into the shelter and threatened the two female directors on duty. The
most divisive debate involved a situation in which one student-director
unintentionally rescinded the warning given to a homeless man by
another student-director.

Although neither the most important nor the most emotional nor
the most divisive, perhaps the debate which most vividly captures the
divide among the shelter staff in 2009 focused on the question of skim
milk versus whole milk. For many years, the Harvard Square Shelter
purchased whole milk because the homeless men and women staying
at the shelter expressed a clear preference for it. In the fall of 2008,
however, supplies director Kelly Parker read an article about a health
risk commonly found in homeless populations referred to as "starving
obese."[1] According to Parker, the homeless are obese at a much higher
rate than other people, and yet the food that most homeless people are
eating is so unhealthy that they are simultaneously more likely to be
malnourished. From Parker's perspective, "We have a responsibility
to supply food that is healthy." Moreover, whole milk turned out to be
more expensive than skim milk, so the less healthy option was actually
costing the shelter more money. On the other hand, several directors
argued that homeless people have so few choices in their lives that it
seemed like a small thing to honor their preference for whole milk. As
Parker noted, the debate came down to the following question: "At what
point is it okay to regulate and say, 'We're going to say what's best for
you, and we know what's good for you?'"

Junior Amanda Mooney noted that, in debates like this one all
winter long, one camp of directors prioritized giving their homeless
guests as much autonomy as possible and another camp of directors
prioritized policies that provided the most beneficial conditions for the
men and women staying at the Harvard Square Shelter. After half an
hour of debate, the decision was made to switch over to skim milk. In
this seemingly small issue, though — an issue which everyone could
agree was by no means high stakes — one can see the two blocs of staff

members who managed to butt heads all winter long. In fact, several directors described the policy debates in 2008–09 as significantly more contentious than those from previous seasons. As the Staff Director, junior Nathan Small was responsible for chairing the weekly policy meetings. According to Small:

> "Last year at our policy meetings, we'd go around on an agenda item and people would say things. And then I would take what people said and try to draw them into some language that everyone was like, 'Yes, okay, that's great.' And it was really about building consensus. And, this year, I felt like it's more about holding two sides at bay. Definitely facilitating meetings has been a little bit more stressful for me this year."

As for what accounts for this difference in tone, Small commented diplomatically that "Our senior class has some really strong personalities. People who are brilliant, care a ton about the shelter and are pretty dogmatic in how they present their opinions. And so I think this led to some head butting this year." Two of these strong personalities belonged to Robert Vozar and Kathryn Tobin.

Vozar and Tobin were both seniors, both economics majors, and both worked spectacularly hard as juniors on the shelter's endowment campaign. As Tobin explained, "The endowment was a sufficiently large cause, and we were sufficiently dedicated to it that we were willing to keep coming back to the table and keep working things out. But absent that motivating goal, I think we both began to see each other's imper fections." From Tobin's perspective, the divide between the two was an ideological one. These two students represented the spokespersons of the two blocs described above: the autonomy of particular individuals versus the best interests of the shelter community as a whole. From Tobin's perspective, "Fundamentally, you work as a director to give people agency. . . . With guests, it's always, when at all possible, allowing people to do things for themselves if they want to, not imposing certain norms." Vozar, for his part, focused on creating an environment in the Harvard Square Shelter that offered safety, comfort, and dignity to the greatest possible number of homeless men and women.

Tobin and Vozar's differing objectives came to a head over the issue of whether Francine should be forced to take a shower. Recall from Chapter 3 that Francine was a homeless woman in her early sixties who had been living on the streets of Harvard Square for more than

20 years. Having eschewed all homeless shelters or services of any kind for decades, the Harvard Square Shelter won the admiration of the entire homeless services community when the shelter's Street Team convinced Francine to come inside in January 2009. Unfortunately, Francine did not shower regularly, and the other men and women staying at the shelter — particularly the other homeless women who shared a bedroom with her — complained to the shelter staff about the odor.

The question came down to whether an individual staying at the shelter could be required to take a shower. As Tobin said, "I just thought that was totally inappropriate and out of sync with the kind of ideology that I wanted the shelter to operate on. Obviously nudity is involved [with a shower], and if someone is uncomfortable, that's just such a removal of agency from the person." For Vozar, the question came down to a question of fairness and utility; requiring one person to take a shower would improve the experience of several dozen other people in the shelter. The debate over this question grew tense, and ultimately the staff decided — by a vote — *not* to require Francine to take a shower.

Similar to the whole milk versus skim milk discussion, it is easy to brush off this debate over Francine's hygiene as a small issue involving a single woman who stayed at the shelter for just a few weeks. At the same time, however, the young adults who participated in this discussion had to make some important decisions about *what* factors were most important to them in doing this work. Reflecting on the disagreement, Tobin asserted, "I don't think Robert and I think the same. I don't think the worlds that we are working for are the same. I think they're radically different." In these discussions over seemingly small matters lie opportunities for students to articulate visions of right and wrong and to compare a personal vision to those of their classmates. This back and forth is an invaluable step in the development of a mature adult identity.[2]

A number of scholars have written about the ways in which social networking websites such as Facebook and MySpace facilitate identity development among teenagers by encouraging them to articulate various aspects of their lives including preferences in music, television, cinema, favorite quotations, and causes with which they identify.[3] In so doing, these networking sites encourage teens to make clear declarations about their beliefs and values. Similarly, the Harvard Square Shelter's weekly policy meetings are a forum in which the young adults who serve as the shelter's supervisors and directors must offer clear declarations — both to themselves and their peers — about what they believe and value. While these discussions are not posted online for all to see, the stakes of the discussions would seem to be much higher. Tobin and Vozar also butted heads all winter over how to address failures. One such failure occurred over the Christmas holiday. Keeping the shelter operating over Harvard's two-week winter break is a perennial challenge because nearly all of the shelter's weekly volunteers head home for the holidays. The shelter's volunteer director is responsible for rounding up enough local students, international students, graduate students, and community groups to keep the shelter running, albeit with a skeleton crew. Unfortunately, in December of 2008, Christmas vacation arrived with the shelter dangerously understaffed for the two-week holiday. Vozar characterized the situation as a "colossal failure," and Tobin described the situation as "a huge problem."

Ultimately, two of the directors who grew up in Cambridge — Nathan Small and Jerry Chen — spent six straight nights at the shelter, and another director, Leo LaSala, flew back early from his vacation in Washington DC to help out. The crisis passed, but, when everyone returned to campus in early January, a debate ignited over how best to address the situation. As Vozar commented, "I have really high standards for myself and other people, and sometimes that comes across as having overly high standards for other people." From his perspective:

"I feel like if we have a colossal failure, we shouldn't sweep it under the rug. We should be open about it and try to learn from the experience. And a lot of people on staff are afraid to, so the two ways in which I'm different from other people on staff in this situation is that I'm not afraid to have it brought up, and I think other people are afraid of offending the volunteer director, but I think that really has to be second order to how did this enormous failure occur?"

In short, Vozar saw value in taking the time to analyze the failure, call the student responsible for the failure to account and take the steps necessary to make sure the situation never occurred again. He also expressed his belief that the volunteer director owed the staff a public apology.

Tobin saw the situation differently. Though equally concerned about the vacation fiasco, she saw little value in publicly embarrassing a classmate. As she explained, "I don't think that's very efficient because I don't think that motivates people to do better. It just makes them ashamed or unhappy." The way Tobin saw it, the other shelter directors had picked up the slack, which was one reason for having such a large staff in the first place.

Ultimately, the majority of directors sided with Tobin, and the issue was dropped. In this debate about responding to failure, however, is a perfect example of an opportunity for the shelter's leaders to consider the most effective and ethical ways to lead an organization. There is little doubt that, upon graduating from Harvard, students such as Tobin and Vozar will go out into the world and apply their perspectives about ethics and leadership to the organizations they join. These perspectives will have been informed by having had to articulate their beliefs to fellow shelter directors and in responding to the perspectives of their peers. Ironically, both Tobin and Vozar expressed interest in pursuing doctorates in economics, so their clashes during the winter of 2009 may be only the beginning of their professional clashes over leadership and policy.

Scholars Clydesdale and Levine would likely argue that these debates about how best to operate the shelter provide the student-leaders with a significant head start over many of their peers in preparing for the future. In his 2008 study of young adults, Clydesdale observed: "Teen employment does little to help American teens identify meaningful future pathways . . . or to evaluate the deeper, longer-term purposes of their work, leisure and financial activities."[4] From Clydesdale's perspective, the employment opportunities available to most teens offer little access to significant responsibility, skill-building, or adults able to serve as professional mentors.

Psychiatrist Mel Levine's 2005 book, *Ready or Not, Here Life Comes*, criticizes the American educational system for not doing enough to prepare its youth for the world of work that lies ahead. Levine asserts that "Secondary schools have to prepare students for what will confront them after college or instead of college. Colleges too should be equipping their students for life after graduation. At present, this need is almost entirely overlooked."[5] The Harvard students leading the Harvard Square Shelter, however, have the opportunity to consider through their debates and discussions the values that are most important to them and also to gain experience in articulating these values, building consensus and working collaboratively. According to Clydesdale and Levine, the opportunities for young Americans to gain such experiences are presently few and far between. Such an opportunity is an invaluable process for young adults to experience, especially as they make the transition from adolescence to emerging adulthood.[6]

Moreover, one of the founding fathers of moral psychology, Lawrence Kohlberg, believed that the key to strengthening people's morality lay in strengthening their ability as moral reasoners.[7] Towards this end, Kohlberg and his colleagues created a series of short vignettes which described different types of moral dilemmas.[8] They used these dilemmas as a mechanism for assessing an individual's moral reasoning ability. An important critique of Kohlberg's work, however, is that individuals may offer one perspective when it comes to a fictional dilemma but act very differently in real life.[9] This critique is sometimes referred to as the judgment-action gap.[10]

There is no judgment-action gap at the Harvard Square Homeless Shelter. The shelter's supervisors and directors have the responsibility every Sunday night in their weekly policy meetings to think through a diverse set of complex issues with *genuine* implications for the men and women staying there. The real-life implications of these debates render them substantially different from Kohlberg's vignettes as well as the mock trials, debate competitions, and investment contests in which many of their university classmates are simultaneously engaging. The opportunity to confront a difficult scenario, debate its implications, come to a decision, and then watch the results of this decision play out is an invaluable process for young adults to experience. Looking back on her work at the Harvard Square Shelter, alumna Amelia Ginsberg remarked that "I don't think I thought this in a conscious way then, but a lot of my most moral and ethical encounters that place produced for me were probably pretty formative in some ways." As Ginsberg suggested, the debates and dilemmas considered by the shelter's student-leaders likely play an important role in the development of moral and ethical understandings that they will carry with them into adulthood.

HOOKED ON A FEELING

The Harvard Square Homeless Shelter also offers its volunteers, and in particular its student-leaders, an opportunity to experience what meaningful work *feels like*. Ward Welburn, who now works as the director of an urban middle school, described the shelter as giving him a "sense of what it was like to do something that was very fulfilling" as well as cluing him in to his "love of active entrepreneurship in getting things done." Upon graduating from Harvard, Welburn turned down a job offer from investment bank Goldman Sachs and found in education an experience akin to his work at the Harvard Square Shelter.

Dr. Aaron Dutka, too, offered the shelter significant credit for his work as a medical doctor specializing in patients with substance abuse problems and HIV/AIDS. Medical school was not on Dutka's radar screen for most of his time at Harvard. A history and literature major, he planned to become a high school history teacher and enrolled in Harvard's undergraduate teacher education program to earn the necessary licensure to pursue that career trajectory. As Dr. Dutka described it, his change in plans came about as a result of an experience at the shelter combined with the words of an inspiring professor:

> "We had patients with HIV and AIDS at the shelter, and you could see how the illness was driven by behaviors, choices like drug use, risky sex practices. So I was interested in HIV and I was interested in the guests at the shelter, and how you could help them, I guess. So that was when I started to think about medicine, and then the kind of final straw was I took 'Literature of Social Reflection' with Robert Coles, and he is a doctor who is a teacher, and I had never really seen that. I hadn't had doctors as role models before, so that kind of confirmed the seed that the shelter planted, which is that I could be a doctor and also do rewarding service that would be intellectually stimulating."

As a history and literature major, Dr. Dutka finished his undergraduate career without having completed the science courses required even to apply to medical school. As he worked his way through those required science courses, he volunteered as a research assistant at an organization called Healthcare for the Homeless, which he described as "the first time I saw doctors doing homeless medicine."[11] All of these different experiences combined to push Dr. Dutka towards the work he does today with substance abusers and HIV patients — work that continues to bring him into contact with a significant number of men and women contending with homelessness. For him, the Harvard Square Shelter truly lies at the foundation of this career trajectory. As he explained it, his experience as a director there provided him a taste of what it felt like to "have it all." By that, Dr. Dutka meant, "I could be a Harvard student and work in a homeless shelter. So from there on, I looked for careers where I could do both. It could be intellectually stimulating, but would fundamentally have service in there at its base."

Dr. Dutka was not the only Harvard alumni who described his career trajectory as a search for the balance he experienced at the Harvard Square Homeless Shelter. Dennis McGonagle is now a professor of religion at an Ivy League university who does research on religious social change movements. The majority of his student are preparing for careers in ministry. In words very similar to Dr. Dutka's, Professor McGonagle said:

"Because University Lutheran was my church community, my activist community and my school community, it was a place where I experienced the possibility of having a balanced commitment to the church, to academia and to social change activism. And, you know, I've pretty much insisted on having all those elements in the mix for me. And my career has just been kind of figuring out what kind of pattern allows me to keep that mix of things."

While the job of professor of religion isn't intrinsically connected to working with the homeless, Professor McGonagle described his work at the shelter as providing a template for the religion-activism-academic balance that he has continually sought out in his professional career. Likewise, alumna Amelia Ginsberg — who does environmental advocacy work — considered that her work at the shelter "has always been something that I think back to as a touchstone of the kind of feeling that your work should give you."

Several 2008–09 shelter directors offered a similar organizing principle for their future job searches. Junior Deanna Galante was by no means certain what type of work she will ultimately pursue but hoped to "have a job that I get the same thing I get out of the shelter." Likewise, senior Leo LaSala said of the Harvard Square Shelter: "I like that atmosphere a lot. I've found it in the best possible way at the shelter. I don't think I'm going to find anything quite like this in the real world, but the closer I get, the happier I think I'll be."

In describing the impact of the Harvard Square Shelter upon participating students, the shelter's founder, Pastor Fred Reisz, noted: "I was delighted to see how their experiences began to fade over by osmosis into their academic work and to a certain extent to even channel their academic work in terms of what they were going to major in or do in their lives." Likewise, Harvard professor and University Lutheran congregant Julie Wilson remarked, "The people that I have known that have been shelter directors, it has been transformative, and it has changed what they have thought about doing after graduation." The ability of the Harvard Square Shelter to lead to these types of insights is particularly important when one considers the assertion by scholar Richard Weissbourd that most universities do "strikingly little" to help students "sort out their role" in the world.[12] Likewise, William Damon reports: "Only about one in five young people in the 12–22 year age range express a clear vision of where they want to go, what they want to accomplish in life, and why."[13] Damon also expresses concern that "Few young people today go about their preparation for adult life with the combination of self-appraisal and purposeful intent that produces a sense of calling."[14] By no means will all of the Harvard students operating the shelter emerge from the experience with a crystal-clear vision of their professional pathway. However, the shelter does provide an opportunity for that vision of the future to grow significantly clearer.

Perhaps the clearest example of the shelter's impact upon career trajectories is alumna Helen Van Anglen, whom Joseph Finn, Executive Director of the Massachusetts Housing and Shelter Alliance, described as a shining example of the shelter's influence. According to Van Anglen, who volunteered at the shelter from 1989 to 1993:

> "One of the things that I loved about the overnight shift was that at two o'clock in the morning you were just talking to people. I was younger than most of the people [and] the power dynamic was so flattened that we could just talk, and over the years, people I knew there were women who let me into their lives."

When she graduated in 1993, Van Anglen wasn't sure what she wanted to do with her life but realized that "What I had was all the stories that the women had told me, and this sense that nobody was talking about the long-term impact of trauma in the lives of homeless women. . . . Nobody was talking about the long-term effects of sexual abuse."

Over the next two years, Van Anglen won several grants that provided the seed money to start a not-for-profit organization that provides shelter and support to homeless women living in crisis. Since its founding in 1996, her organization has worked with nearly 300 women a year, offering resources that include shelter, counseling, a legal clinic, a health clinic, and a wellness program. On the organization's website, one can unequivocally read echoes of Van Anglen's experiences at the

Harvard Square Shelter. For example, the description of the organization's history begins with the explanation that the organization "grew out of the hopes and stories of homeless women attempting to access programs in the Cambridge, Massachusetts area."[15] In this explanation, one can envision Van Anglen as a college student in the basement of the University Lutheran Church talking late into the night with the homeless women staying there.

In 2011, Van Anglen's organization will commemorate the fifteenth anniversary of its founding. Van Anglen has won numerous awards for her social activism, and the organization has served as a national model for serving women victimized by domestic violence and sexual abuse. After 11 years, Van Anglen left the organization to embark on a new social services venture, but three Harvard Square Shelter alums — Ward Welburn, Joshua Villanueva, and Aaron Dutka — sit on the organization's Board of Advisers and continue to support an organization that addresses issues about which they all became intimately familiar in the basement of the University Lutheran church.

Clearly, the men and women described here have gone on to utilize in their professional lives the lessons and experience they drew from their volunteer work at the shelter. The 2008–09 Harvard Square Shelter directors, however, showed every sign of following in their predecessor's footsteps. Like Dr. Aaron Dutka, a number of students were considering careers in medicine. Junior Larry Yoon entered Harvard thinking he wanted to be a doctor but admitted that "it was really about the prestige, about having the 'Dr.' in front of your name, the MD after my name, and being well off." And, in fact, one of his initial motivations for becoming involved with the Harvard Square Shelter was the recognition that he needed some community service on his resume for the medical school application process. Through his involvement with the shelter and his founding of the Street Team, however, Yoon's commitment to medicine changed. Citing how much he has gained from interacting with the homeless on a weekly basis, Yoon expressed a newfound interest in primary care medicine: "I want to work with people, see people over and over again." In this same interview in April 2009, Yoon further explained that, now, "There's a part of me that's just very grassroots. I just want to open up a health clinic for the homeless, a free clinic somewhere in another city, and maybe I could also be working abroad. I've been thinking about Latin America or the developing world for a bit of time." Yoon's whole framework for thinking about his role in the medical world has changed.

Junior Amanda Mooney, the daughter of two doctors, entered Harvard with medical aspirations as well. Like Yoon, Mooney always saw the shelter as a valuable way to gain experience that will be useful to a future career in medicine. Going back to her work as a breakfast shift volunteer, she described as useful the opportunity to practice "be[ing] able to talk just very naturally to people I might not have very much in common with off the cuff." Then, as a shelter supervisor, she described the value of overnight shifts in which you have to summon up "enough energy to deal with someone when all you can think about is, 'Oh my God, I just want to sleep.'" Mooney described her work as a director as "a little bit analogous" to the work of a physician — "this constant stream of people coming up to you and [asking], 'Can you come and get this? Can you do this?' And you just try to deal with those the best you can."

In an earlier chapter, Mooney was described as one of the Harvard students who became "addicted" to the shelter, and that tremendous investment in the shelter has influenced her career plans as well. As she said at the conclusion of the 2008-09 shelter season:

> "Kind of a big light bulb happened around February because I'd been directing for a semester and just thinking about these issues and in particular for the work contract program and just thinking, 'Oh my gosh, how are they going to get off this carousel? And where's the primary care? Where's any sense of prevention or follow up?' And then, all of a sudden, the light bulb went off. I'm like, I can do that. And so actually tomorrow I start at Boston Health Care for the Homeless. Just helping out once a week."

As promised, Mooney began volunteering at the same organization that helped alumnus Aaron Dutka transition from the shelter to a career in homeless medicine. Of course it is far too early to know if Mooney will stay on this pathway over the final years of her undergraduate career and then medical school, but, like Dutka, the seed was planted at the Harvard Square Homeless Shelter.

Two other current students may follow in alumna Anusha Ghosh's footsteps by allowing the shelter to propel them towards a career in public service law. As described in an earlier chapter, South Dakotan Melissa Sanguinetti made it to Harvard as a result of her participation in the federal government's Congressional Page Program.[16] In contrast to several of the other students working at the shelter, however,

Sanguinetti became disenchanted by politics during her first three years of college. The work she observed in Washington DC as a congressional page and as an intern for a South Dakota Senator felt "just too slow for me and too disconnected from what was actually going on to be satisfying." In contrast, Sanguinetti explained that, at the Harvard Square Shelter, "Somebody comes in and they're hungry and you feed them." She appreciated the shelter's directness and immediacy and, as a result, expressed a newfound interest in public service law.

As a means of exploring this interest, Sanguinetti began volunteering in December 2008 in the housing unit of Boston Legal Services. Very similar to alumna Anusha Ghosh who now works as an immigrant rights attorney, Sanguinetti described her belief that she needs a concrete skill-set in order to be useful to the homeless population she has encountered at the shelter:

> "If you really want to be useful, you need to have tools and knowledge and credibility to do something pro-active in their lives. And I think that's kind of where I arrived at legal stuff, and the other day when I was able to have not a ton of solidly good legal advice — but enough to say, 'Oh these five instances are violations of tenant rights, and you should definitely bring those up in housing court,' I was like, wow, that's the most useful thing I've learned since I've been at Harvard!"

It seems entirely possible that Sanguinetti's introduction to direct service at the shelter and continuation of that learning at Boston Legal Services will propel her towards a career in public service law upon graduation.

Wellesley College sophomore Charlotte Wu described a parallel interest in pursuing public service law. In an interview at the start of the shelter season in November 2008, Wu described an interest in law school, but admitted to being uncertain about public service law versus work in the private sector:

> "I want to work as an attorney for a non-profit, but just the financial aspects of it are very daunting. And all my professors are saying, 'Perhaps, Charlotte, you should consider going into corporate law and then once you can pay off all your debts and become a little more stable, then go into the non-profit and public sector law that you really want to do.'"

By the conclusion of a winter of overnight shifts at the Harvard Square Shelter, however, this indecision had melted away. As Wu said, "I'm more certain than ever that I want to go into public service. Just going into public service and working in the public sector. I've even thought so far as to go and work for non-profits who deal with the rights of homeless people." Towards this end, Wu applied for a summer job with the Office of Clinical and Pro Bono Programs at Harvard Law School. She, too, credited the shelter with helping to provide greater clarity to her future professional pathway:

> "[Prior to volunteering at the shelter] I didn't really know which cause I wanted to champion. And I feel like homelessness really hit home for me, especially with the economic crisis that's going on and a lot of my friend's parents who are being laid off. And realizing that homelessness is very real, a tangible reality. That is something I want to continue to work with."

As she grows more deeply involved in the shelter over the final two years of her college career, one can imagine Wu's commitment to pursuing public service law only growing deeper.

Of course, not all of the shelter's directors and supervisors saw themselves pursuing professional work that directly involves homelessness. Following her graduation from Harvard in June of 2009, Lissette McDonald began a job doing medical research at the University of San Francisco. However, she noted that "Being at the shelter really got me interested in psychology and specifically clinical psychology in that, I think, through my time at the shelter, I've seen a spectrum of mental issues." Junior Jerry Chen said at the conclusion of the 2009 shelter season that "It's really impacted my thinking on what I'm going to do after college. Not necessarily working with homelessness, but it makes me realize how being on policy group is the most interesting thing to me — how policies are made, on what basis they're justified." Chen speculated that he could imagine himself getting involved in healthcare policy, which he has "learned more about at the shelter and become more frustrated with."

Following his graduation from Harvard in 2009, senior Leo LaSala began teaching high school in Philadelphia through Teach for America and has contemplated starting a charter school further down the road. LaSala, whose senior thesis focused on college students' beliefs about the American dream, explained that "I always knew I wanted to do something with education because I feel like it's such a crucial part of both the ideology behind the inequality in this country and also the way that people are supposed to pull themselves up by their bootstraps." In other words, LaSala conceived of education as the lever through which he is best suited to address poverty and inequality. Likewise, Antonia Garcia-Brown — who did a weekly overnight shift in the fall of 2008 and then staffed the Resource Advocacy desk in the spring of 2009 — always envisioned herself pursuing a career as an elementary school teacher; however, Garcia-Brown explained in the spring of 2009 that her work at the shelter had led her to begin contemplating a career in social work as well. As she described it, through her work at the shelter connecting homeless men and women to relevant resources, "It sort of became utterly appealing to me to be able to work with someone to get what they needed for one period of time."

And of course large numbers of shelter volunteers and directors will end up pursuing careers with less socially responsible foci. In 2007, approximately 50 percent of the Harvard senior class entering the work force began positions in the finance and management consulting industries. In 2008, despite the scarcity of jobs in these sectors as a result of an economic recession, nearly 40 percent of Harvard's senior class, again, chose jobs in finance and consulting.[17] Unquestionably, shelter volunteers, supervisors, and directors have contributed to that percentage. Even those students entering the financial sector, however, will have opportunities over the course of their lives to influence society's treatment of the homeless and to advocate for social justice. As the CASPAR Shelter's Meghan Goughan noted:

"I assume most at Harvard are going to go on to jobs where they have some relative position of power, influence, even if it's just, 'Hey, I vote.' And so when something comes up about cutting funding, they can go back, 'Okay, this is what that would mean. If funding is cut for homeless services, that means there's 20 less beds and on any given night that's 20 more people outside.' That's where I think the biggest carry-over is, that ultimately they end up being ambassadors for people experiencing homelessness."

Over the past 26 winters, the Harvard Square Shelter has offered food, shelter, conversation, and resources to hundreds of men and women contending with homelessness. And during those same 26 years, the shelter has offered an equal number of Harvard students a chance to deepen their understanding of the world, to develop skills they will bring with them into the workforce, and to reflect upon the most relevant domains towards which to direct these skills. This symbiosis makes the Harvard Square Homeless Shelter a unique organization — and one with important implications for the delivery of both effective social service and a quality university education.

CONSTRUCTIVE FAILURES

While Robert Vozar, Kathryn Tobin, and the rest of the shelter staff engaged in heated debates this past winter about how to respond to failure, the leadership of the University Lutheran Church had long since developed its own perspective on the failures that will inevitably occur when a group of college students are charged with managing a complex organization. As University Lutheran congregant Julie Wilson commented, "Our role is to mentor students. . . . We keep in mind that our mission is [only] indirectly to serve the homeless. That was our initial mission, but now our mission is to support the development of students in this work." This attitude towards student development was evident in the church's attitude towards the shelter and sanitation codes.

In interviews in early 2009, three different members of the University Lutheran leadership expressed their belief that the shelter might soon run into trouble with Cambridge health inspectors. Church congregant Selma Brooks noted that "The biggest challenge [for students] is that they have to realize that when people are living in a group setting, cleanliness and order are very important." Pastor Donald Larsen acknowledged that one of the challenges for the students is "keeping the place clean, keeping the kitchen clean, dealing with food preparation according to health code, and staying on top of things." Congregant Julie Wilson went so far as to say, "Maybe what happens is you just have to fail an inspection once and close the shelter for a couple nights, and they will understand that the city and the church are really serious about some of the basic health practices."

As if by clockwork, in March 2009, the Cambridge health inspector visited the shelter and promptly shut the kitchen down. Senior Leo LaSala was the director on duty. According to LaSala:

"Basically we had a number of very small — 17 or so — vio-
lations: things blocking the door, surface not wiped down
properly. The real kicker was a mouse ran through the legs of
the health inspector. We have seen mice on and off. There's a
lot of food around. It's very hard to get rid of mice. But the
mouse came, and that was the end of that. So we were shut
down."

Initially, the health inspector planned to close down the entire shelter
and evacuate the space, but she ultimately agreed to only close down
the kitchen and allow the shelter's 30 homeless guests to continue to
use the sleeping and living areas. LaSala and his co-director ordered
dozens of pizzas for dinner that night and — in a move reminiscent
of the shelter's beginnings — a number of local restaurants sent over
donations of food. That night, and all the next day, it was all hands on
deck. As LaSala recalled, "We went into crisis mode. Absolutely. . . .
Everyone kind of dropped what they were doing and showed up. And
we spent the whole day cleaning." The University Lutheran adminis-
trator pitched in, and the shelter was re-inspected (and passed) the
following morning.

One might say the University Lutheran leadership pursued a strategy that fell between Robert Vozar and Kathryn Tobin's perspectives
on failure. The church leadership foresaw the failed health inspection
coming and recognized that facing some real consequences might offer
the students a valuable lesson on some of the less appealing (but crucial) facets of operating a homeless shelter. At the same time, when the
failure occurred, there was little in the way of reprimand from Pastor
Larsen or the church leadership — just support in getting the kitchen
reopened as quickly as possible. An important piece of what makes
the Harvard Square Shelter such a tremendous learning experience
for its participants, then, is the ability of the shelter's landlord — the
University Lutheran Church — to recognize the inevitability *and the
value* of the occasional failure.

TEAMWORK

The Harvard Square Homeless Shelter also offers its volunteers a vehicle
for considering the future through their day-to-day responsibilities
and challenges. Specifically, in its day-to-day operation, the shelter's

college-aged supervisors and directors have an opportunity to consider the facets of leadership, management, direct service, and policy-making that do and do not appeal to them. Educator Michael Fullan has stated that "The ability to collaborate — on both a large and small scale—is becoming one of the core requisites of postmodern society."[18] The Harvard Square Shelter, with its flat leadership structure, provides an ideal laboratory for students to practice working on a team, a skill not always emphasized in their academic schooling.

Perhaps the biggest teamwork challenge for the Harvard Square Shelter staff is consistency. With 14 directors and 14 supervisors managing the shelter's dinner shifts and overnight shifts in teams of two, it is a significant challenge for all 28 staff members to apply the shelter's rules and policies consistently. As senior Leo LaSala explained, "Each night there's only two of us there at any given time, but to the guests we're all the same. We're all staff. So each one of us sort of represents everyone." Perhaps not surprisingly, inconsistent enforcement of shelter policies is the biggest criticism of the Harvard Square Shelter by the homeless men and women who stay there. One homeless man, Frank Green, complained, "How do we know what their rules are? They change each shift. And even if they do have them, with that many people involved, nobody is going to interpret it the same way." Green's point is a valid one. Supervisor Drew McGinty, for example, admitted that "I like being the good cop" and that he regards some of the other shelter directors as "tight asses." Likewise, director Deanna Galante acknowledged: "I hate giving warnings" and that "a lot of the time the warnings I should be giving and don't give are . . . because I tend to talk a lot with the guests, and I think I might let them say more than others would." The perennial attempt to maintain consistency, then, is one way in which the shelter staff is able to practice acting as a cohesive team.

Because there is no hierarchy among the shelter's 14 directors, individual staff members can become frustrated when they feel they are being marginalized or disrespected. Junior Larry Yoon noted that, in the shelter's weekly policy meetings, "Some people have louder voices than others, and even though it's flat, it's more like what you make of it. Like how big of a role you want to take." The policy meetings, then, provide an opportunity for staff members to consider how best to make their voices and perspectives heard. Yoon, for example, noted that "I'm definitely more quiet. It's not like I don't talk . . . I voice my opinions when it comes to things that are significant, and [if] I feel like someone is saying something egregiously wrong." Likewise, several newer directors discussed the process of learning how to express their authority within the shelter. For example, junior Amanda Mooney said, "I'm a new director, and I'm paired up with a veteran director . . . which means that sometimes she bosses me around during a shift." Over the course of the winter, Mooney had to learn how to interact with her co-director as an equal rather than a subordinate. Senior Lissette McDonald described a similar frustration that involved the homeless men and women staying at the shelter:

> "It was also frustrating when I was working at the shelter and they would say, 'I want to talk to a director' and I would say, "I *am* a director.' And they were like, 'No, I want to talk to this person,' and it was like, 'Okay, you can talk to this person.' And it was really frustrating."

Particularly frustrating for McDonald was that, often, these requests seemed to fall along gender lines with homeless men perceiving the shelter's male directors to be the "real" directors. McDonald, too, had to learn to assert her authority within the shelter while her male co-directors had to take care not to play into the stereotypes of the homeless men staying at the shelter.

A flat leadership structure also means there is no one positioned to reprimand a staff member shirking his or her responsibility. For example, two different directors, Kathryn Tobin and Kelly Parker, expressed frustration that a co-director with whom they both worked in 2009 wasn't pitching his weight. As Parker remarked, "He would come at 7:20 p.m., and the shelter opened at 7 p.m. And every time he would do a, 'I don't feel well,' so that was a little bit stressful." Likewise, Tobin — who worked with this same director — expressed her disappointment that "He was not invested at all in the shelter, and it was just very disheartening to be left alone at the end of the shift to write notes, and if things came up, then dealing with them alone." As junior Nathan Small noted, a challenge in these types of situations was that there was no single individual who could say to the neglectful director, "You need to do these three things in order to fulfill your job." In short, then, shelter guest Frank Green may have been accurate when he declared that hiring 28 CEOs wouldn't be the most efficient way to run a company and causes all sorts of challenges in a homeless shelter as well. Nonetheless, such a flat leadership structure does serve the function of giving each new batch of supervisors and directors perhaps the most extensive experience of their lives at working in a team setting. And recall alumnus Dr. Aaron Dutka's hypothesis that no other structure could really work for a student-run shelter. As he noted, "The judgment of any one 20 or 21 year old is probably not up to the challenge of running an organization like that. But the collective judgment of that group, I think, really did make that possible." In short, working in a team may prevent the shelter's leadership from making truly egregious mistakes and also offer these young adults practice at a skill — collaboration — that has grown increasingly important in most professional realms.

CONFIDENCE

Through all of these opportunities to work on a large, egalitarian team; to debate the shelter's policies and practices; and to grapple with successes and failures, the Harvard Square Homeless Shelter provides Harvard students with a remarkable stage for learning how to lead. Harvard professor and University Lutheran congregant Julie Wilson referred to the shelter as "a laboratory for creating the next generation." Alumna Helen Van Anglen noted that "It gave me a sense of, 'I could do stuff.'" She doubted she would have had the self-confidence to begin her non-profit organization for homeless women were it not for her work at the Harvard Square Shelter. Ward Welburn, who went on to found an independent school that provides a free private school education to low-income youth, also cited the shelter as providing him with "responsibilities and leadership challenges that were really, really helpful at a young age." As Welburn said, "I use the shelter a lot when I talk about what justifies a place like Harvard. It's that Harvard in a hundred different ways gives kids opportunities at a very young age that they have no right having and which can have a tremendous impact on their future." In this comment, Welburn alluded to opportunities at Harvard to do research alongside brilliant professors, to write for student publications, and to intern in some of the most beautiful art museums in the country. While several of these opportunities require the resources of an elite university such as Harvard, the leadership opportunities available at the Harvard Square Shelter require only the presence of a social issue in need of attention and the commitment of an organization like the University Lutheran Church to put up with constructive failures in service to a greater good.

As they came to the end of their time at Harvard and as directors of the shelter, both Robert Vozar and Kathryn Tobin — despite the tension along the way — appreciated the tremendous confidence the shelter experience had instilled in them. Vozar remarked, "I feel like I've gotten a tremendous sense of empowerment having this institution which we run." Speaking particularly about the success of the endowment campaign, Tobin added:

> "You can have an idea, and you can get people excited about it, and you can form a team, and it will be hard and it will be difficult, but you can get there. You can do it. It was crazy that we thought we could raise the money in the time we had. It was ridiculous, and I had no fundraising experience, and Robert had no fundraising experience at all. And we started, and we finished, and it was a lot harder than that. But, yeah, I hope I think that way in the future — that yes it can be done."

As mentioned, psychologist Albert Bandura defines self efficacy as a belief in one's ability to accomplish a particular goal.[19] The stronger an individual's sense of self-efficacy, the more willing he or she is to take on and expend effort to overcome obstacles. Echoing Bandura's findings are studies of college student activists,[20] civil rights activists[21] and Holocaust rescuers[22] that have found these people to be highly efficacious individuals. Bandura described four mechanisms for strengthening an individual's self efficacy, and the most effective of these mechanisms is what he calls "mastery experience."[23] The Harvard Square Homeless Shelter offers its student-leaders a mastery experience in leading a complex organization and, in so doing, strengthens their confidence in their leadership and management abilities. Whether or not these young adults continue to work towards combating homelessness upon graduating from college, their heightened sense of self-efficacy increases their ability to overcome obstacles and challenges in whatever careers they ultimately pursue.

Chapter 9

Enough Committed Fleas

For the past 25 years, the Harvard Square Shelter has stood alone as the only student-run homeless shelter in the United States.[1] Former shelter guest Fred Slomiak asserted that "There should be a shelter at every major university in the country." According to Slomiak, such an opportunity would be "unbelievable for the students" and would result in a greater number of professionals "who understand the issues [of homelessness] whether they go into politics, city planning, healthcare [or] counseling psychology." And while the number of student-run homeless shelters has been fixed at one for over 25 years now, undergraduates from the University of Pennsylvania visited the Harvard Square Homeless Shelter in 2009 with the goal of learning more about establishing such a model in Philadelphia. Likewise, a student group from the University of Florida contacted several of the Harvard Square Shelter directors with questions about the feasibility of such a model in Gainesville, Florida. Such interest is a welcome sign.

For such replication to occur, however, there first need to be 30–50 young adults at a particular university or cluster of universities willing to take on the time and responsibility for keeping a homeless shelter operating night after night after night for an entire winter. And then there needs to be a new batch of young adults ready to take their place the winter after that. And then the winter after that, or until a critical mass of Americans decide that homelessness is an unacceptable state for our poorest neighbors to have to endure.

Each night at the Harvard Square Homeless Shelter is divided into three shifts: the dinner shift 7–11 p.m., the overnight shift 11 p.m.–6:30 a.m., and the breakfast shift 6:30–8:30 a.m. With nearly 3.3 million college-aged Americans participating in a variety of community service opportunities every year, the dinner and breakfast shifts would seem to be no problem.[2] Any college campus worth its salt should be able to come up with 20 students willing to volunteer four hours a week to staff the dinner shifts and 20 more students willing to volunteer two hours a week (albeit early in the morning) to fill the breakfast shifts. But how about the more significant commitments: the overnight volunteers and then the students willing to take the helm for each of those shifts as supervisors and directors?

Perhaps some cause for concern is that a high percentage of those 3.3 million young adults participating in community service each year constitute one-time or occasional volunteers. In a study of community service at the high school level using a large national data-set, Richard Niemi and colleagues found that while 50 percent of high school students reported participation in a community service activity in the past year, that figure drops to 30 percent once students who only participated "once or twice" are excluded.[3] Moreover, these scholars found that the percentage of high school students who report participating in more than 35 hours of community service in the past year is just 14 percent. If the teenagers participating in *required* community service are taken out of the mix, the figure is even lower.

As for college-aged students, the Center for Information and Research on Civic Learning and Engagement (CIRCLE) reported in 2004 that, among 19–22 year olds, 36 percent participated in some form of community service in the past year. However, only 14 percent characterized themselves as volunteering regularly.[4] The median time commitment for this age group was 36 hours per year. For one of the Harvard Square Shelter's overnight volunteers in 2009, the annual commitment that accompanied a weekly overnight shift was approximately 110 hours per year. For one of the shelter's supervisors or directors, the annual volunteer commitment averaged approximately 250 hours per year. Clearly, then, the existence of a Harvard Square Homeless Shelter requires a small but dedicated cohort of young adults willing to go far beyond the typical levels of engagement of their peers. Does such a cohort exist on university campuses across the United States, or are the young adults described in these pages — students at one of the world's most elite institution of higher learning — a special breed?

While the motivations of the Harvard students operating the shelter have come up in previous chapters, here we delve more deeply into the types of experiences and values that led the supervisors, directors, and volunteers from the 2008–09 academic year to take on the responsibility of keeping the Harvard Square Homeless Shelter operating for its twenty-sixth winter.

URGINGS OF PEERS

The most common thread that emerged from interviews with 22 shelter volunteers, supervisors, and directors was that their initial involvement in the Harvard Square Homeless Shelter had come at the urging of another student — often an upperclassman. More specifically, 13 of the interviewed young adults described their volunteer work at the shelter as motivated, in large part, by the suggestion of a peer. For example, senior Leo LaSala explained that "One of my friends was a director at the time, and said, 'You should really, really apply to be a supervisor.' I wasn't sure I had the time for it, and he was like, 'No, totally go for it. You'll be fine.'" Senior Lissette McDonald recalled that one of the veteran directors, Jill, "really encouraged me to become a supervisor and take that next step. . . . I didn't picture myself being enough of a leader to take that role, but Jill really encouraged me to apply for it." Junior Jerry Chen described how one of his close friends, Nathan Small, who was already a shelter director, pushed him to get more involved as well. As Chen said, "He was just like, 'You should really come work at the shelter, be a supervisor' and I said, 'Okay, give up a night of my week? You're crazy!' But then I started thinking more about it, and I realized, 'The question is not really why, but why not?'"

Several of the first-time volunteers described the urging of peers as integral to their involvement with the shelter as well. For example, Harvard freshman Nancy Mellor described how one of her friends went to an information session about volunteering at the shelter and reported to Mellor that this was a service opportunity that was "truly well organized and sincere in its mission. She was really ardent about me going to it." Junior Lester Pearsons said that volunteering at the shelter was "on the back burner . . . [until] one of my good friends told me he had been involved with it, and it had been a good experience, so I thought I'd take a shot at it." Senior Hope Franklin commented similarly that "I was sort of intrigued but hadn't done anything about it. And then one of my roommates this year is one of the directors, and she encouraged me to do it."

Perhaps what is most notable about these explanations is that none of these young adults arrived at Harvard determined to seek out a service opportunity or certain that they were ready to make a deep commitment to combating homelessness. Rather, their involvement came about, in large part, through the suggestion of a peer. This pattern of involvement mirrors findings by other scholars. For example, one national survey of youth and adult volunteerism found that only 18 percent of the teens and adults surveyed reported seeking out service opportunities on their own.[5] The majority of volunteers described themselves as having been asked to participate by family members, friends, teachers, classmates, and colleagues. Likewise, in his study of college students who participated in the 1964 Freedom Rides, McAdam found that "Personal ties served to pull many of the applicants into the project."[6] Another study found that youth and adults who are asked to participate in volunteer work are four times more likely to do so than youth and adults who are not asked to participate.[7]

In short, the willingness of the Harvard students volunteering at the shelter to take on such a heavy responsibility was significantly influenced by already-involved peers. Aside from this single commonality, however, what emerged most strongly from interviews with these young adults was the *diversity* of experiences that they credited with fueling their commitment to the shelter. In the pages that follow, I describe the impact of early service experiences, religious beliefs, service-oriented parents, experiences of hardship, strong mentors, powerful academic experiences, and opportunities to witness inequity. For each of these factors, six to nine students credited the experience with having influenced their commitment to the Harvard Square Homeless Shelter. One obvious conclusion that can be drawn from this diversity is that there are many different pathways which can lead to a deep commitment to service work and social action. Here, I describe each of these pathways in turn.

SERVICE-ORIENTED PARENTS

Nine students described their commitment to the shelter as having been inspired in part by their service-oriented parents. For example, senior Robert Vozar commented:

"My parents are pretty lefty and opposed to conspicuous consumption. I think that they read E. Digby Baltzell's *Puritan Boston and Quaker Philadelphia*, and they lived in Philly, but they're from Boston now. They believe in hard work and public service. They're Jewish, not Puritan, but [believe in] hard work, public service, and be really modest about your accomplishments."

Here, Vozar offered a description of the philosophy by which his parents live, and, in fact, when Vozar arrived at Harvard, he described it as "very disconcerting to see so much opulence. The formals and certain social events that felt just wasteful, extravagant." In many ways, Vozar's involvement with the Harvard Square Shelter served as a means of honoring his parents' values rather than those of his new university.

Senior Kelly Parker's parents are an optometrist and university professor who have enjoyed substantial professional success; however, Parker noted that, when it came to raising their daughters, they reserved their praise for good deeds rather than good grades. According to Parker, "Their idea [was] that pride should be for something that you do, not for something you get like a grade."

Senior Elyse Margolis grew up in Manhattan where her father works as a high-powered literary and talent agent, and Margolis, herself, attended the prestigious Horace Mann School. Despite this privileged upbringing, Margolis described her parents as taking her along on community service experiences beginning when she was a toddler:

"We used to collect money on the street on Saturdays once a month for a food pantry on the Upper West Side called the Riverside Food Pantry with my mom and dad. They'd stand in different places, and I'd stand with one of them. And I was sort of the cute child attraction aspect."

Margolis — whose thesis focused on changes in affordable housing opportunities over the past 30 years — described plans to pursue a career in government working on anti-poverty public policy. She saw her volunteer work at the shelter as both a continuation of the service she had begun with her parents at an early age as well a means of "seeing firsthand the people that I'm trying to impact."

Junior Amanda Mooney described her parents, both of whom work as family doctors, as role-models for her commitment to community service. She recalled the experience of "go[ing] on rounds with my mom, and patients would say, 'Your mom is an angel, she is wonderful!' So they've taught me by example." As described in earlier chapters, Mooney planned to pursue a career in medicine herself, and decided during the winter of 2009 that she wanted to focus her medical career on treating the homeless. As a result, she began an internship in the spring of 2009 with Boston's Healthcare for the Homeless.[8] Mooney credited her parents with not only guiding her by example but also explicitly teaching her that she was lucky to have been born into a loving, economically secure family and that it is important to take steps to give back.

Numerous scholars report on the connection between volunteerism and being raised by service-oriented parents. In her national study on volunteerism and philanthropy, Virginia Hodgkinson found that three out of four adults whose parents participated in community service are currently performing regular community service themselves.[9] In contrast, less than one in four adults whose parents did *not* do volunteer work are currently performing any type of regular community service. Other scholars have found that college students who participate in community service are more likely than non-volunteering students to have been raised by parents who themselves performed regular community service.[10] As scholar Joan Grusec commented, "One of the major ways in which children acquire the value systems of society is through identification. By identifying with their parents, they adopt parental attitudes and behaviors, including those related to altruism."[11]

MENTORS

Nine students cited mentors other than their parents as having significantly influenced their commitment to volunteering at the Harvard Square Shelter. Kathryn Tobin, Charlotte Wu, and Nathan Small all described influential teachers. For example, senior Kathryn Tobin described the influence of a high school history teacher who billed himself as "the last socialist in Fargo, North Dakota." According to Tobin, "I basically adopted this high school teacher's views on most subjects and . . . he was very formative in impressing [upon me] that poverty is not someone's fault." Sophomore Charlotte Wu described a high school English teacher who introduced her to community organizing through a documentary about Saul Alinsky and also, according to Wu, led her to see the dichotomous nature of her California high school in which half the student body was being prepared for college and the other, less affluent half was not. Wu said, "He opened my eyes to things that were going on in my own school that I really wouldn't have noticed."

Junior Nathan Small — who grew up in Cambridge — explained that his high school social studies teacher literally brought him to the Harvard Square Homeless Shelter:

"My sophomore year of high school, I had a teacher for World History who had been an undergraduate at Harvard and had gone on to teach at Cambridge Rindge & Latin School, and he had been a director on staff at the shelter when he was an undergraduate and continued to work there after leaving Harvard in a volunteer role. And the year before me, he had started taking kids from his class into the shelter to cook dinner and hang out. And so when he raised the opportunity for us when I was in his class . . . I was like, hey this is a cool opportunity to do something in my neighborhood, and I get to go with my friends and a teacher I really admire and respect."

According to Small, as a result of this inspiring teacher, his commitment to the Harvard Square Shelter began in his sophomore year of *high school*. Looking back, Small characterized himself as having been powerfully influenced by a teacher "who was just so committed to students and to the work he did at the shelter." Small believed that observing his teacher in action "really made me committed to the idea that whatever I want to do with my life, it's important to me that it's service-related or service-oriented in some way."

Sophomore Liam Murphy described his godfather as a mentor who motivated his commitment to community service. Murphy's godfather was a successful ophthalmologist with his own practice in Oklahoma City, and every year he and his wife spent several weeks in Peru on a mission trip in which Murphy's godfather treated impoverished Peruvians suffering from cataracts and other eye diseases. During high school, Murphy accompanied his godparents on one of these trips to Peru and came away with a deeper commitment to service and a new aspiration of pursuing a career in medicine and, ultimately, global health.

In these and other examples, the young adults keeping the Harvard Square Shelter running during the winter of 2009 pointed to mentor figures who had inspired and encouraged their commitment to service work. A number of scholars have pointed to the importance of such role-models.[12] As noted in Chapter 6, scholars have also pointed to the reluctance of contemporary young adults to cite *public* figures they admire.[13] In previous generations, young adults could turn to activists such as Cesar Chavez, Rosa Parks, Albert Schweitzer, Robert Kennedy, and Edward Abbey for inspiration. In a world when the foibles and failures of our public figures are routinely exposed, however, these young people seem to be even more reliant on the older figures within their own sphere — parents, teachers, relatives, and community members — for encouragement to pursue work in service to others.

WITNESSING INEQUITY

Eight students also cited opportunities during their childhood to witness inequality as pivotal to their motivation for volunteering at the Harvard Square Homeless Shelter. As a result of his parents' work for the World Bank and International Monetary Fund, senior Leo LaSala lived in Singapore for three years during his early adolescence and traveled extensively with his family around Southeast Asia. He said:

> "I think when you see mass poverty, you realize more clearly the sort of structural things that can lead to poverty occurring. You look at India, and you look at Bangladesh, and you say the reason there is mass poverty there is because the climate is terrible, and the place is ravaged by natural disasters constantly."

Upon returning to the United States for high school and then college, LaSala brought with him a belief that "There's a lot more contingency and luck involved in determining where you end up . . . and that influenced me to work at the shelter."

Senior Kelly Parker, whose father is a professor at Harvard, grew up just outside Boston, but, in high school, she and her older sister spent a summer volunteering at an under-resourced public school in Guatemala. Prior to the trip, Parker described herself as a typical high school student more focused on her friends and schoolwork than the wider world. However, the experience of spending time in a developing country was deeply impactful. She recalled:

"These people were living in the filled-in area of a dump. And the eight year olds were working in the dump. Kids in my class would say, 'I'm sorry I didn't come to class yesterday. My mom was sick, so I had to go collect the trash.' And then they'd sell it to recycling companies. It deepened my understanding of how much disparity there is in the world."

Having witnessed firsthand a slice of the world's inequalities, Parker began volunteering with the Harvard Square Homeless Shelter in the first semester of her freshman year at Harvard. She spent summers teaching in Ecuador and working with Sudanese immigrants in Egypt. In spite of these powerful experiences, Parker credited that first summer in Guatemala with having the greatest impact upon her worldview by opening her eyes to the existence of such tremendous suffering and inequity.

Junior Lester Pearsons, who is British, related how English teenagers often spend a "gap" year between high school and university. During his own year of traveling, Pearsons spent time doing volunteer work in Tanzania and Cambodia. In a small mountain community in Tanzania, Pearsons helped to build a cottage for local women to use as a work-space for producing garments. In Cambodia, he assisted at an orphanage. Pearsons commented:

"I've been fortunate to work and travel a lot around some very poor countries. And it was really that that's influenced my desire to go into global health and to make my life about improving conditions for people. I don't think we're ever going to have equality, but I think that equality of opportunity is something we can strive for."

Clearly, Pearsons, too, was deeply impacted by the experience of having witnessed poverty firsthand. Through both his current work at the shelter and his future career aspirations, he sought to play a role in addressing the disparities he has witnessed.

EXPERIENCES OF HARDSHIP

Similar to the transformative experiences described above are experiences of hardship. Several researchers have identified experiences of early hardship as playing a role in the development of a commitment to service work and activism.[14] In their classic study of social activists, Colby and Damon reported that many of the activists in their study had grown up in poverty or experienced various types of discrimination or early loss.[15] Seven of the Harvard students interviewed as part of this study described similar examples of hardship as having impacted their commitment to volunteerism. For example, as described in an earlier chapter, junior Nathan Small lost his mother in his senior year of high school and credited his work at the Harvard Square Shelter with serving as "the most constant thing in my life for the past six years in terms of what I do, my friends, even my family, where I live, where I spend my time." Two other shelter volunteers described the experience of growing up as racial minorities as having deepened their commitment to helping others.

Though never homeless himself, junior Liam Murphy did experience poverty similar to that he witnesses at the shelter. The son of an unemployed father and a mother who worked as a bank cashier, Murphy explained that "I grew up in a poor family. We were never homeless, but we definitely had a lot of difficulty." He admitted that he is only able to attend Harvard as a result of a full tuition scholarship. As for why he volunteered at the Harvard Square Shelter, Murphy stated simply: "There were times that my family needed help like this."

Another volunteer, Hope Franklin, described a familiarity with poverty as well. "Growing up, my family was very poor. We were on food stamps. My parents were both sort of struggling their way through graduate school. I have three siblings, so I just have these very stark memories of a house with no heat." Franklin went on to describe memories of self-consciousness about going to school in worn-out clothing and shoes. Though her family's financial situation improved as she entered high school, Franklin believed those childhood experiences "allowed me to feel a little bit more compassion but also understanding of what individuals are going through."

A number of other Harvard Square Shelter volunteers — several of whom were the children of immigrants — described childhood brushes with poverty as well. Senior Drew McGinty, whose parents divorced when he was eight years old, described himself as having "grown up on both sides of the tracks." For 11 years, he and his brother spent the first half of every month with their father who was "climbing the corporate ladder" and the second half of the month with their mother who "had to move to the ghetto" and sometimes "had to eat less because her car had broken down." Former shelter guest Lucy Draper remarked that, in her annual speech to an audience of incoming volunteers, "There is always one person who has been homeless in the group in one form or another. Foster kid, their family was homeless. There are lots of kids at Harvard, who because of the scholarships, in fact do not come from a wealthy background." For a number of the Harvard Square Shelter's volunteers, their own early experiences of hardship deepened their sense of empathy and desire to play a role in supporting struggling fellow citizens.

ACADEMIC EXPERIENCES

Six students described academic or intellectual experiences that have influenced their commitment to service work and activism. Both sophomore Christopher Kitts and junior Louis Landau described as influential the reading they did in preparation for high school debate tournaments. For Kitts, this influential reading focused on genocide in various parts of the world, and he noted: "Once you become aware there's this world out there that is different from the privilege that you enjoy, then you start to ask the question, if there are people in Africa, are these also people down the street from me that are also in that different situation?" Likewise, junior Louis Landau explained that preparation for high school debate tournaments resulted in his reading a good deal of philosophy. He commented that "John Rawls' *A Theory of Justice* is a book I really like." According to Rawls, "All goods — liberty and opportunity, income and wealth — are to be distributed equally unless an unequal distribution of any or all of these goods is to the advantage of the least favored."[16] In short, Rawls — and now Landau — see society as having an obligation to work to improve the circumstances of the least fortunate. Landau characterized his work at the shelter as playing a small role in that endeavor.

Another student, sophomore Antonia Garcia-Brown, considered that her commitment to social action arose in part from her interest during high school in several feminist Internet blogs:

> "In the beginning, I was very narrowly focused on the feminist aspect of them, but after a while I started paying attention to the fact that a lot of those bloggers were saying you couldn't just be focused on social justice for one group. You had to be

focused on social justice for everyone. And that includes a lot of groups that people otherwise ignore."

The homeless might be described as one such invisible group, and it was in part her recognition of this invisibility that led Garcia-Brown to work both a weekly overnight shift and a Resource Advocacy shift during the winter of 2009.

Senior Elyse Margolis described an influential sociology course she took during her freshman year of college. Embedded within the course was a unit on inequality:

> "It was about the relationship between class and crime, and class and health, and class and the political system. And our professor gave us very straightforward facts that were all intuitively not surprising, but the real numbers and the explicitness really stuck with me. And made me want to learn more about it. And I guess there was sort of a domino effect that got me to the point where I am now."

By "the point where I am now," Margolis was referring to her volunteer work at the shelter, her thesis on 40 years of affordable housing policy, and her aspirations of doing anti-poverty public policy work upon her graduation. Each of these students, then, cited a particular academic or intellectual experience as having played an important role in their current commitment to the Harvard Square Homeless Shelter. In so doing, these students offered support for a branch of my own earlier research on the role that academic experiences can play in deepening a commitment to service work and social action.[17] Likewise, Ann Colby and her colleagues have reported: "Colleges and universities can also transform students' interpretive frames, for better or for worse, through traditional academic coursework. . . . A powerful course can open students' eyes to global economic interdependence or the influence of opportunity structures on individual achievement."[18]

RELIGION

A number of scholars have found religious faith to have a positive effect upon people's commitment to volunteer work. Teenagers who consistently attend religious services are three times more likely to participate in community service than teenagers who do not attend religious services.[19] Likewise, adults who consistently attend religious services are four times more likely than their non-attending peers to perform community service.[20] Approximately 80 percent of the activists in Colby and Damon's study of moral exemplars attributed their commitment to social action to their religious faith.[21] It was somewhat surprising, then, that only six of the 22 Harvard Square Shelter volunteers in this study described their volunteer work as having been influenced by their religious beliefs. The shelter's affiliation with the University Lutheran Church — if only as the shelter's landlord — made this finding even more surprising.

Two students, junior Larry Yoon and freshman Nancy Mellor, described their religious faith as the primary influence upon their dedication to the Harvard Square Shelter. Yoon, a junior, thought that his deepening involvement with the shelter "coincided with me delving into my faith a little more. Like my spiritual walk. Like essential questions that a lot of people have when they come to college. What's my purpose? Why am I here? Why did God put me here?" As for why he chose the Harvard Square Shelter over dozens of other community service opportunities, Yoon referenced the story from the New Testament of the Good Samaritan. In this parable, a man who has been robbed and badly injured is ignored by two passersby but is ultimately taken in by the Good Samaritan who nurses the wounded man back to health and treats him with respect and hospitality. Yoon characterized his work at the shelter as "the most obvious way to live out Jesus' call to be like a Good Samaritan."

Likewise, freshman Nancy Mellor characterized her Catholic faith as "probably my number one factor behind the majority of my decisions." While Mellor has struggled to honor her church's views on issues such as birth control, she appreciates Catholicism for being "very, very service-oriented." As Mellor remarked:

"I think that's simply had an impact on my view of the world. Like I need to help people, and all people are people, and, again they're innately good, so therefore I need to help them because it's the right thing to do, because that's what Christ would have done. And that's what we need to do in His reflection."

Here, Mellor, too, characterized her religious beliefs as a primary force motivating her volunteer work.

Other students cited their religious faith as playing an important, if not central, role in their volunteerism. Senior Leo LaSala believed that his commitment to the shelter came from "a little bit of religion and a little bit of philosophy outside of religion. Because there's an implicit sort of reward for service in the Catholic understanding of it. It's something that God looks well on, but I think I'm more of a Kantian duty-oriented person in that regard." Here, LaSala explained that he can point to both his religious faith *and* Kantian philosophy to justify community service as an intrinsically good action to undertake.

Both junior Christopher Kitts and senior Kelly Parker considered their Jewish upbringing as integral to their commitment to service. Kitts characterized success as creating a balance in one's life between service to oneself and service to others, and said, "The sense of communal responsibility [I feel] is something that I derive from my religious community." Likewise, Parker observed:

> "The only thing that's really central to Judaism is this idea of community and this idea of being indebted to other people. Orthodox Judaism will tell you to pray one way, and Reform Judaism will tell you to pray another way. But every stream of Judaism is going to tell you, you need to do some form of service."

For each of these students, then, their religious faith played an important role in motivating their commitment to the work they carry out at the Harvard Square Homeless Shelter.

EARLY SERVICE EXPERIENCES

Perhaps not surprisingly, one of the best predictors of community service participation in college is earlier involvement in community service opportunities. A number of scholars have reported that participation in community service in high school is the single best predictor of community service involvement in college.[22] In explaining this connection, Daniel Hart and colleagues have suggested that young adults "often infer what kind of persons they are from the actions they are involved in; self-attributions in many situations, then, follow from, rather than precede, actions."[23] In other words, when children or adolescents are given the opportunity to participate in community service experiences, they come to see this participation as a personality trait they possess.

Given these scholars' findings, it was somewhat surprising that only six of the shelter's volunteers described themselves as having partici-pated in meaningful community service experiences prior to college. Already described in this chapter were senior Kelly Parker teaching in Guatemala; junior Lester Pearsons' work in Tanzania and Cambodia; and senior Elyse Margolis' solicitations for a New York City food pantry alongside her parents. Three other students described important early service experiences as well.

Senior Drew McGinty, though not Catholic himself, attended a Jesuit high school with a department devoted entirely to community service. One of the school's annual projects was a canned food drive that yielded tens of thousands of cans. In his senior year, McGinty served in a leadership position for this canned food drive, which he described as an important experience for him. As McGinty said of the Jesuits:

> "They made me do community service, but at a deeper level, they really encouraged personal growth through service. They really encouraged loving doing something for the good of others. And they took this general feeling and just spread it throughout the school and made all these kids like want to become better people . . . I don't know if there's an objective good, but I think there's objective goodness. And I think you can sort of embody some of that. My high school had a lot to do with me thinking like that just because of the way it was championed."[24]

Upon arriving at Harvard, McGinty saw the Harvard Square Shelter as an opportunity to continue doing the good work that had been an important aspect of his high school experience.

Wellesley College sophomore Charlotte Wu also described an early service experience as crucial to her current commitment to the shelter. During high school, Wu participated in an internship program offered by the Orange County (California) Human Relations Commission. The purpose of the organization was to minimize incidents of hate crimes going on in Orange County through education and outreach. As a result of her internship, Wu — who was from the middle class community of Irvine — had the opportunity to visit Orange County's wealthy, predominantly White communities like Newport Harbor as well as poorer, predominantly minority communities like Santa Anna and Anaheim.

Through visiting these disparate communities, Wu described her growing recognition of "the stark differences in schools and the quality of the communities and some of the situations they have." As she explained, "Some of the people in Anaheim worked so hard, and yet they'd never become so successful or have everything that a kid in Newport Harbor did without ever having to do anything for themselves." At two speaker symposiums that the Commission held each year, Wu noted that one could even see the differences in opportunity in the quality of the school buses which transported the teenagers from different communities. The opportunity to witness these disparities fueled Wu's commitment to pursuing opportunities that allowed her to combat inequity.

Clearly, a number of the current volunteers at the Harvard Square Homeless Shelter engaged in service experiences as children that played a role in their seeking out community service opportunities in college. Perhaps more surprising, however, was the number of students who described their community service experiences prior to college as quite limited. For example, senior Hope Franklin — whose mother actually ran the local soup kitchen in her hometown of Amherst, Massachusetts — noted that "Interestingly, I didn't work there very much. . . . I suppose I didn't do much growing up in the way of your sort of traditional community service. That is surprising looking back to me actually." Likewise, junior Amanda Mooney said, "I don't know if I really did any community service in high school. I was spending all my time doing music and theater." Having described her parents as working to instill in her a sense of the importance of giving back, Mooney added that "I'm very surprised, just reflecting back, that they didn't push me to reach out to others during high school."

Junior Jerry Chen observed that, during high school, "I did things, but I don't think I ever felt very strongly about them. I was like, I've got to do this to get into college." One of his early volunteer experiences involved offering piano lessons to cancer patients at a local hospital, but Chen admitted: "I guess I was just too young to adopt such a huge responsibility. I literally just flaked out more than a couple of times, and I feel really bad about it, but it makes me realize how little I cared." On a similar note, junior Larry Yoon said:

"I was part of the volunteer club, but I actually wrote a big paper on it. The name of the club was 'The Who Club' W-H-O. We Help Others. I wrote a paper on saying it should actually be 'We Help Ourselves.' After reflecting on my motivations, and why am I doing this, [I realized] I guess I'm doing this because I kind of want to put it on my resume so I can get into a better college."

Yoon, too, saw community service during high school as a chance to pad his college application rather than an opportunity to reduce inequity or effect change.

Sophomore Christopher Kitts noted that "One of the reasons why I wanted to get involved in the shelter was I didn't do a lot of community service in high school. I traveled nationally for debate team, and I was really busy for that." He explained that part of his motivation in volunteering at the shelter was that, prior to college, "I spent my whole life doing things that were to some extent for me. You know to kind of satisfy my own curiosity, my own passions and interests. And so I felt a responsibility to give back for the good fortune that I've had thus far." A number of other students offered similar descriptions of their lack of community service experience during high school. Ambitious and intelligent, the majority of these young adults focused their early teenage years on academics, music, theater, athletics, debate, and other competitive endeavors.

While it is surprising to see that the Harvard Square Shelter represented an entirely new pursuit for so many of its volunteers, it is also useful to recognize that operating a student-run shelter does *not* require a campus full of students who have been steeped in community service experiences or social justice ideology from the womb. Rather, there are clearly a wide variety of experiences — and combinations of experiences — that motivated these 22 young adults to commit so much of their time and energy to the success of the Harvard Square Shelter.

REVISING THE AMERICAN DREAM

Despite the diversity of their experiences, a second commonality among the majority of Harvard Square Shelter volunteers was the *impact* of their varied experiences upon their beliefs about the American dream.

Specifically, 18 of the 22 students engaged in running the shelter expressed significant doubts about the veracity of the American dream. For example, junior Melissa Sanguinetti considered that "the argument that people are poor because they don't work hard enough is so offensive to me." Senior Kathryn Tobin asserted: "I think that this illusion that the individual is autonomous and is responsible entirely for their future and for their development of their own talent is ridiculous and absurd and damaging." Senior Leo LaSala observed:

"There's this thing that goes with American capitalism, there's this meritocracy, and if you're at the bottom, it's because you deserve to be there, just as if you're at the top, you deserve to be there. I believe there's a lot more contingency and luck involved in determining where you end up."

Junior Nathan Small expressed his perspective:

"I don't believe that, for everyone, hard work will always pay off. . . . I think that sometimes you can't just do it on your own. No matter how hard you work, you need to get a boost from someone else or someplace else to make it, and not everyone gets that boost."

While it may not sound as if these young adults are espousing particularly radical beliefs, it is important to recognize that their perspectives diverge substantially from the majority of their fellow Americans. Numerous scholars have found that Americans, as a whole, prioritize individualistic factors in their explanations for economic inequality.[25] In other words, wealthy individuals are credited with possessing intelligence and willpower while poor individuals are blamed for the absence of these qualities. In their classic book entitled *Beliefs about Inequality*, Kluegel and Smith found that 70 percent of Americans agreed with the statement, "Everyone who works hard can get ahead."[26] Other scholars have found that the majority of Americans believe that poverty is caused by "lack of effort" on the part of the poor.[27] Likewise, a 2006 World Values Survey demonstrated that 71 percent of Americans believed the poor could escape poverty if they worked hard enough.[28] In short, the majority of Americans espouse a deep belief in the American dream. The above comments by shelter volunteers, then, about the influence of "contingency and luck" upon one's social positioning represent a quite different lens than the one through which the typical American examines homelessness.

An important question is whether the comments of these Harvard Square Shelter volunteers represent perspectives they have developed *as a result* of their work at the shelter. And, in fact, there seems to be little doubt that the experience of working closely with men and women contending with homelessness served to strengthen these young adults' doubts about the American dream.[29] Interestingly, however, eight of the ten volunteers new to the shelter in 2008–09 expressed doubts about the veracity of the American dream in their interviews at the beginning of the winter before working a single shift at the shelter. For example, junior Lester Pearsons, a new volunteer, described an experience from his earlier travels through Africa to explain his beliefs about inequality:

> "I remember when I was in Rwanda, I met this guy who told me that his parents and five of his siblings had been killed in the genocide. And this guy spoke four languages without any problem, and he was a very friendly guy, and he was athletic. He had all the same qualities that someone here at Harvard might have, and he absolutely had no chance of raising himself in society at all. He had no opportunities, no support. And that is just one example. There are more people closer to that end of the spectrum than the Harvard end of the spectrum."

Here, Pearsons offered evidence from his travels to dispute the notion that talent and ability are the sole determinants of success. Likewise, junior Louis Landau — who described the influence of reading various philosophers in preparation for debate competitions — observed that "Different people are born in different situations, and they start out that way, which is unjust." Sophomore Antonia Garcia-Brown added:

> "I don't understand people who think poor people don't work hard. I'm like, you go work an eight-hour shift at McDonald's, and tell me how much you like that, and how easy you think that is. Or go try to pick berries in the fields for 12 hours and tell me that they're being lazy."

Sophomore Charlotte Wu thought that "Everyone comes here as the land of opportunities and there are all of these ideals running around, but I really think the playing field isn't even." Freshman Nancy Mellor observed that "Where I'm from there's definitely a sentiment that all homeless people are lazy . . . And I don't agree with that." It would seem, then, that a virtual prerequisite for the deep commitment demonstrated by the Harvard Square Shelter's volunteers is a worldview that acknowledges structures and situations to be as or more responsible for homelessness than the individual choices of the homeless themselves.

THE NECESSARY INGREDIENTS

There are many different pathways by which the Harvard students profiled here arrived at the Harvard Square Homeless Shelter. For some, the primary motivation was their religion while for others it was the influence of a respected mentor. Several students cited the importance of early experiences with community service while others described the impact of their own experiences with hardship. What each of these pathways has in common, however, is that they seemed to instill in these young adults what philosopher Nel Noddings refers to as an "ethic of care."[30] Gilligan describes an ethic of care as a conception of morality centered upon one's responsibilities and relationships with others.[31] For all of these students — whether influenced by religion, readings, parents, or prior community service — the result was a belief that they had a role to play in alleviating the struggling of others. As sophomore Christopher Kitts noted, "I think good adults are people who are conscious of the world around them and take actions in one way or another to correct the problems of that world."

One might argue that keeping the Harvard Square Shelter up and running all winter long requires a critical mass of young adults who possess three critical ingredients: an ethic of care, questions about the American dream, and a peer to solicit their involvement. For a shelter like the Harvard Square Shelter to remain open night after night requires young adults who witness the homeless men and women in Harvard Square and feel a sense of care and responsibility for their well-being. Alumnus Joshua Villanueva noted that, during his days as a state senator, raising support for the homeless was difficult because "some of us, even if we wouldn't admit it, don't think those folks are quite as human." The young adults operating the Harvard Square Shelter were fully convinced of the humanity of the homeless men and women who stay there.

These young adults were also able to question a dangerous corollary to the American dream — namely, that, in this land of opportunity, a homeless person must have done something wrong to deserve his or her homelessness. Though coming from different parts of the country, from various socioeconomic levels, and holding different political ideologies, the majority of the Harvard students operating the shelter did not regard the homeless as *to blame* for their homelessness.

Despite their ethic of care and doubts about the American dream, it would seem that the majority of the young adults described in these pages needed one final push in the form of a solicitation from an upperclassman or peer. With the dizzying array of extracurricular opportunities available to most college students, the voice of a respected peer was necessary to rise above all of the other noise. Importantly, then, the shelter does not seem to require its student-leaders to be the second coming of Jane Addams or the red-diaper babies of sixties beatniks. Activist and Children's Defense Fund founder Marian Wright Edelman once said, "You just need to be a flea against injustice. Enough committed fleas biting strategically can make even the biggest dog uncomfortable and transform even the biggest nation."[32] It seems likely that there are enough "committed fleas" on college campuses across the United States to sustain many more Harvard Square Homeless Shelters and, in so doing, play an important role in transforming our nation's fight against poverty and homelessness.

Chapter 10

Something that
Lives On

The National Alliance to End Homelessness estimates that on any given night 744,000 people go homeless in the United States.[1] An additional 39 million Americans are living below the poverty line, and 14 million of those poor Americans are children.[2] Such a state of affairs in the world's wealthiest nation is deeply concerning if one agrees with Harvard alumnus Franklin Delano Roosevelt's assertion that "The test of our progress is not whether we add more to the abundance of those who have enough; it is whether we provide enough for those who have too little."[3] The preceding nine chapters have demonstrated that the student-run model in operation at the Harvard Square Homeless Shelter for more than a quarter century provides crucial support for the homeless men and women who have "too little" while simultaneously adding meaning, purpose and direction to the lives of Harvard students who "have enough."

POWERFUL EFFECTS FOR THE HOMELESS

The first half of this book sought to demonstrate that the Harvard students who volunteer at the Harvard Square Homeless Shelter are in a unique developmental period that allows them to provide several types of support to homeless men and women that older, professional service workers *cannot*. Take, for example, the passion and idealism which the volunteers bring to their dinner, overnight, and breakfast shifts at the shelter. Perhaps the greatest example of what such passion and idealism can accomplish is Lex Obain's improbable route to college. Recall that Lex was a homeless teenager originally from the Ivory Coast who spent much of the past year at the Harvard Square Shelter. Several of the college-aged volunteers he met there shepherded Lex all of the way through the college admissions process. They helped him study for the SATs, bought him a suit for interviews and edited his personal statements. When Lex was awarded a full-tuition scholarship to Hamilton College in December of 2008, these students rented a van for all of Lex's belongings, piled in, and helped him move into his new home. These students and Lex now fire text messages and Facebook comments back and forth between Cambridge, Massachusetts and upstate New York. Where virtually any seasoned professionals would have, quite reasonably, established some professional distance with a client like Lex, the young adults volunteering at the Harvard Square Shelter simply dove in headlong.

Another trait unique to emerging adulthood is the enthusiasm with which the shelter's college-aged volunteers sought to connect with the homeless men and women staying there. One of the shelter's primary draws for its volunteers is the opportunity to learn more about homelessness through conversations with those staying at the shelter. This motivation means that most of the shelter's volunteers are not only willing but excited to sit, listen, and respond to the stories and insights that the men and women staying at the shelter choose to offer. This willingness and enthusiasm provides a tremendous resource for the shelter's homeless guests. As Joe Presley recalled, "There were times when I just wanted to give up, and they would sit there, and they'd talk to me."

More seasoned professionals are rarely available for long blocks of time to sit and listen to one of their homeless clients, and, on the occasions that they can engage in such conversation, their years of listening to nearly identical stories make some level of skepticism and guardedness inevitable. The Harvard students volunteering at the shelter, on the other hand, are honored to be seen as confidantes and genuinely engaged by the stories which they experience as fresh and eye-opening. Moreover, because they are typically many years younger than the homeless guests with whom they are speaking, this difference in age and experience gives the homeless men and women at the shelter an opportunity to assume the role of teacher or mentor — even if the advice they have to offer is simply to avoid particular mistakes and temptations.

For Fred Slomiak, the "definitive moment" in his journey out of homelessness occurred when a young woman volunteering at the Harvard Square Shelter asked him to how to play chess. As Slomiak explained, in teaching this bright young woman the rules of chess, he experienced for the first time in years a sense of having something to contribute to the world. It was that feeling of self-worth that allowed him to move forward.

The youth and inexperience of the college students operating the shelter also lead them to be fearless in trying out new strategies and approaches to combating homelessness. Certainly there is substantial value in seasoning and experience, but seasoning and experience can also have the effect of stifling innovation. In 2008, for example, two shelter directors — Larry Yoon and Mark Lee — decided that the shelter did not have to limit itself to aiding the homeless men and women *inside* the Harvard Square Shelter. There were scores of homeless people in Harvard Square who were not accessing the shelter's resources, and Yoon and Lee decided to bring those resources to them. They founded the Street Team that went out into Harvard Square six nights a week from 9 to 10 p.m. distributing sandwiches and blankets, referring homeless men and women to the shelter, and offering a few minutes of company and conversation.

Virtually everyone who has worked in professional settings has had the experience of suggesting a new idea or strategy only to be told: "Oh, we tried that in 1989, and it didn't work." At the Harvard Square Homeless Shelter, the constant turnover of college students means that the most veteran of the shelter's supervisors and directors may have just four years of experience. Naturally, there are drawbacks to such a novice management team, and institutional knowledge is routinely lost. However, there is also an upside to *not* knowing what isn't supposed to work. If the college students on the Street Team had known that the homeless woman Francine had rejected offers of help for longer than most of them had been alive, perhaps they would have walked right past her. Instead, their perseverance allowed an elderly homeless woman to come in from the cold. In his 1984 Presidential campaign, President Ronald Reagan, then 73 years old, famously joked that he would not exploit the "youth and inexperience" of his 56-year-old opponent, Walter Mondale. Perhaps counter-intuitively, however, there are several ways in which the youth and inexperience of the college

students operating the shelter make them uniquely suited to working
with a marginalized community such as the homeless.

POWERFUL EFFECTS FOR THE
HARVARD STUDENTS

The second half of this book focused on the tremendous opportunities
and growth that working at the Harvard Square Homeless Shelter
affords its college-aged volunteers. First, a number of the shelter's
volunteers described the importance to them of having something in
their lives that feels real and purposeful. For example, Harvard freshman Ashwin Ganguli asserted that "There's so much work [in college],
but none of it is really significant in the real sense. So I definitely felt
like I needed a place where I can help make a difference." Likewise,
sophomore Liam Murphy said, "It was awesome to go there and do
something real and substantial rather than sitting in my room and
playing a few hours of Halo." Ganguli, Murphy, and a number of other
Harvard students recognized a need within their own lives for meaningful work and interactions. In this way, they are living out the advice
that humanitarian Albert Schweitzer once offered to an audience of
young people. Schweitzer said, "I don't know what your destiny will
be, but one thing I know: the only ones among you who will be really
happy are those who have sought and found how to serve."[4]

The students volunteering at the shelter also voiced their appreciation of the way in which their weekly shelter shifts lifted them
temporarily out of the "Harvard bubble" in which the competition
for grades, fellowships, summer jobs, and popularity can become all
consuming. Perhaps ironically, the Harvard Square Shelter serves as a
form of shelter for its college student volunteers as well. As Harvard
junior Jerry Chen noted, "You go there, and you adopt a new life.
School doesn't matter right now. People outside the shelter don't matter.
That party you wanted to go to doesn't matter . . . Everything else just
becomes less important."

Chen was by no means the only student who characterized the
shelter as his "safe haven" at Harvard. Junior Nathan Small, who lost
his mother a year before coming to Harvard, explained that the shelter
"really has been the most constant thing in my life for the past six years
in terms of what I do, my friends, even my family, where I live, [and]
where I spend my time." Small was just one of many students who

described the shelter as playing an important role to him as a community within Harvard.

Volunteering there also had a powerful impact upon the worldviews of the shelter's volunteers, supervisors, and directors. For the volunteers, the shelter "put a face" on homelessness. Prior to beginning her volunteer work at the shelter, Harvard senior Hope Franklin acknowledged that "I don't think of homeless people as individuals. I sort of think of them as an aggregate homeless population rather than the woman named Sally who has a mental health issue. So I think there's some level of anonymity, facelessness to homelessness which I think will change." Interviewed again at the end of the shelter season, Franklin described her shock at some of the men and women she had met during her weekly breakfast shift. "If you'd passed these people on the street, you wouldn't know they were homeless or struggling." The most significant example in her mind was a homeless man who worked during the day as a tour guide for Boston's Duck Boat tours. Meeting him left Franklin wondering about the residential status of many of the other people with whom she interacts on a daily basis.

For the college students who served as the shelter's supervisors and directors, their intimate involvement in the lives of the homeless guests allowed a deeper understanding of homelessness to emerge. Or, as shelter alumnus Joshua Villanueva remarked, working as a shelter director served to "complexify my understanding of how homelessness connects to a wide spectrum of issues." Several of the shelter's current and former leaders discussed their newfound awareness of the relationship between homelessness and lack of affordable housing. For example, Rusty Sadow described his realization through his work at the Harvard Square Shelter that guests "could hold a job, they could work 40 hours a week, but that wasn't going to pay the rent." Other shelter directors described similar realizations about the connections between homelessness and America's healthcare, educational system, and welfare policies. For example, sophomore Liam Murphy described his discovery of Catch-22s in Massachusetts welfare policy whereby individuals receiving disability payments would forfeit those payments if they accumulated more than $2,000 in savings. Such a policy created a disincentive for saving and all but guaranteed a homeless man receiving disability payments would remain homeless into perpetuity. In short, as a result of their close and frequent interactions with a marginalized community, Murphy and a number of the other Harvard students developed a deeper, more nuanced understanding of the complex set of challenges facing the men and women staying at the shelter. The shelter also offered its volunteers opportunities to reflect upon the skills they will bring with them into the professional world and the domain in which they would like to apply these skills. Several former volunteers explained that, upon graduating from college and entering the work force, they sought out employment opportunities that offered a sense of meaning and stimulation similar to that they had experienced at the Harvard Square Shelter. For example, Amelia Ginsberg, a shelter alumna who now does environmental advocacy work, related how she has always thought back to her experience at the Harvard Square Shelter "as a touchstone of the kind of feeling that your work should give you." Likewise, current junior Deanna Galante expressed a hope of one day finding a profession "that I get the same thing I get out of the shelter."

Other former volunteers like Dr. Aaron Dutka described how his interest in pursuing a career in medicine was sparked by his interactions with homeless men and women in the shelter contending with HIV/AIDS. Likewise, Harvard senior Robert Vozar talked of plans to pursue a PhD in economics with the goal of applying a researcher's tools to evaluations of social policies. Through his work at the shelter, Vozar found a way to direct his academic interest in economics to a domain that he found meaningful and relevant. Psychologist William Damon has reported this level of focus to be highly unusual among young adults.[5] Yet the experience of working at the shelter seemed to play a substantial role in allowing the Harvard students working there to reflect upon the skills they possess and the domains in which they would like to put these skills to work.

POWERFUL EFFECTS FOR SOCIETY

Robert Kennedy famously said, "Each time a man stands up for an ideal, or acts to improve the lot of others, or strikes out against injustice, he sends a tiny ripple of hope . . . and those ripples build a current which can sweep down the mightiest walls of oppression and resistance."[6] If three-quarters of a million Americans going homeless every night constitutes an injustice, a third way in which the Harvard Square Homeless Shelter plays an important role in the world is by increasing the size and frequency of Kennedy's "ripples of hope."

For the past 25 years, Harvard's graduating class has included 30 to 80 students who had volunteered weekly at the Harvard Square Shelter.

As volunteer Lester Pearsons noted, he and his classmates emerged from these weekly shifts with an understanding of homelessness beyond the stereotype of "the typical old man with a beard sitting on the side of the street." Like many other shelter volunteers, Pearsons was ready to serve as what CASPAR's Meghan Goughan referred to as an ambassador for people experiencing homelessness. Or as Philip Mangano said, "As long as you're directly involved with the people who are being oppressed in one way or another, you have a better sense of what to do when the possibility of ending that wrong is available to you."

As graduates of perhaps the most elite university in the world, many of the Harvard students who spent time in the basement of the University Lutheran Church will be positioned to play a role in fostering a more equitable society. In his 2008 book entitled *Unequal Democracy*, Princeton political scientist Larry Bartels utilized the voting records of United States senators to gauge the impact upon senators' votes of their constituents' policy preferences.[7] What Bartels found was that the preferences of a senator's affluent constituents (those with incomes in the top third of the income distribution) exerted approximately 50 percent more weight upon that senator's voting record than the preferences of middle-class constituents. Bartels also reported that the policy preferences of a senator's lower-class constituents (those with incomes in the bottom third of the income distribution) exerted no discernable influence at all upon their senator's votes. As Bartels noted of these poorest constituents, "Far from being considered as political equals, they were entirely *unconsidered* in the policy-making process."[8]

Bartels' research offers evidence of the disparate political influence held by the homeless men and women in the Harvard Square Shelter versus the students who volunteer there. Without a powerful lobbying group, the resources to make influential political donations or even a high turnout at the polls, the three-quarters of a million homeless persons in the United States are effectively *unrepresented* in the political process. In contrast, many of the Harvard students volunteering at the shelter will likely go on to lucrative careers in business, medicine, and law, or to positions of influence in journalism, academia, and government. In so doing, they will exert a disproportionately large effect upon the decisions of their elected representatives when important votes influencing America's response to poverty and homelessness come to the table (or if those issues even come to the table at all). The Harvard students described in these pages who spent scores — and in some cases, hundreds — of hours in the basement of the University Lutheran

Church are, in the words of former guest Lucy Draper, in the unusual position of "really understanding homelessness and who people really are, and what it takes to end it." One hopes they will use their disproportionate influence upon our nation's political system to do so.

The shelter's weekly volunteers come away from their experience with a deeper sense of who the homeless really are; however, the shelter's supervisors and directors come away with an understanding of the complex ways in which homelessness interacts with a variety of other social issues. For many of the shelter's current and former leaders, this understanding has motivated their desire to address these issues through careers in government and public service. Joshua Villanueva sought elected office as a state senator while Rusty Sadow has spent the past decade as a community organizer, first working on affordable housing issues and later on increasing voter turnout. Helen Van Anglen founded an organization committed to supporting women contending with homelessness and domestic violence while Ward Welburn founded an independent, tuition-free middle school for low-income children in Boston.

Current student-leaders like Amanda Mooney and Larry Yoon plan to attend medical school and focus their expertise on the homeless and other low-income patients while Christopher Kitts, Nathan Small, and Jerry Chen expressed interest in doing policy work related to homelessness. For Chen, the lever he sees as most connected to combating homelessness is healthcare, while Small can see himself focusing on education policy. Sophomore Christopher Kitts may follow alumnus Joshua Villanueva's path into elected office out of a belief that America's "tremendous structural problems" require greater attention from our nation's politicians.

What is particularly remarkable about the careers of hundreds of shelter alumni and the aspirations of current volunteers is their disjunction with the reports from social scientists that contemporary young adults express little interest in government or public service.[9] Psychologist William Damon reports: "There has never been a time in American history when so small a proportion of young people between the ages of twenty and thirty have sought or accepted roles in governmental or civic organizations."[10] Damon and other social scientists fear that the United States is on the verge of a crisis of leadership, and yet many of the talented young adults involved in leading the Harvard Square Homeless Shelter are planning on careers in government and public service rather than more lucrative careers in the financial sector.

In part, through their work at the shelter, they discovered the importance of doing meaningful work and identified professional arenas where they can continue to do so.

In summary, for more than 25 years, hundreds of Harvard students have graduated from Harvard and entered the next stage of their lives with a more intimate understanding of homelessness than the vast majority of their fellow Americans. This deeper understanding has unquestionably influenced the career trajectories of many of these young adults and almost certainly for others their willingness and ability to serve as advocates for Americans contending with homelessness and poverty. The combined influence of these several hundred alumni of the Harvard Square Homeless Shelter may well cause a small ripple in the efforts to forge a more equitable America, but now imagine an America with many more Harvard Square Homeless Shelters. In New York, Philadelphia, Detroit, St. Louis, Washington DC, San Francisco, Los Angeles, Chicago, Seattle, and every other American city with a sizable student and homeless population. Imagine the combined influence of perhaps tens of thousands of educated young Americans for whom the term "homelessness" conjures up not stereotypes but the memories of specific men and women with whom they have met, conversed, and shared a meal. The combined influence of such a group might be a tidal wave of support for what may be America's most marginalized *and unrepresented* constituency.

Attempts by the University Lutheran congregation to engage students in reflection about their work at the Harvard Square Shelter met with only limited success. Moreover, Harvard University offers no formal mechanism for supporting students in drawing connections between their academic work and their volunteer work at the Harvard Square Shelter. If student-run shelters begin multiplying across the country, imagine the nearly unlimited opportunities for learning, dialogue, and discussion. With or without the support of their universities, one can imagine students quickly reaching out to each other through Facebook and other Web 2.0 technologies to compare notes on successes, challenges, dilemmas, crises, and policy questions within their various shelters as well as to share their ruminations on larger societal issues and potential career trajectories. Such interconnections could take the *learning* in service-learning to a level far beyond what is currently occurring at the Harvard Square Homeless Shelter.

CAVEATS

By no means does this volume represent an argument for all homeless shelters in the United States to be turned over to college students. Many of the men and women contending with homelessness in the United States are also contending with significant problems involving substance abuse and mental illness, and nearly *all* homeless Americans are contending with the challenge of accessing the full menu of supports and resources to which they are entitled. Complex challenges like these absolutely require the support of professionals.

In fact, perhaps where the Harvard students running the shelter ran into the greatest difficulties in 2008–09 was when they tried to encroach upon the role of professional caseworkers and social workers rather than serving as a bridge *to* these professionals. In the shelter's Work Contract program, for example, the Harvard students had significant difficulty in 2009 with the criteria that established eligibility for the program.

For the past 15 years, the program has provided a long-term bed to homeless people who are employed, able to save $200 a week, and are willing to work with students towards achieving permanent housing. As one of the directors of the program, Amanda Mooney, explained, "People are applying to us, giving very personal information, being interviewed, and then we have to say yes or no, and giving up a bed to somebody for eight weeks is a very big deal. So it's a very charged program and a very charged application process."

The Work Contract program became even more emotionally charged during the winter of 2009. As a result of the economic crisis, so few homeless people were employed that the shelter's student-directors agreed to take into the program individuals whose monthly *disability* payments amounted to more than $200 a week. They also took into the program a homeless man who was self-employed as a house painter, which meant that his weekly salary fluctuated above and below the $200 threshold.

According to Mooney, in December and then again in January, "There was a kind of guest uprising." One of the leaders of that revolt, Frank Green, believed that many of the men and women in the Work Contract program were no more employed than he was. He complained of the students: "They weren't verifying anything. They had six beds tied up for ten weeks, and nobody worked. Not a one of them worked. Everybody walked out after their ten weeks and went to another shelter." Green was by no means the only person who held this perspective. Mooney said, "I can't tell you how many times people took me aside and said so and so's conning you. You know, open your eyes." Another homeless man told her that one of the men in the Work Contract program was deceiving her about his employment and savings by going to the bank and "pulling little ATM receipts out of the waste bin." Mooney admitted: "Who knows if it's true or not?" Challenges like these led Dr. Aaron Dutka — one of the original Work Contract directors in 1991 — to express uncertainty whether students possess the expertise to be case managers.

One can contrast the challenges of the Work Contract program with the success of the shelter's Resource Advocacy program. Rather than serving as case managers, the Harvard students staffing the shelter's Resource Advocacy table sought to connect men and women in the shelter to organizations and professionals who could help them attain identification, healthcare, social security, subsidized housing, eyeglasses, and a host of other resources. Anyone staying in the shelter may utilize the services of the resource advocacy table, and, as a result, the program elicits only gratitude from the homeless men and women at the shelter.

The Work Contract program, then, may represent an example of a resource for the homeless that requires the expertise of professional social workers rather than the energy and enthusiasm of college students. An even clearer example might be therapy for homeless veterans of the Vietnam, Persian Gulf, and Iraq Wars— a demographic that constitutes one in four of America's homeless.[11] Moreover, as a "dry" homeless shelter, the students managing the Harvard Square Shelter reserve the right to breathalyze or drug test any individual seeking a bed and to refuse entry to anyone who proves to be intoxicated or high. Of course, homeless men and women contending with drug and alcohol addictions still require shelter and other services, but the challenges posed by this more volatile population may extend beyond the capabilities of college-aged volunteers.

And, naturally, in addition to these limitations in expertise, there also exists a segment of the homeless population that wants nothing to do with idealistic college students. Former guest Joe Presley noted that the Harvard Square Shelter "is not for everybody. You have to be prepared for students to sit down with you, and it's a shock." What many homeless men and women appreciate about the shelter is a temporary escape from feelings of invisibility. For homeless individuals *not* interested in dropping that invisibility, however, another, larger shelter may suit them better.

Clearly, then, replacing all existing homeless shelters with replications of the Harvard Square Homeless Shelter would be neither practical nor effective. And, yet, as this book has sought to demonstrate, for a particular segment of the homeless population, the Harvard Square Shelter offers a number of valuable opportunities and experiences that simply do not exist in more traditional shelters. In advocating for the establishment of student-run homeless shelters in major cities across the country then, I imagine something akin to the school-choice that teenagers in my hometown of Boston, Massachusetts experience as they move from middle school to high school. Specifically, the rising ninth graders in the Boston Public Schools have more than 20 different high schools from which to choose. The Boston Arts Academy has students spending as much time on the arts as academics while the Health Careers Academy has focused its curriculum around the daily experiences, challenges, and skills required in the health professions. Ninth graders entering the Boston Latin School experience a traditional Great Books curriculum while the curriculum for ninth graders entering Fenway High School is based upon the essential question: Who built America?

There are a number of teens who would thrive at the Boston Arts Academy but flounder at Boston Latin School and vice versa. Men and women contending with homelessness are no different. For homeless men like Fred Slomiak and Lex Obain, the Harvard Square Homeless Shelter proved transformative in offering the support they needed to begin the climb out of homelessness. For other men and women contending with homelessness in Boston, the Harvard Square Shelter may not be the right match. It is rare in life that one size fits all, but there would be tremendous value for the homeless, for the students, and for society if more American cities could add a student-run homeless shelter to their arsenal of strategies for combating homelessness. And, with an annual budget of $45,000 a year, a student-run, all-volunteer shelter operates for less than the salary of a single employee at traditional homeless shelters.

The final caveat is that it is important to note here that I am *not* advocating for more volunteerism among college students. At last count, more than 3.3 million Americans between the ages of 18 and 24 were participating in some form of community service, and nearly seven out of ten college students characterized their university as offering

community service opportunities.[12] In short, record numbers of young
people are already participating in community service. Rather, what this
book has sought to capture are some of the ways in which a *student-run*
homeless shelter — a homeless shelter in which college students are
truly the managers and decision-makers — offers unique benefits to
both participating students and the homeless people who stay there.

LOOKING AHEAD

Joseph Finn, the Executive Director of the Massachusetts Housing and
Shelter Alliance, said, "There's a revolution that's going on, and I think
that the revolution is around the delivery of services in our society
today. And there's a focus on more of a residential-based, community-
based approach." What Finn is describing here is the Housing First
philosophy championed by homeless czar Philip Mangano and others that calls for placing homeless men and women into permanent
housing and then providing supports that allow them to live indepen-
dently.[13] According to Finn, "Shelters as these large acceptable housing
niches for the poorest, most disabled people in our society, I believe
that idea is on its way out." Is the Harvard Square Homeless Shelter on
its way to being an anachronism?

It would be a wonderful day in the United States if suddenly no more
homeless shelters were necessary. Unfortunately, Cambridge's State
Representative Alice Wolf is doubtful about Finn's vision becoming
reality in the near future. According to Wolf, the success of the Housing
First model requires a substantial increase all across the country in
units of affordable and subsidized housing. The combination of the
current economic recession and spiraling national debt leads both
Representative Wolf and Harvard Professor Julie Wilson to question the
likelihood of substantial increases in affordable housing construction
in the next ten years.

Moreover, Philip Mangano acknowledged that a perennial challenge to the Housing First model lies in three phenomena he refers
to as NIMBY, NOPE, and BANANA. NIMBY is short for "Not in my
backyard," and refers to the tendency of middle-class and affluent
individuals to resist the construction of low-cost housing in *their*
neighborhoods. NOPE and BANANA are even more fervent versions
of NIMBY. NOPE is short for "Not on Planet Earth," and BANANA
is short for "Build Absolutely Nothing Anywhere Near Anyone." In

short, central to the Housing First philosophy is placing homeless men and women into low-cost apartments and homes embedded within functioning communities, but such plans often face fierce opposition from the residents of these communities.

As Harvard Square Shelter alumnus and former state senator Joshua Villanueva asserted at a recent forum on combating homelessness:

"It's pretty easy to get funding to help first-time homebuyers. It's a little harder to advocate for transitional housing funds for people who are homeless. Because some of us, even if we wouldn't admit it, don't think those folks are quite as human."

According to Villanueva, the Harvard students who have volunteered at the shelter have the potential to be uniquely effective in countering such claims because they can attest to the "human-ness" of the homeless men and women they know personally. Paradoxically, then, the Housing First philosophy for combating homelessness — which calls for a shift away from homeless shelters as a mechanism for combating homelessness — might be significantly aided over the next decade by an increase in the number of student-run homeless shelters across the country. As described above, if more Harvard Square Shelters existed, tens of thousands of educated young adults who graduate from college each year, would move into professions and communities across the United States, and serve as ambassadors for the homeless men and women that Mangano and Finn want to move into residential communities.

Imagine a town meeting in an affluent suburban community to discuss the building of affordable housing units for currently homeless men and women. Now imagine that same meeting with one or two community members who can speak about their experiences at a shelter like the Harvard Square Shelter. Joshua Villanueva suggests that "The experience of working in a shelter, and the obligation that comes with it, is to bring others to the awareness of our shared humanity." For middle-class Americans to embrace — or at least, accept — the presence in their communities of men and women struggling to pull themselves out of homelessness, there need to be many more young adults like the students described in these pages who are prepared to raise their neighbors' awareness of our shared humanity.

Even Joseph Finn, who sees his work at the Massachusetts Housing and Shelter Alliance as focused on ending the use of homeless shelters as a mechanism for combating homelessness, acknowledged that

"You'll always have at this point in time some need for some kind of emergency, short-term residential response for people." Likewise, Philip Mangano sees a future role for the Harvard Square Shelter as "a short triage that leads to stable, permanent housing." In other words, while the Housing First philosophy seeks to provide a new form of support for those who have been homeless for years, there will always be a need for emergency, short-term shelter for individuals who suddenly find themselves without a place to stay, but who will move back into permanent housing within a year's time. These are the men and women the college students at the Harvard Square Homeless Shelter are most equipped to support, and so, even if the Housing First vision described by Philip Mangano and Joseph Finn becomes a reality, there will remain a useful niche for student-run shelters to fill.

Harvard Professor Julie Wilson raised the possibility that the student-run model that characterizes the Harvard Square Homeless Shelter could be utilized to serve other marginalized communities as well. For example, Professor Wilson wondered whether a similar set-up could be useful in working with youth currently in the foster care system. The noteworthy success of this year's shelter volunteers in working with an older teenager like Lex Obain lends some credence to this possibility. Perhaps similar to the homeless men and women who come to the Harvard Square Shelter, children thrust into the short term foster care system would benefit from a living situation where their nightly supervisors are enthusiastic, idealistic, and academically driven college students. Professor Wilson also noted that "I think domestic violence is a huge issue, and a lot of shelters won't let you take [along] young boys." She speculates about the possibility of a student-run model that provides shelter to women fleeing domestic violence situations without forcing them to separate or make different arrangements for their children. The feasibility of these and other possibilities would, of course, require substantial thinking, planning and research, but, in the spirit of the outside-the-box thinking that characterizes the Harvard Square Homeless Shelter, it is important to consider the full range of possibilities that the student-run model might yield.

CONCLUSION

Several Harvard students and homeless people described the experience of spending the night at the Harvard Square Shelter as an egalitarian one. Former guest Lucy Draper recalled her wonderment that "these kids actually treated me as an equal if not more than an equal." She described as integral to her ascent out of homelessness that "they didn't dwell on my homelessness. We talked about food, cooking, food salvaging, and then it went kind of from there to other stuff like books." Likewise, Helen Van Anglen said, "One of the things I loved about the overnight shift was that at two o'clock in the morning you were just talking to people. . . . I was younger than most of the people, [so] the power dynamic was so flattened that we could just talk." A current student, senior Hope Franklin, concurred that the shelter felt like "a place where I sort of dropped the Harvard identity." And University Lutheran Pastor Donald Larsen described a student who had recently come to talk to him about a similar feeling:

> "She sat down with guests during meal time, and another student sat down, and they got involved in some conversation about where they had been. And they were talking to some guest from Sierra Leone, and it suddenly dawned on her that the conversation had developed in such a way that distinctions between volunteers and guests had been completely forgotten. And she was almost overcome by it. She said that she has come to realize out of that experience that service is a form of immortality because in giving of yourself to another, and in giving of yourself in a context that becomes mutual, something happens that lives on."

This volunteer's phrase — "Something happens that lives on" — offers perhaps the most concise summary yet of the argument put forth in these pages. On any given night, for the homeless men and women sleeping at the shelter, for the Harvard students working the overnight shift, and for the "real world" that awaits them all at 8 o'clock the next morning, something has happened at the Harvard Square Homeless Shelter that lives on. Philip Mangano has said that he hopes his grandchildren will one day have to go to a museum to learn about the disgrace that homelessness once was.[14] A lot will need to happen for such a museum to come into being, but the Harvard Square Homeless Shelter — and the potential for more such shelters — have a role to play in that museum's construction.

Appendix

Research Methods

*S**helter* is the result of a year-long qualitative study of the Harvard Square Homeless Shelter during the 2008–09 academic year. The seeds for this project were sown in May 2008 when I sat down in Harvard's Eliot House with four of the Harvard Square Shelter's student-directors and expressed my interest in carrying out a research study that investigated the impact of the Harvard Square Homeless Shelter upon its college-aged volunteers and homeless guests. The student-directors generously agreed to lend their support to the study, and I spent much of the summer and fall of 2008 developing a research proposal and research design.

RESEARCH DESIGN

For nearly a decade now, my research has focused on the civic development of adolescents and young adults. Typically, I take a mixed-methods approach, using both quantitative methods such as multiple-choice surveys and qualitative methods such as one-on-one interviews. I initially did design a quantitative survey, which I planned to administer to all of the Harvard Square Shelter's volunteers at the beginning and conclusion of the 2008–09 academic year. Within this survey tool, I included items that had been adapted from existing measures of "Beliefs about Homelessness," "Attributions for Poverty," and "Attitudes towards Community Service." However, I ultimately decided that this survey tool could not provide me with a meaningful understanding of the impact of the Harvard Square Shelter upon participating college students. Because there was no natural comparison group to whom I could also administer the survey, I would have no way of knowing whether changes on these measures demonstrated by the shelter volunteers were due to their volunteer work at the Harvard Square Shelter; their experience living in an urban setting; or simply the experience of being in college. As noted in Chapter 3, numerous scholars have demonstrated that young adults experience spikes in their commitment to activism and social justice during the college years, so a simple demonstration of positive changes on a pre–post survey tool would not have effectively shed light on the impact of the shelter upon its college-aged volunteers. As a result, I decided to take a qualitative approach to studying the effects of the Harvard Square Homeless Shelter.

STUDY PARTICIPANTS

Triangulation of data in the social sciences refers to the utilization of two or more research methods to test a particular result.[1] As noted above, in many of my earlier research endeavors, I have utilized *both* quantitative surveys and qualitative interviews to gauge the impact of a particular intervention or experience. While such triangulation was not feasible with this study of the Harvard Square Shelter, I determined that it would be important to conduct qualitative interviews with several different constituencies of the shelter in order to understand more fully the impact of the volunteer experience upon participating college students and the guest experience upon the homeless men and women who stay there. Towards this end, I sought to conduct interviews with individuals from each of the following five constituencies:

1. First-time Harvard Square Shelter volunteers
2. Harvard Square Shelter "staff" (i.e. student-leaders)
3. Harvard alumni who had volunteered at the Harvard Square Shelter during college
4. Homeless and formerly homeless men and women who had stayed at the Harvard Square Homeless Shelter as "guests"
5. Stakeholders who interacted professionally with the college students operating the Harvard Square Homeless Shelter

FIRST-TIME SHELTER VOLUNTEERS

This study involved interviews with ten college-aged students for whom the 2008–09 academic year represented their first year volunteering at the Harvard Square Homeless Shelter. Nine of these students attended Harvard College, and one attended Wellesley College. Six were women, and four were men. Among these ten students were three freshmen, three sophomores, two juniors, and two seniors. Eight were born in the United States, and two were international students (coming from England and India respectively). Seven identified as White, one as Asian American, one as Indian, and one as Puerto Rican.

I identified these ten participants by attending the two volunteer trainings held by the Harvard Square Homeless Shelter in October of 2008 and introducing myself and my research project to the assembled students. With the assistance of the shelter's volunteer director, I then contacted first-time volunteers via email and requested their participation in the study. In choosing among the approximately 40 new volunteers during the 2008–09 academic year, I sought a diverse sample in terms of gender, age, ethnicity, etc. A brief description of each of these ten students is presented below. All are referred to by pseudonyms.

- Anna Robinson was a freshman at Harvard College during the 2008–09 academic year who identified as White and had grown up just outside Boston, Massachusetts. Robinson had heard about the Harvard Square Homeless Shelter during high school and decided to get involved during her freshman year at Harvard by signing up for an overnight shift.
- Antonia Garcia-Brown was a sophomore at Harvard in 2008–09 who identified as Puerto Rican and had grown up in New York City. Garcia-Brown signed up for an overnight shift at the start of her sophomore year and then switched to a Resource Advocacy shift for the spring semester.
- Ashwin Ganguli was a freshman at Harvard College in 2008–09 who identified as Indian and had grown up in Bangalore, India. A computer science major, Ganguli signed up for an overnight shift at the start of his freshman year and applied to become a shelter supervisor for the spring semester of his freshman year.
- Charlotte Wu was a sophomore at Wellesley College in 2008–09 who identified as Asian American and had grown up in southern

California. She became involved in the shelter through her older brother (a Harvard undergraduate) by signing up for a weekly overnight shift.

- Elyse Margolis was a senior at Harvard who identified as White and had grown up in New York City. A social theory major, Margolis signed up for a dinner shift at the shelter.
- Hope Franklin was a senior at Harvard College who identified as White and had grown up in western Massachusetts. An environmental science major, Franklin signed up for a breakfast shift at the shelter at the urging of a roommate involved with the shelter.
- Lester Pearsons was a junior at Harvard who identified as White and had grown up outside London, England. A history major, Pearsons signed up for a dinner shift at the shelter at the urging of a friend.
- Liam Murphy was a sophomore at Harvard in 2008–09 who identified as White and had grown up in rural Oklahoma. At the start of his sophomore year, he signed up to participate in both a dinner shift and a Resource Advocacy shift.
- Louis Landau was a junior at Harvard who identified as White and had grown up in Cleveland, Ohio. A math major, Landau signed up for an overnight shift at the shelter at the start of his junior year.
- Nancy Mellor was a freshman at Harvard College in 2008–09 who identified as White and had grown up in rural Ohio. She signed up for an overnight shift at the shelter at the start of her freshman year and added a shift at the shelter's Resource Advocacy table midway through her freshman year.

SHELTER STAFF

This study also involved interviews with 13 college students who served as "staff" (supervisors or directors) at the Harvard Square Homeless Shelter during the 2008–09 academic year. All 13 were students at Harvard College. Seven of the students were men, and six were women. Among these 13 students were six juniors, six seniors, and one sophomore. All 13 were born in the United States. Eleven identified as White and two as Asian American.

I identified these participants by attending one of the weekly staff meetings of the Harvard Square Homeless Shelter in November of

2008 and introducing myself and my research project. I then contacted individual staff members via email and requested their participation in the study. In choosing among the 28 staff members during the 2008–09 academic year, I sought a diverse sample in terms of gender, age, ethnicity, etc. A brief description of each of these 13 students is presented below. All are referred to by pseudonyms.

- Amanda Mooney was a junior at Harvard in 2008–09 who identified as White and had grown up in suburban Michigan. A pre-med major, Mooney served as one of the shelter's Work Contract program directors during the 2008–09 academic year.
- Christopher Kitts was a sophomore at Harvard in 2008–09 who identified as White and had grown up in suburban Michigan. A government major, Kitts served as an overnight supervisor during the 2008–09 academic year.
- Deanna Galante was a junior at Harvard in 2008–09 who identified as White and had grown up in Maine. A government major, Galante served as one of the shelter's Resource Advocacy program directors during the fall semester of the 2008–09 academic year. She was studying abroad in the spring semester.
- Drew McGinty was a senior at Harvard in 2008–09 who identified as White and had grown up in Cincinnati, Ohio. McGinty served as a shelter supervisor during the fall semester of the 2008–09 academic year but graduated from Harvard in January of 2009 and moved to New York City.
- Jerry Chen was a junior at Harvard in 2008–09 who identified as Asian American and had grown up in Cambridge, Massachusetts. A biology major, Yang served as the shelter's "Computer" director during the 2008–09 academic year and also played a significant role in managing the shelter's Street Team.
- Kathryn Tobin was a senior at Harvard in 2008–09 who identified as White and had grown up in Fargo, North Dakota. An economics major, Tobin served as one of the shelter's Work Contract program directors during the 2008–09 academic year and also played a major role in the shelter's endowment campaign.
- Kelly Parker was a senior at Harvard in 2008–09 who identified as White and had grown up just outside Boston, Massachusetts. Parker served as the shelter's "Supplies" director during the 2008–09 academic year.

- Larry Yoon was a junior at Harvard in 2008–09 who identified as Asian American and had grown up in Chicago, Illinois. A pre-med major, Yoon served as the shelter's Street Team director during the 2008–09 academic year.
- Leo LaSala was a senior at Harvard in 2008–09 who identified as White and had grown up in Washington DC, Singapore, and Ireland as a result of his parents' work for an international development organization. LaSala served as one of the shelter's "Administrative" directors during the 2008–09 academic year and played a significant role in the shelter's endowment campaign.
- Lissette McDonald was a senior at Harvard in 2008–09 who identified as White and had grown up in Montpelier, Vermont. A psychology major, McDonald served as the shelter's "Volunteer" director during the 2008–09 academic year.
- Melissa Sanguinetti was a junior at Harvard in 2008–09 who identified as White and had grown up in rural South Dakota. A religion major, Sanguinetti served as an overnight supervisor during the fall semester of the 2008–09 academic year before studying abroad in the spring semester.
- Nathan Small was a junior at Harvard in 2008–09 who identified as White and had grown up in Cambridge, Massachusetts. A social theory major, Small served as the shelter's "staff director" during the 2008–09 academic year and also worked on the shelter's endowment team. Small had become involved with the shelter as a high school student and continued his involvement upon matriculating to Harvard.
- Robert Vozar was a senior at Harvard in 2008–09 who identified as White and had grown up in Massachusetts. An economics major, Vozar served as one of the shelter's "Administrative" directors during the 2008–09 academic year and also played a major role in the shelter's endowment campaign.

HOMELESS AND FORMERLY HOMELESS HARVARD SQUARE SHELTER "GUESTS"

This study also involved interviews with eight homeless or formerly homeless men and women who had spent time as "guests" at the Harvard Square Homeless Shelter. Of these eight participants, seven were men and one was a woman. This ratio reflects the proportion of men to women on a nightly basis at the shelter (typically 23–26 men and 2–3 women). Of these eight participants, six identified as White, one as African American, and one as African. Two participants were in their sixties, one in his fifties, three in their forties, one in his early twenties, and one was 19 years old. Three of these participants were currently homeless, and five were formerly homeless.

I was put in touch with four of these participants (all formerly home-less) by Harvard Square Shelter staff as well as by professionals working with Boston and Cambridge's homeless population. The other four par-ticipants I met and interviewed by "hanging out" at the Au Bon Pain in Cambridge's Harvard Square, a restaurant which allows homeless men and women to loiter.[2] By approaching several individuals who appeared to be homeless and explaining that I was interested in interviewing men and women who had stayed at the Harvard Square Homeless Shelter, I was directed to four more individuals (three currently homeless, one formerly homeless) who had stayed or were currently staying at the Harvard Square Shelter. A brief description of each of these eight individuals is presented below. All are referred to by pseudonyms.

- Frank Green was a currently homeless man in his forties who identified as White. He spent much of the 2008–09 winter at the Harvard Square Homeless Shelter.
- Fred Slomiak was a formerly homeless man in his sixties who identified as White. He was homeless for several years in the mid to late 1990s and stayed at the shelter during this time as a participant in the Work Contract program.
- Joe Presley was a formerly homeless man in his fifties who identified as African American. He stayed at the shelter during a period of homelessness in the early 1990s. He now manages an organization that provides support to men and women contend-ing with homelessness.
- Lex Obain was a formerly homeless man in his early twenties who identified as African and had immigrated to the United States in 2006. He experienced two years of homelessness in 2007–09 and spent much of 2008 as a guest at the shelter before matriculating to Hamilton College.
- Lucy Draper was a formerly homeless woman in her forties who identified as White. She experienced two years of homelessness in the late 1980s. Although she refused to sleep in homeless

shelters during this period, she came to the shelter in the evenings for dinner, warmth, and conversation. Draper now directs a non-profit organization committed to helping individuals contending with homelessness.

- Mike Andretti was a currently homeless man who identified as White and was 19 years old. He spent much of the 2008–09 winter at the shelter.

- Ralph McGann was a formerly homeless man in his early fifties who identified as White. He stayed at the shelter during periods of homelessness in the mid-1980s, the early 1990s, and for a brief period in 2002. He now has a room at a local YMCA.

- Ray Diaz was a currently homeless man in his late sixties who identified as White. Diaz had been homeless for more than 20 years and has spent significant time at the shelter over the past 15 winters.

HARVARD SQUARE SHELTER ALUMNI

This study also involved interviews with ten men and women who had volunteered at the Harvard Square Shelter during their undergraduate years at Harvard College. Five of these participants were men, and five were women. Three of these participants were in their early thirties, four were in their late thirties, and three were in their early forties. Seven identified as White, one as Latino, one as Southeast Asian, and one as bi-racial.

In seeking out shelter alumni, I sought a balanced number of men and women as well as individuals who ranged in age from their early thirties to their early forties. The individuals in their early forties were present for the earliest years of the Harvard Square Homeless Shelter. I deliberately excluded more recent alumni from this sample (i.e. individuals in their early and middle twenties) because I wanted to interview participants who could reflect upon the impact of the shelter upon their personal and professional trajectories. I feared that more recent alumni would still be too enmeshed in the process of career exploration and training to be able to reflect effectively upon the shelter's impact upon them.

In order to identify this sample, I sought nominations from professional stakeholders who had interacted with the Harvard Square Shelter over its 26-year history. These stakeholders included past and present pastors of the University Lutheran Church and professionals working in homeless services in Boston and Cambridge, Massachusetts. I then contacted each of the individuals below and requested their participation in a one-on-one interview about their experience volunteering at the shelter. All of the individuals below are referred to by pseudonyms. A brief description of each of these individuals is presented below.

- Aaron Dutka was a White man in his late thirties who volunteered at the Harvard Square Homeless Shelter from 1990 to 1993. He is now a doctor in Boston, Massachusetts who focuses on treating individuals contending with substance abuse problems and HIV/AIDS.
- Amelia Ginsberg was a White woman in her early thirties who volunteered at the shelter from 1994–1998 while she was an undergraduate at Harvard College. She currently works for an environmental advocacy not-for-profit organization.
- Anusha Ghosh was a Southeast Asian American in her early thirties who volunteered at the shelter from 1997 to 2001 while she was an undergraduate at Harvard College. She now works as an immigrants-rights attorney in New York City.
- Dennis McGonagle was a White man in his early forties who volunteered at the shelter from 1985 to 1989 while he was an undergraduate at Harvard College. During this time, he was also a member of the University Lutheran congregation. McGonagle is now a professor of religion at an Ivy League university.
- Helen Van Anglen was a White woman in her late thirties who volunteered at the shelter from 1989 to 1993 while she was an undergraduate at Harvard College. After completing her studies at Harvard, Van Anglen went on to found a multi-service program for women who are homeless or in crisis.
- Joshua Villanueva was a Cuban American man in his early forties who volunteered at the shelter from 1986 to 1988 while he was an undergraduate at Harvard College. Villanueva went on to become a state representative and state senator.
- Kristin Sommers was a bi-racial woman in her mid-thirties who volunteered at the shelter from 1993 to 1997. She works as a primary care doctor at a public hospital in Seattle, Washington.
- Lana Zielinski was a White woman in her early forties who volunteered at the shelter from 1984 to 1988 while she was

an undergraduate at Harvard College. She works as a project manager in Boston at a laboratory focused on epidemiological research.

- Rusty Sadow was a White man in his early thirties who volunteered at the shelter from 1996 to 2000. He works as a community organizer in Washington DC.
- Ward Welburn was a White man in his late thirties who volunteered at the shelter from 1988 to 1992 while he was an undergraduate at Harvard College. He serves as the director of an urban middle school for low-income youth.

PROFESSIONAL STAKEHOLDERS

This study also involved interviews with 11 individuals who interacted with the Harvard Square Homeless Shelter in a professional capacity. I identified these participants by seeking out individuals associated with the University Lutheran Church as well as professional services for the homeless in Cambridge, Massachusetts and Boston, Massachusetts. The eight individuals who were interviewed as a result of their professional backgrounds are identified by name while pseudonyms are utilized for the three participants who were interviewed as a result of their voluntary roles as members of the University Lutheran congregation. A brief description of each of these individuals is presented below:

- Alice Wolf is a state representative for Cambridge in the Massachusetts state legislature. The Harvard Square Homeless Shelter sits in her district.
- Donald Larsen began serving as the pastor of the University Lutheran Church in 2003 and was the pastor during the 2008–09 academic year when this study was carried out.
- Fred Reisz co-founded the Harvard Square Homeless Shelter in 1983 in his role as pastor of the University Lutheran Church. He then served as the University Lutheran pastor for the first 10 years (1983–93) of the church's partnership with the shelter. He left the University Lutheran Church in 1993 in order to assume the presidency of the Lutheran Theological Southern Seminary in South Carolina.
- Julie Wilson is a professor of social policy at the John F. Kennedy School of Government at Harvard University with a particular

research interest in poverty policy. She is also a long-time member of the University Lutheran Church.

- Joseph Finn began serving as the Executive Director of the Massachusetts Housing and Shelter Alliance in 2003 and was in this role during the 2008–09 academic year when this study was conducted. Prior to this role, Finn served as the Executive Director of Shelter Inc., another homeless shelter in Cambridge, Massachusetts.

- Meghan Goughan is the Assistant Director of the CASPAR Homeless Shelter in Cambridge, Massachusetts during the 2008–09 academic year. She also served as a resource to the Harvard Square Shelter staff members operating the Shelter's Street Team program.

- Philip Mangano served from 2002 to 2009 as Executive Director of the United States Interagency Council on Homelessness. Prior to this role, Mangano served for 12 years as Executive Director of the Massachusetts Housing and Shelter Alliance.

- Stewart Guernsey co-founded the Harvard Square Homeless Shelter in 1983 while he was a graduate student at Harvard Divinity School. Guernsey went on to do anti-poverty work in Boston and Cambridge from 1983 to 1991. He then returned to his native Mississippi where he continues to practice poverty and civil rights law.

- Selma Brooks was a deacon in the University Lutheran Church during the 2008–09 academic year when this study was conducted. In this role, she served as a liaison between the congregation and the Harvard Square Shelter. Brooks also organized a monthly visit to the shelter for University Lutheran congregants.

- Terry Tebow was President of the Board of Directors of the Harvard Square Homeless Shelter Corporation during the 2008–09 academic year, a fundraising group established by members of the University Lutheran Church to support the shelter. Tebow was also a member of the congregation in 1982 when the shelter was founded.

- Wendy Burrell was a student at the Harvard Divinity School during the 2008–09 academic year. She was appointed by the University Lutheran Church to lead regular reflection sessions for the undergraduates volunteering at the shelter.

DATA COLLECTION

I conducted in-depth qualitative interviews with each of the 53 individuals described above. The professional stakeholders, shelter alumni, homeless, and formerly homeless individuals all participated in one interview apiece. The ten first-time Harvard Square Shelter volunteers and 13 shelter staff members were all interviewed at both the beginning of the shelter season (October or November 2008) and again at the conclusion of the shelter season (March or April 2009). In all, 73 interviews were conducted. Three shelter staff members were not interviewed in the spring; two of these students were studying abroad for the spring semester, and one had graduated from Harvard College in January of 2009 and moved out of state.

All 73 of these interviews lasted approximately an hour and a half apiece and were audio-recorded. For all of these interviews, the protocol was sufficiently structured to ensure that questions posed to the participants were open-ended, clear, and not overly complex.[3] However, the protocol also allowed me the flexibility to pose probes or follow-up questions.[4]

FIRST-TIME VOLUNTEERS

The initial interview for first-time shelter volunteers conducted in the fall of 2008 focused on the following topics:

- students' motivation for volunteering at the shelter
- students' expectations for the experience
- students' beliefs about the causes of homelessness
- students' beliefs about the impact of community service
- students' earlier experiences with community service
- students' beliefs about success and future career aspirations
- the formative influences upon students' worldview and self-concept

The follow-up interview for first-time shelter volunteers conducted in the spring of 2009 focused on the following topics:

- what students most enjoyed/least enjoyed about the volunteer experience

- what students found meaningful about the volunteer experience
- what students found surprising about the volunteer experience
- opportunities for interaction and conversation with homeless "guests"
- opportunities for interaction and conversation with other students
- comparisons between this and earlier volunteer experiences
- the impact of the volunteer experience upon students' beliefs about homelessness, poverty, and the American dream
- the impact upon future career aspirations

SHELTER STAFF

The initial interview for 2008–09 shelter staff members conducted in the fall of 2008 focused on the following topics:

- current role in shelter leadership
- how student initially became involved with the shelter
- conversations with homeless men and women that have been influential
- particularly challenging nights at the shelter
- the decision to become a part of the shelter leadership
- challenges associated with managing the shelter
- balancing the dual role of shelter manager and college student
- descriptions of a debate about how to operate the shelter
- future career aspirations

The follow-up interview for 2008–09 shelter staff members was conducted in the spring of 2009 and focused on the following topics:

- a challenge that occurred this year at the shelter
- impact of shelter upon other aspects of student's life
- an interaction with a shelter "guest" that stands out this year
- a great moment/challenging moment in working with the other staff-members
- advantages/disadvantages to a flat leadership structure
- impact of this past winter upon beliefs about homelessness and poverty
- impact of this past winter upon beliefs about community service

- experience of managing the shelter's volunteers
- how student imagines he/she will look back on the shelter ten years in the future

SHELTER ALUMNI

Interviews with men and women who had served as Harvard Square Shelter volunteers during their undergraduate years at Harvard College were interviewed throughout the 2008–09 academic year. Interviews with these individuals focused on the following topics:

- role within the leadership structure at the shelter
- particular interactions with homeless "guests" that were influential
- impact of shelter upon beliefs about homelessness and poverty
- impact of shelter upon career aspirations
- impact of shelter upon adult development
- impact of shelter upon experience at Harvard
- impact of shelter upon beliefs about social responsibility

HOMELESS AND FORMERLY HOMELESS SHELTER "GUESTS"

Interviews with men and women who had stayed (or were currently staying) at the Harvard Square Homeless Shelter as "guests" were interviewed throughout the 2008–09 academic year. Interviews with these individuals focused on the following topics:

- how Harvard Square Shelter compared to other homeless shelters
- initial impressions of Harvard Square Shelter
- what other shelters could learn from Harvard Square Shelter
- what Harvard Square Shelter could learn from other shelters
- impression of students volunteering at the shelter
- interaction or conversation with student that stands out
- beliefs about what student-volunteers get out of the volunteer experience

PROFESSIONAL STAKEHOLDERS

Interviews with men and women who interacted with the Harvard Square Homeless Shelter in their capacities as professionals were interviewed throughout the 2008–09 academic year. The protocol for these interviews was adapted for each individual participant; however, the following topics were included in all ten interviews:

- initial impression of Harvard Square Homeless Shelter
- what is impressive about the shelter
- what the students do *not* do well
- what the shelter has to contribute to the conversation on combating homelessness
- what students get out of the volunteer experience at the shelter
- how homeless men and women experience the Harvard Square Shelter in comparison to other shelters

DATA ANALYSIS

All 73 of the qualitative interviews were recorded and transcribed verbatim. Participants were assigned pseudonyms to ensure confidentiality. Each of these interview transcripts was then coded using etic and emic codes drawn from existing scholarship on identity development, community service-learning, adolescent development, emerging adulthood, moral development, and civic engagement. Upon completing the coding and categorizing of the transcribed interviews, I constructed matrices that juxtaposed the themes and patterns emerging from the data with the relevant scholarship.[5] Finally, narrative profiles were developed for all 53 individuals who participated in qualitative interviews.[6]

It is important to acknowledge that I worked as a volunteer and staff member at the Harvard Square Homeless Shelter during my own years as an undergraduate at Harvard College from 1995 to 1999. As I have previously written, this experience was a formative component of my own development from adolescence into emerging adulthood.[7] That said, of the 53 individuals who participated in this study, I had only previously met four of the participants (the four alumni who overlapped with my own undergraduate years). Moreover, I was not close friends with any of these four participants or in contact with any of them in the years prior to carrying out this study.

It was in large part due to my prior experience at the Harvard Square Shelter that I chose to investigate the impact of the shelter primarily through qualitative interviews with various shelter constituencies rather than substantial participant observation within the shelter itself. Having already spent literally scores of evenings inside the shelter during my own undergraduate years, I felt that I possessed a strong sense of the rhythm of an evening there and the types of interactions that take place between volunteers and homeless guests. I was primarily interested, then, in how current and former shelter volunteers and the homeless men and women staying at the shelter *understood* these interactions and their perceptions of the *effects* of these interactions. Likewise, I was interested in how external stakeholders conceived of the *impact* of the shelter upon both homeless men and women who stayed there and college students who volunteered there. For this reason, the majority of the data collected for this study came from qualitative interviews with 53 students, alumni, stakeholders, homeless, and formerly homeless guests. I conducted five sessions of participant observation within the shelter during the 2008–09 academic year and attended a number of shelter-related events and meetings. The narrative that comprises Chapter 1 comes directly from my field notes from one of these participant observation sessions — a full night (6 p.m.–9 a.m.) spent at the Harvard Square Shelter in December 2008.

In short, then, although I undertook this project more than a decade removed from my own undergraduate days, it was clear that my own prior experiences as a volunteer at the Harvard Square Homeless Shelter had the potential to impact my interpretation and analyses of this study's qualitative data. In order to reduce the threat of researcher bias to interpretive validity, I reflected upon my own biases and impact by writing analytic memos on these subjects throughout the data collection and data analysis process. I also shared code lists, transcripts, analytic memos, and data analysis with colleagues at the Harvard Graduate School of Education and Boston University and solicited their feedback both to cross-check my coding and to offer alternatives to my conclusions.[8] I also conducted member checks to receive feedback from several of my study's participants on my interpretations and conclusions.[9] As a result of these various measures, I believe the findings and analyses from this study can be regarded as valid and verifiable. And I am hopeful that these findings may serve as a catalyst for the replication of the Harvard Square Homeless Shelter's student-run model in major cities across the United States.

Notes

CHAPTER 1: PRIVILEGE AND POVERTY

1 All of the college students, former students, homeless men and women, and formerly homeless men and women in this book are referred to by pseudonyms.

2 The Harvard Square Homeless Shelter has periodically experimented with dividing up the shifts in different ways. For example, the period 7–11 p.m. has been divided into two different shifts: a dinner shift 7–9 p.m. and an evening shift 9–11 p.m.

3 In order to protect the identity of both Harvard students and homeless men and women described in this narrative who had not elected to participate in this study, I have deliberately altered a number of their identifying characteristics and minor details of the night's events and conversations.

4 See the Appendix on Research Methods for a more thorough description of this study's research methodology and interview protocols.

5 J. Tanner. Recentering during emerging adulthood: a critical turning point in life span human development. In: J. Arnett and J. Tanner (eds.). *Emerging adults in America: coming of age in the 21st century* (Washington DC: American Psychological Association, 2006); J. Arnett. *Emerging Adulthood: the winding road from the late teens through the twenties* (Oxford: Oxford University Press, 2004).

6 J. Arnett. Emerging adulthood: a theory of development from the late teens through the twenties. *American Psychologist*, 55 (2000).

7 E. Erikson. Youth, fidelity and diversity. In: E. Erikson (ed.) *The Challenge of Youth* (New York: Anchor Books, 1965).

8 See E. Erikson. *Identity, Youth and Crisis* (New York: W.W. Norton, 1968).

9 See J. Edelwich and A. Brodsky. *Burn-out: stages of disillusionment in the helping professions* (New York: Human Sciences Press, 1980).

10 See L. Finkelstein, T. Allen, and L. Rhoton. An examination of the role of age in mentoring relationships. *Group & Organization Management*, 28, 2 (2003); see also J. Youniss and M. Yates. *Community Service and Social Responsibility in Youth* (Chicago: The University of Chicago Press, 1997).

11 R. Evans. *The Human Side of School Change: reform, resistance, and the real-life problems of innovation* (San Francisco: Jossey Bass, 1996).

12 See D. Deutsch and P. Knobler. *Often Wrong but Never in Doubt: unleash the business rebel within* (New York: Harper Business, 2005).

13 On a typical winter night at the Harvard Square Homeless Shelter, the student-directors complete their shifts at 11 p.m. as well and are replaced by two students who serve as "overnight supervisors." However, because this particular evening occurred so close to Harvard's winter break, the Harvard Square Shelter was operating on a special "vacation" schedule in which the two directors on duty stayed for the entire night.

14 S. Harter. Self and identity development. In: S. Feldman and G. Elliott (eds.). *At the Threshold: the developing adolescent* (Cambridge, MA: Harvard University Press, 1990); S. Parks. *Big Questions, Worthy Dreams* (San Francisco: Jossey-Bass, 2000); J. Youniss and M. Yates. *Community Service and Social Responsibility in Youth* (Chicago: The University of Chicago Press, 1997).

15 See R. Gaztambide-Fernandez. *The Best of the Best: becoming elite at an American boarding school* (Cambridge, MA: Harvard University Press, 2009).

16 See W. Damon. *The Path to Purpose: helping our children find their calling in life* (New York: Simon & Schuster, 2008).

17 See Gaztambide-Fernandez. *The Best of the Best* (2008).

18 See E. Pascarella and P. Terenzini. *How College Affects Students: a third decade of research* (San Francisco: Jossey-Bass, 2005).

19 See Youniss and Yates. *Community Service and Social Responsibility in Youth*, 1997.

20 S. Seider. Tiers of understanding at the Harvard Square Homeless Shelter. *Journal of College & Character*, 10, 6 (2009).

21 T. Clydesdale. *The First Year Out: understanding American teens after high school* (Chicago: The University of Chicago Press, 2007).

22 See R. Bringle and J. Hatcher. Implementing service-learning in higher education. *Journal of Higher Education*, 67, 2 (1986).

23 See A. Astin and L. Sax. How undergraduates are affected by service participation. *Journal of College Student Development*, 39 (1998).

24 See K. Sternas, P. O'Hare, K. Lehman, and R. Milligan. Nursing and medical student teaming for service learning in partnership with the community: an emerging holistic model for interdisciplinary education and practice. *Holistic Nursing Practice*, 13, 2 (1999).

25 For a relevant consideration of the role of "declarations" in the adolescent identity development process, see S. Stern. *Instant Identity: girls and the culture of instant messaging* (New York: Peter Lang Publishing, 2007).

26 M. Cunningham and M. Henry. *Homelessness Counts* (Washington DC: National Alliance to End Homelessness, 2007).

27 S. Fiske. Look twice. *Greater Good*, 5, 1 (2008).

28 Ibid., p. 2.

29 Damon. *The Path to Purpose*, 2008; S. Macedo, Y. Alex-Assensoh, J. Berry, M. Brintnall, D. Campbell, L. Fraga, L, et al. *Democracy at Risk: how political choices undermine citizen participation and what we can do about it* (Washington DC: Brookings Institute Press, 2005); R. Putnam. *Bowling Alone: the collapse and revival of American community* (New York: Simon & Schuster, 2000).

30 See A. Terry and J. Bohnenberger. Service-learning: fostering a cycle of caring in our gifted youth. *Journal of Secondary Gifted Education*, 15 (2003).

31 Interview with P. Mangano, January 2009.

32 See J. Blau. Service-learning: not charity, but a two-way street. In: J. Ostrow, G. Hesser, and S. Enos (eds.), *Cultivating the Sociological Imagination: concepts and models for service-learning in sociology* (Washington, DC: American Association for Higher Education, 1999).

33 Interview with Professor J. Wilson, December 2008.

CHAPTER 2: THE CADILLAC OF HOMELESS SHELTERS

1 From 1983 to 1997, the Harvard Square Homeless Shelter was referred to as the University Lutheran Homeless Shelter. The name was changed to the Harvard Square Homeless Shelter in 1997 to reflect the shelter's standing as an independent entity separate from the University Lutheran Church. For simplicity's sake, the shelter is referred to as the Harvard Square Homeless Shelter throughout the book.

2 P. Koegel, M. Burnam, and J. Baumohl. The causes of homelessness. In: J. Baumohl (ed.). *Homelessness in America* (Phoenix: Oryx Press, 1996), pp. 24–34.

3 The first large-scale attempt to determine the size of the homeless population in the United States was not conducted until 1983 (R. Wasson, Guidelines for a classroom presentation on homelessness: a demand and supply curve analysis. *The Journal of Economic Education*, 29, 3, 1998). In 1983, the U.S. Department of Housing and Urban Development determined that between 250,000 and 300,000 Americans were homeless on any given night. (U.S. Housing and Urban Development. *A Report to the Secretary on the Homeless and Emergency Shelters*, 1984). By 1989, that figure would balloon to 500,000 (M. Burt and B. Cohen. *America's Homeless: numbers, characteristics, and programs that serve them*, Washington DC, The Urban Institute, 1989).

4 History of Christ Church Cambridge. Retrieved on January 29, 2009 from www.cccambridge.org/who_history.php.

5 C. Jencks. *The Homeless* (Cambridge, MA: Harvard University Press, 1994).

6 A. Melia. Renovated UniLu shelter ready to reopen. *Harvard Crimson*. November 4, 1999.

7 A. Powell. University Lutheran homeless shelter to undergo renovations. *Harvard University Gazette*, December 17, 1998.

8 C. Wen, P. Hudak, and S. Hwang. Homeless people's perceptions of welcomeness and unwelcomeness in healthcare encounters. *Journal of General Internal Medicine*, 22, 7 (2007), 1012.

9 M. Price. More than shelter. *Monitor on Psychology*, 40, 11 (2009), p. 61.

10 Please see the Appendix on Research Methods for a more thorough description of this study's research methodology and interview protocols.

CHAPTER 3: DOING PASSION WELL

1 This excerpt from Lex Obain's college application essay was published in 2009 in the *Boston Globe*. The citation is withheld to protect Obain's identity.

2 W. Fischman, B. Solomon, D. Greenspan, and H. Gardner. *Making Good: how young people cope with moral dilemmas at work* (Cambridge, MA: Harvard University Press, 2004); P. Cookson and C. Persell. *Preparing for Power: America's elite boarding schools* (New York: Basic Books, 1985).

3 For a more thorough consideration of these reflection sessions, see S. Seider, S. Gillmor, J. Leavitt, and S. Rabinowicz. Puzzling over community service and reflection. *Journal of College & Character*, 10, 7 (2009).

4 J. Arnett. Emerging adulthood: a theory of development from the late teens through the twenties. *American Psychologist*, 55 (2000).

5 J. Arnett. *Emerging Adulthood: the winding road from the late teens through the twenties* (Oxford: Oxford University Press, 2004).

6 Arnett. Emerging adulthood (2000), 10.

7 Arnett. *Emerging Adulthood* (2004), 15.

8 R. Evans. *The Human Side of School Change: reform, resistance, and the real-life problems of innovation* (San Francisco: Jossey Bass, 1996).

9 Arnett. Emerging adulthood (2000), 10.

10 Arnett. Emerging adulthood (2000), 7.

11 J. Twenge. *Generation Me: why today's young Americans are more confident, assertive, entitled — and more miserable than ever before* (New York: Free Press, 2006).

12 A. Colby and W. Damon. *Some Do Care: contemporary lives of moral commitment* (New York: The Free Press, 1992), 16.

13 E. Pascarella and P. Terenzini. *How College Affects Students* (San Francisco: Jossey-Bass, 1991), 277.

14 J. Tanner. Recentering during emerging adulthood: a critical turning point in life span human development. In: J. Arnett and J. Tanner (eds.). *Emerging Adults in America: coming of age in the 21st century* (Washington DC: American Psychological Association, 2006), 48.

15 L. Sax, A. Astin, W. Korn, and K. Mahoney. *The American Freshman: national norms for fall 1999* (Los Angeles: Higher Education Research Institute, 1999).

16 R. Dahl. Adolescent brain development: a period of vulnerabilities and opportunities. *Annals of N. Y. Academy of Sciences*, 1021 (2004), 30.

17 Ibid., p. 30.

18 H. Giroux. Border pedagogy and the politics of postmodernism. *Education and Society*, 9, 1 (1991).

19 M. Price. More than shelter. *Monitor on Psychology*, 40, 11 (2009), 58.

20 For further investigation of this question, see W. Damon. *The Path to Purpose: helping our children find their calling in life*. (New York: Simon & Schuster, 2008).

21 For further discussion of triggering events, see H. Haste. Social and moral cognition. In: H. Haste and D. Locke (eds.) *Morality in the Making: action and social context* (Chichester, UK: John Wiley & Sons Ltd, 1983).

22 For further consideration of the impact of insular suburban communities on prosocial development, see S. Seider. "Bad things could happen": How fear impedes the development of social responsibility in privileged adolescents. *Journal of Adolescent Research*, 23, 6 (2008).

23 G. Clary and M. Snyder. A functional analysis of altruism and prosocial behavior: the case of volunteerism. In: M. Clark (ed.), *Review of Personality and Social Psychology* (Newbury Park: Sage, 1991), 125.

24 G. Brewer, S. Selden, and R. Facer. Individual conceptions of public service motivation. *Public Administration Review*, 60 (2000).

25 Ibid., p. 260.

26 Ibid., p. 259.

27 For a discussion of the surge of homelessness in the United States in the 1980s, see J. Baumohl, *Homelessness in America* (Phoenix: Oryx Press, 1996).

28 E. Erikson. Youth, fidelity and diversity. In: E. Erikson (ed.) *The Challenge of Youth* (New York: Anchor Books, 1965).

29 E. Erikson. *Childhood and Society* (New York: Norton, 1963).

30 S. Parks. *Big Questions, Worthy Dreams*. (San Francisco: Jossey-Bass, 2000), 1.

31 Clary and Snyder. A functional analysis of altruism and prosocial behavior, (1991) 125.

32 Ibid, p. 125.

33 Erikson. *Youth and Society* (1968), 31.

34 Erikson. *The Challenge of Youth* (1965), 24.

35 S. Seider. Frame-changing experiences: a key to the development of a commitment to service-work and social action in young adults. *Journal for Civic Commitment*, 4, 2 (2006); S. Seider. Frame-changing experiences and the freshman year: catalyzing a commitment to service-work and social action. *Journal of College and Character*, 8, 2 (2007); S. Seider. Catalyzing a commitment to community service in emerging adults. *Journal of Adolescent Research*, 22, 6 (2007).

36 Clary and Snyder. A functional analysis of altruism and prosocial behavior (1991).

37 Erikson. *Childhood and Society* (1963).

38 Clary and Snyder. A functional analysis of altruism and prosocial behavior (1991); Brewer, Selden, and Facen. Individual conceptions of public service motivation (2000).

39 Clary and Snyder. A functional analysis of altruism and prosocial behavior (1991).

40 Parks. *Big Questions, Worthy Dreams* (2000).

41 For further discussion of burn-out in the service professions, see C. Maslach and M. Leiter. *The Truth about Burnout* (San Francisco: Jossey-Bass, 1997).

42 For further consideration of this issue, see W. Bennis and R. Thomas. *Geeks & Geezers: how era, values, and defining moments shape leaders* (Boston: Harvard Business School Press, 2002).

43 See B. Farber. A critical perspective on burnout. In: B. Farber (ed.). *Stress and Burnout in the Human Services* (New York: Pergamon, 1983).

44 Arnett. Emerging adulthood (2000).

45 A. Omoto, M. Snyder, and S. Martino. Volunteerism and the life course: investigating age-related agendas for action. *Basic and Applied Social Psychology*, 22 (2000).

46 For example, see C. Kadushin. Social distance between client and professional. *The American Journal of Sociology*, 67, 5 (1991).

47 Arnett. *Emerging Adulthood* (2004); Tanner. Recentering during emerging adulthood (2006).

48 For a further discussion of the impact of volunteers in working with the homeless, see K. Hirsch. *Songs from the Alley* (New York: Anchor, 1990).

49 See J. Hightower and S. DeMarco. *Swim Against the Current: even a dead fish can go with the flow* (New York: John Wiley & Sons, 2008), 214.

CHAPTER 4: SEEKING CONNECTIONS

1 J. Arnett. Emerging adulthood: a theory of development from the late teens through the twenties. *American Psychologist,* 55 (2000); E. Erikson. *Childhood and Society.* (New York: Norton, 1963).

2 E. Erikson. Youth, fidelity, and diversity. In: E. Erikson (ed.). *The Challenge of Youth* (New York: Anchor Books, 1965).

3 J. Marcia. Development and validation of ego-identity status. *Journal of Personality and Social Psychology,* 3, 5 (1966), 551–558; J. Marcia. Identity in adolescence. In: J. Adelson (ed.). *Handbook of Adolescent Psychology* (New York: Wiley, 1980), pp. 159–87.

4 G. Francies. The volunteer-needs profile: a tool for reducing turn-over. *Journal of Volunteer Administration,* 1 (1983); A. Omoto, M. Snyder, and S. Martino. Volunteerism and the life course: invest-igating age-related agendas for action. *Basic and Applied Social Psychology,* 22 (2000).

5 G. Clary and M. Snyder. A functional analysis of altruism and prosocial behavior: the case of volunteerism. In: M. Clark (ed.), *Review of Personality and Social Psychology* (Newbury Park: Sage, 1991).

6 A. Bandura. Self-efficacy: toward a unifying theory of behavioral change. *Psychological Review,* 84, 2 (1977).

7 A. Bandura. *Social Foundations of Thought and Action: a social cognitive theory* (Englewood Cliffs: Prentice-Hall, 1982).

8 M. Price. More than shelter. *Monitor on Psychology,* 40, 11 (2009).

9 Ibid.

10 Ibid, p. 58.

11 Ibid, p. 58.

12 Erikson. *Childhood and Society* (1963).

13 J. Youniss and M. Yates. *Community Service and Social Responsibility in Youth* (Chicago: The University of Chicago Press, 1997).

14 M. Yates and J. Youniss. Community service and political-moral identity in adolescents. *Journal of Research on Adolescence,* 6, 3 (1996), 272.

15 E. Metz, J. McLellan, and J. Youniss. Types of voluntary service and adolescents' civic development. *Journal of Adolescent Research,* 18 (2003), 201.

16 E. Erikson. *Identity, Youth, and Crisis.* (New York: Norton, 1968).

17 E. Erikson. Youth, fidelity, and diversity (1965).

18 G. Clary and M. Snyder. A functional analysis of altruism and prosocial behavior: the case of volunteerism (1991).
19 W. Deresiewicz. The disadvantages of an elite education. *American Scholar*, 77, 3 (2008), 2.
20 T. Clydesdale. *The First Year Out* (Chicago: The University of Chicago Press, 2007), 147.
21 M. Krumer-Nevo. The arena of othering: a life-story with women living in poverty and social marginality. *Qualitative Social Work: Research and Practice*, 1, 3 (2002).
22 For more on the positive role of volunteers in working with the homeless, see K. Hirsch, *Songs from the Alley* (New York: North Point Press, 1998).
23 J. Russell. The word is their bond. *The Boston Globe*. July 5, 2009. B1.
24 L. Watson. *The Centre for Restorative Justice*. Retrieved November 1, 2009 from www.sfu.ca/cfrj/quotes.html.
25 E. Erikson, *Identity, Youth, and Crisis* (1968).

CHAPTER 5: OUTSIDE THE BOX

1 *Spare Change News* and *What's Up Mag*. Two street papers together as one. Retrieved June 1, 2009 from http://sparechangenews. blogspot.com.
2 Vision & Mission of *Spare Change News*. Retrieved January 1, 2009 from http://sparechangenews.net.
3 J. Quigley and S. Raphael. Is housing unaffordable? Why isn't it more affordable? *Journal of Economic Perspectives*, 18, 1 (2004); J. Quigley, S. Raphael, and E. Smolensky. Homelessness in America, homelessness in California. *The Review of Economics and Statistics*, 83, 1 (2001).
4 D. Lyons. Foreword to Working Paper No. W01–007: Homeless in California, *Program on Housing and Urban Policy Working Paper Series* (2001), iii.
5 E. Mansur, J. Quigley, S. Raphael, and E. Smolensky. Examining policies to reduce homelessness using a general equilibrium model of the housing market. *Journal of Urban Economics*, 52 (2002).
6 Overview of MassHealth Services. Official Website of the Massachusetts Office of Health and Human Services. Retrieved November 1, 2009 from www.mass.gov/.

7 G. Fabrikant. Harvard and Yale report losses in endowment. *New York Times*, September 10, 2009.
8 J. Arnett. *Emerging Adulthood: the winding road from the late teens through the early twenties* (Oxford: Oxford University Press, 2004), 8.
9 J. Arnett. Emerging adulthood: a theory of development from the late teens through the twenties. *American Psychologist*, 55 (2000), 8.
10 R. Evans. *The Human Side of School Change: reform, resistance, and the real-life problems of innovation* (San Francisco: Jossey Bass, 1996).
11 Ibid., p. 30.
12 Ibid., p. 30.
13 Ibid., p. 97.
14 Ibid., p. 100.
15 E. Erikson. *Identity, Youth, and Crisis* (New York: Norton, 1968); J. Marcia. Development and validation of ego-identity status. *Journal of Personality and Social Psychology*, 3, 5 (1966).
16 R. Evans. *The Human Side of School Change* (1996).
17 M. Gladwell. Million dollar Murray. *The New Yorker*. February 11, 2006.

CHAPTER 6: SHELTERED *FROM* THE IVORY TOWER

1 For further discussion of the social effects of community service on college students, see D. Giles and J. Eyler. The impact of a college community service laboratory on students' personal, social, and cognitive outcomes. *Journal of Adolescence*, 17 (1994).
2 For further discussion of the role of personal relationships in the academic success of college students, see M. Jacobi. Mentoring and undergraduate academic success: a literature review. *Review of Educational Research*, 61, 4 (1991).
3 For further discussion of achieving a sense of purpose through community service, see W. Damon. *The Path to Purpose: helping our children find their calling in life* (New York: Simon & Schuster, 2008).
4 For further discussion of the relationship between religious faith and participation in community service, see R. Wuthnow. *Acts of Compassion: caring for others and helping ourselves* (Princeton: Princeton University Press, 1991).
5 M. Yates and J. Youniss. A developmental perspective on community service in adolescence. *Social Development*, 5 (1996).

6 W. Deresiewicz. The disadvantages of an elite education. *American Scholar*, 2008. Retrieved on March 1, 2009 from www.the americanscholar.org.

7 Ibid, p. 1.

8 For further discussion of this phrase at elite boarding schools, see R. Gaztambide-Fernandez. *The Best of the Best: becoming elite at an American boarding school* (Cambridge, MA: Harvard University Press, 2009).

9 For further discussion of the positive effects of volunteerism on physical and mental health, see P. Thoits and L. Hewitt. Volunteer work and well-being. *Journal of Health and Social Behavior*, 42, 2 (2001).

10 E. Erikson. *Identity, Youth and Crisis* (New York: W.W. Norton, 1968).

11 E. Erikson. *Childhood and Society* (New York: Norton, 1963), 261.

12 K. Keniston. *Young Radicals: notes on committed youth* (New York: Harcourt Brace and World, 1968); E. Pascarella and P. Terenzini. *How College Affects Students: a third decade of research* (San Francisco: Jossey-Bass, 1991); A. Waterman and C. Waterman. A longitudinal study of changes in ego identity status during the freshman year of college. In: R. Lerner and L. Hess (eds.). *Development of Personality, Self and Ego in Adolescence* (New York: Garland Publishing, 1999).

13 Deresiewicz. The disadvantages of an elite education (2008), 2.

14 Ibid, p. 2.

15 For further discussion of stress and high achieving young adults, see D. Pope. *Doing School: how we are creating a generation of stressed out, materialistic, and miseducated students* (New Haven: Yale University Press, 2001).

16 Harvard Crimson Editorial Board. A break fit for Harvard brains. *Harvard Crimson*, 2000. Retrieved on March 1, 2009 from www.thecrimson.com.

17 For more on universities as "total institutions," see E. Goffman. *Asylums: essays on the social situation of mental patients and other inmates* (New York: Anchor, 1961).

18 For further discussion of the insularity of Harvard students, see S. Seider. Lessons from a hunger strike at Harvard. *Journal of College and Character*, 9, 3 (2008).

19 Harvard Student Agencies. *The Unofficial Guide to Life at Harvard 2008–2009* (Cambridge, MA: Harvard Student Agencies, 2008).

20 J. Youniss, J. McLellan, Y. Su, and M. Yates. The role of community service in identity development: normative, unconventional, and deviant orientations. *Journal of Adolescent Research*, 14, 2 (1999), 250.

21 For a further discussion of privilege as identity rather than simply class status, see A. Howard. *Learning Privilege: lessons of power and identity in affluent schooling* (New York: Routledge, 2008); see also R. Douthat. *Privilege: Harvard and the education of the ruling class* (New York: Hyperion, 2005).

22 K. Arenson. Harvard: no tuition for parents making under 60K annually. *The MIT Tech*, 2006, Retrieved on February 1, 2009 from http://tech.mit.edu/.

23 For further discussion of working-class students contending with the impact of attending an elite university, see E. Aries and M. Seider. The interactive relationship between class identity and the college experience: the case of lower income students. *Qualitative Sociology*, 28, 4 (2005).

24 The U.S. House of Representatives Page Program, 2009, Retrieved on March 15, 2009 from http://pageprogram.house.gov.

25 For further discussion of the relationship between elite college students and their relationships with their hometowns, see Aries and Seider. The interactive relationship between class status and college students (2005).

26 For further discussion of the role of social class and public service motivation, see S. Seider. "Surprisingly relevant to life": The impact of philosophy and theology on the public service motivation of emerging adults. (Presentation at 4th Annual Conference on Emerging Adulthood, Atlanta, GA, 2009).

27 Erikson. *Identity, Youth and Crisis* (1968).

28 S. Harter. Self and identity development. In: S. Feldman and G. Elliott (eds.). *At the Threshold: the developing adolescent* (Cambridge, MA: Harvard University Press, 1990), 362.

29 M. Csikszentmihalyi and R. Larson. *Being Adolescent: conflict and growth in the teenage years* (United States: Basic Books, 1984), 250.

30 Ibid., p. 260.

31 For further discussion of the value of manual labor, see M. Crawford. *Shop Class as Soulcraft: an inquiry into the value of work* (New York: Penguin Press, 2009).

32 A. Omoto, M. Snyder, and S. Martino. Volunteerism and the life course: investigating age-related agendas for action. *Basic and Applied Social Psychology*, 22 (2000).

33 M. Csikszentmihalyi and R. Larson. *Being Adolescent* (1984), 263.

34 Damon. *The Path to Purpose* (2008), xiii.

35 Ibid., p. 33.

36 P. Baltes, U. Lindenberger, and U. Standinger. Life span theory in developmental psychology. In: W. Damon and R. Lerner (eds.). *Handbook of Child Psychology, Vol. 1: theoretical models of human development*, 6th ed., (New York: Wiley, 2006); D. McAdams. Generativity in midlife. In: M. Lachman (ed.). *Handbook of Midlife Development* (New York: John Wiley, 2001).

37 Parks. *Big Questions, Worthy Dreams* (2000), 90.

38 Erikson. Youth, fidelity, and diversity (1965).

39 Ibid., p. 24.

40 D. McAdam. *Freedom Summer* (New York: Oxford University Press, 1988), 137.

41 See J. Blau. Service-learning: not charity, but a two-way street. In: J. Ostrow, G. Hesser, and S. Enose (eds.). *Cultivating the Sociological Imagination: concepts and models for service-learning in sociology* (Washington DC: American Association for Higher Education, 1999).

42 C. Flanagan. Volunteerism, leadership, political socialization, and civic engagement. In: R. Lerner and L. Steinberg (eds.). *Handbook of Adolescent Psychology* (Hoboken, NJ: Wiley, 2004); A. Omoto, M. Snyder, and S. Martino. Volunteerism and the life course: investigating age-related agendas for action. *Basic and Applied Social Psychology*, 22 (2000).

43 G. Clary and M. Snyder. A functional analysis of altruism and prosocial behavior: the case of volunteerism. In: M. Clark (ed.). *Review of Personality and Social Psychology* (Newbury Park: Sage, 1991).

44 Harvard Student Agencies. *The Unofficial Guide to Life at Harvard* (2009).

45 W. Fischman, B. Solomon, D. Greenspan, and H. Gardner. *Making Good: how young people cope with moral dilemmas at work* (Cambridge, MA: Harvard University Press, 2004), 168.

46 L. Sax, A. Astin, W. Korn, and K. Mahoney. *The American Freshman: national norms for fall 1999* (Los Angeles: Higher Education Research Institute, 1999).

47 McAdam. *Freedom Summer* (1989), 190.

48 V. Hodgkinson. Key factors influencing caring, involvement and community. In: P. Schervish, V. Hodgkinson, and M. Gates (eds.).

Care and Community in Modern Society: passing on the tradition of service to future generations (San Francisco: Jossey-Bass, 1995); S. Oesterle, M. Johnson, and J. Mortimer. Volunteerism during the transition into adulthood. *Social Forces*, 82, 3 (1998).

49 A. Bandura. *Social Foundations of Thought and Action: a social cognitive theory* (Englewood Cliffs: Prentice-Hall, 1986), 94.

50 A. Colby, T. Ehrlich, E. Beaumont, and J. Stephens. *Educating Citizens: preparing America's undergraduates for lives of moral and civic responsibility* (San Francisco: Jossey Bass, 2003), 140.

51 P. Gibbon and P. Gomes. *A Call to Heroism: renewing America's vision of greatness* (Boston: Atlantic Monthly Press, 2002); S. Seider and H. Gardner. The fragmented generation. *Journal of College & Character*, 10, 4 (2009).

52 Fischman, Solomon, Greenspan, and Gardner. *Making Good* (2004), 168.

CHAPTER 7: THE BEST CLASS AT HARVARD

1 For more on stereotypes about the homeless, see A. Whaley and B. Link. Racial categorization and stereotype-based judgments about homeless people. *Journal of Applied Social Psychology*, 28 (1998).

2 A. Koppelman. Conservatives angry over Michelle Obama's trip to homeless shelter. *Salon.com*. March 6, 2009.

3 L. Ross. The intuitive psychologist and his shortcomings: distortions in the attribution process. In: L. Berkowitz (ed.). *Advances in Experimental Psychology* (San Diego: Academic Press, 1977).

4 B. Weiner. *An Attributional Theory of Motivation and Emotion* (New York: Springer-Verlag, 1980).

5 It should be noted that Sanguinetti attributed this theory of the "volunteer cycle" to a former student-director.

6 S. Fiske. Look twice. *Greater Good*, 5, 1 (2008), 1.

7 For more on the role of volunteerism in putting a face on homelessness, see S. Seider. Tiers of understanding at the Harvard Square Homeless Shelter. *Journal of College & Character*, 10, 6 (2009).

8 For more on the role of elder care, see D. Wolf, V. Freedman, and B. Soldo. The division of family labor: care for elderly parents. *Journal of Gerontology Series B*, 52 (1997).

9 D. McAdam. *Freedom Summer* (New York: Oxford University Press, 1988), 187.

10 E. Erikson. *Childhood and Society* (New York: Norton, 1963).

11 E. Erikson. Youth, fidelity and diversity. In E. Erikson (ed.) *The Challenge of Youth.* (New York: Anchor Books, 1965).

12 S. Parks. *Big Questions, Worthy Dreams* (San Francisco: Jossey-Bass, 2000), 95.

13 Ibid, p. 95.

14 E. Erikson. *Childhood and Society* (1963).

15 D. McAdam. *Freedom Summer* (1988), 200.

16 J. Pryor, S. Hurtado, V. Saenz, J. Santos, and W. Korn. *The American Freshman: forty year trends* (Los Angeles: Higher Education Research Institute, 2007).

17 W. Damon. *The Path to Purpose: helping our children find their calling in life* (New York: Simon & Schuster, 2008), 55.

18 T. Clydesdale. *The First Year Out: understanding American teens after high school* (Chicago: The University of Chicago Press, 2008), 188.

19 A. Astin, L. Vogelgesang, E. Ikeda, and J. Yee. *How Service Learning Affects Students* (Los Angeles: Higher Education Research Institute, 2000); T. Batchelder and S. Root. Effects of an undergraduate program to integrate academic learning and service. *Journal of Adolescence,* 17, 4 (1994); A. Colby. Intersections of political and moral development. *Journal of College & Character,* 10, 1 (2008); S. Seider, S. Catalyzing a commitment to community service in emerging adults. *Journal of Adolescent Research,* 22, 6 (2007).

20 See D. Soo and M. Hartley. *Emergent and Contested Conceptions of Community Engagement at American Colleges and Universities* (San Diego: 2009 Annual Meetings of the American Educational Research Association, 2009).

21 For an overview of the "Justice" course, see www.justiceharvard. org.

22 J. Rawls. *A Theory of Justice* (Cambridge, MA: Harvard University Press, 1971).

23 M. Gladwell. Million dollar Murray. *The New Yorker,* February 13, 2006.

24 For more on Dr. Paul Farmer, see T. Kidder. *Mountains Beyond Mountains: the quest of Dr. Paul Farmer, the man who would heal the world* (New York: Random House, 2003).

25 T. Clydesdale. *The First Year Out* (2008), 40.

26 J. Youniss and M. Yates. *Community Service and Social Responsibility in Youth* (Chicago: The University of Chicago Press, 1997).

27 L. Dolte, K. Cramer, N. Dietz, and R. Grimm. *College Students Helping America* (Washington, DC: Corporation for National and Community Service, 2006); J. Pryor et al. *The American Freshman: forty year trends* (2007).

CHAPTER 8: LEARNING TO LEAD

1 See W. Edmundson and P. Sikhatme. Food and work: poverty and hunger? *Economic Development and Cultural Change*, 38, 2 (1990).

2 E. Erikson. Youth, fidelity and diversity. In: E. Erikson (ed.). *The Challenge of Youth* (New York: Anchor Books, 1965).

3 D. Boyd. Why youth [heart] social network sites: the role of networked publics in teenage social life. In: D. Buckingham (ed.). *Youth, Identity, and Digital Media* (Cambridge, MA: MIT Press); S. Stern. *Instant Identity: girls and the culture of instant messaging* (New York: Peter Lang Publishing).

4 T. Clydesdale. *The First Year Out: understanding American teens after high school* (Chicago: The University of Chicago Press), 113.

5 M. Levine. *Ready or Not, Here Life Comes* (New York: Simon & Schuster, 2005), 218.

6 J. Arnett. Emerging adulthood: a theory of development from the late teens through the twenties. *American Psychologist*, 55 (2000).

7 L. Kohlberg. *The Philosophy of Moral Development: moral stages and the idea of justice.* (New York: HarperCollins, 1981).

8 L. Kohlberg. *The Psychology of Moral Development: the nature and validity of moral stages* (New York: HarperCollins, 1984).

9 M. Hauser. *Moral Minds: how nature designed our universal sense of right and wrong* (New York: Ecco, 2006).

10 J. Stephens and H. Nicholson. Cases of incongruity: exploring the divide between adolescents' beliefs and behaviors related to academic cheating. *Educational Studies*, 34, 4 (2008).

11 See Boston Healthcare for the Homeless Program. *Who We Are.* Retrieved on November 1, 2009 from www.bhcp.org.

12 R. Weissbourd. *The Parents we Mean to Be* (Boston: Houghton Mifflin, 2009), 166.

13 W. Damon. *The Path to Purpose: helping our children find their calling in life* (New York: Simon & Schuster, 2008), 8.

14 W. Damon. *The Path to Purpose* (2008), 46.

15 Both the name of the organization and the URL of its website are withheld to protect the identity of Helen Van Anglen.

16 See the U.S. House of Representatives Page Program. Retrieved on November 15, 2009 from http://pageprogram.house.gov.

17 D. Faust. Baccalaureate Address 2008. Retrieved on August 1, 2009 from http://harvardmagazine.com.

18 M. Fullan. *Leading in a Culture of Change: being effective in complex times* (San Francisco: Jossey Bass, 2001).

19 A. Bandura. Self-efficacy mechanism in human agency. *American Psychologist*, 37, 2, (1982).

20 K. Keniston. *Young Radicals: notes on committed youth* (New York: Harcourt Brace, 1968).

21 D. McAdam. *Freedom Summer* (New York: Oxford University Press, 1988).

22 S. Oliner and P. Oliner. *The Altruistic Personality: rescuers of Jews in Nazi Europe* (New York: Free Press, 1992).

23 A. Bandura. Self-efficacy mechanism in human agency (1982), 195.

CHAPTER 9: ENOUGH COMMITTED FLEAS

1 Although it is difficult to confirm that the Harvard Square Homeless Shelter is the *only* student run shelter in the United States, a thorough search for other student-run shelters turned up no results. Moreover, none of the individuals associated with the University Lutheran Church and Harvard Square Homeless Shelter over the past 25 years could report ever hearing of another student-run homeless shelter.

2 L. Dolte, K. Cramer, N. Dietz, and R. Grimm. *College Students Helping America* (Washington, DC: Corporation for National and Community Service, 2006).

3 R. Niemi, M. Hepburn, and C. Chapman. Community service by high school students: a cure for civic ills? *Political Behavior*, 21, 1 (2000).

4 Center for Information and Research on Civic Learning and Engagement. Volunteering/community service (2004). Retrieved July 1, 2009 from www.civicyouth.org.

5 V. Hodgkinson. Key factors influencing caring, involvement, and community. In: P. Schervish, V. Hodgkinson, and M. Gates (eds.).

Care and Community in Modern Society: passing on the tradition of service to future generations (San Francisco: Jossey-Bass, 1995).

6 D. McAdam. *Freedom Summer* (New York: Oxford University Press, 1988), 64.

7 S. Oesterle, M. Johnson, and J. Mortimer. Volunteerism during the transition into adulthood. *Social Forces*, 82, 3 (1998).

8 See Boston Healthcare for the Homeless Program. *Who We Are.* Retrieved on November 1, 2009 from www.bhcp.org.

9 V. Hodgkinson, Key factors influencing caring, involvement, and community (1995).

10 T. Fitch. Characteristics and motivations of college students volunteering for community service. *Journal of College Student Personnel*, 28, 5 (1987); T. Tierney and A. Branch. *College Students as Mentors for At-Risk Youth* (Philadelphia: Public/Private Ventures, 1992).

11 J. Grusec. Socialization processes and the development of altruism. In: J. Rushton and R. Sorrentino (eds.). *Altruism and Helping Behavior: social, personality, and developmental perspectives* (Hillsdale, NJ: Erlbaum, 1981), 69.

12 D. Hart, M. Yates, S. Fegley and G. Wilson. Moral commitment in inner-city adolescents. In: M. Killen and D. Hart (eds.). *Morality in Everyday Life: developmental perspectives* (Cambridge, UK: Cambridge University Press, 1995); K. Keniston. *Young Radicals: notes on committed youth* (New York: Harcourt Brace, 1968); J. Piliavin and H. Charng. Altruism: a review of recent theory and research. *Annual Review of Sociology*, 16 (1990).

13 W. Fischman, B. Solomon, D. Greenspan, and H. Gardner. *Making Good: how young people cope with moral dilemmas at work* (Cambridge, MA: Harvard University Press, 2004); P. Gibbon and P. Gomes. *A Call to Heroism: renewing America's vision of greatness* (Boston: Atlantic Monthly Press, 2002).

14 W. Fischman, D. Schute, B. Solomon, and G. Lam. The development of an enduring commitment to service work. In: M. Michaelson and J. Nakamura (eds.). *Supportive Frameworks for Youth Engagement* (New York: Jossey-Bass, 2001).

15 A. Colby and W. Damon. *Some Do Care: contemporary lives of moral commitment* (New York: The Free Press, 1992).

16 J. Rawls. *A Theory of Justice* (Cambridge, MA: Harvard University Press, 1971).

17 S. Seider. Catalyzing a commitment to community service in emerging adults. *Journal of Adolescent Research*, 22, 6 (2007); S. Seider.

Frame-changing experiences and the freshman year: catalyzing a commitment to service-work and social action. *Journal of College and Character*, 8, 2 (2007); S. Seider. Frame-changing experiences: a key to the development of a commitment to service-work and social action in young adults. *Journal for Civic Commitment*, 4, 2 (2006).

18 A. Colby, T. Ehrlich, E. Beaumont, and J. Stephens. *Educating Citizens: preparing America's undergraduates for lives of moral and civic responsibility* (San Francisco: Jossey Bass, 2003), 109.

19 V. Hodgkinson. Key factors influencing caring, involvement and community (1995).

20 Ibid.

21 A. Colby and W. Damon. *Some Do Care* (1992).

22 M. Johnson, T. Beebe, J. Mortimer, and M. Snyder. Volunteerism in adolescence: a process perspective. *Journal of Research on Adolescence*, 9 (1998); L. Sax and A. Astin. The benefits of service: evidence from undergraduates. *Educational Record*, 78, 3–4 (1997).

23 Hart et al., Moral commitment in inner-city adolescents (1995), 326.

24 For more on the role of Jesuit education and community service, see S. Seider, S. Gillmor, J. Leavitt, and S. Rabinowicz. Puzzling over community service and reflection. *Journal of College & Character*, 10, 7 (2009).

25 C. Cozzarelli, A. Wilkinson, and M. Tagler. Attitudes toward the poor and attributions for poverty. *Journal of Social Issues*, 57 (2002); E. Ladd, and K. Bowman. *Attitudes Toward Economic Inequality* (New York: AEI Press, 1998); G. Mantsios. Class in America. In: M. Kimmel and A. Foster (eds.). *Privilege: a reader* (New York: Westview Press, 2003).

26 J. Kluegel and E. Smith. *Beliefs About Inequality: Americans' views of what is and what ought to be* (New York: de Gruyter, 1986).

27 J. Schwarz and T. Volgy. *The Forgotten Americans* (New York: W.W. Norton, 1992).

28 E. Gudrais. Unequal America. *Harvard Magazine*, July–August (2008).

29 In contrast, other research has found that isolated academic study of homelessness does not strengthen adolescents' doubts about the American dream. See S. Seider (in press). The role of privilege *as* identity in adolescents' beliefs about homelessness, opportunity, and inequality. *Youth & Society*.

30 N. Noddings. *Educating Moral People: a caring alternative to character education* (New York: Teachers College Press, 2002).
31 C. Gilligan. *In a Different Voice* (Cambridge, MA: Harvard University Press, 1982).
32 D. McFall. Sisters center for wisdom: illuminating the value of values. *Spelman Messenger*, 117 (2004), 22.

CHAPTER 10: SOMETHING THAT LIVES ON

1 M. Cunningham and M. Henry. *Homelessness Counts*. Washington DC: National Alliance to End Homelessness (2007).
2 U.S. Census Bureau (2009). Poverty 2008. Retrieved November 10, 2009 from www.census.gov/hhes/www/poverty/poverty08/pov08hi.html.
3 F. Roosevelt. Second inaugural address. Retrieved March 31, 2008 from http://avalon.law.yale.edu/20th_century/froos2.asp.
4 J. Brabazon. *Albert Schweitzer: a biography* (Syracuse, NY: Syracuse University Press, 2000).
5 W. Damon. *The Path to Purpose* (New York: Free Press, 2008).
6 C. Heymann. *RFK: candid biography of Robert F. Kennedy* (New York: Arrow Books, 1999).
7 L. Bartels. *Unequal Democracy: the political economy of the new gilded age* (Princeton: Princeton University Press, 2008).
8 Ibid., p. 254.
9 S. Macedo, Y. Alex-Assensoh, J. Berry, M. Brintnall, D. Campbell, L. Fraga et al. *Democracy at Risk: how political choices undermine citizen participation and what we can do about it* (Washington DC: Brookings Institute Press, 2005); R. Putnam. *Bowling Alone: the collapse and revival of American community* (New York: Simon & Schuster, 2000).
10 W. Damon. *The Path to Purpose* (New York: Free Press, 2008), 174.
11 R. Rosenheck, C. Leda, L. Frisman, J. Lam, and A. Chang. Homeless veterans. In: J. Baumohl (ed.). *Homelessness in America* (Phoenix: Oryx Press, 1996).
12 L. Dolte, K. Cramer, N. Dietz, and R. Grimm. *College Students Helping America* (Washington, DC: Corporation for National and Community Service, 2006); J. Pryor, S. Hurtado, V. Saenz, J. Santos, and W. Korn. *The American Freshman: forty year trends* (Los Angeles: Higher Education Research Institute, 2007).

13 M. Gladwell. Million dollar Murray. *The New Yorker*, February 13, 2006.
14 25th Anniversary of the Harvard Square Homeless Shelter. John F. Kennedy School of Government. March 5, 2008. Retrieved on September 1, 2009 from http://www.iop.harvard.edu.

APPENDIX: RESEARCH METHODS

1 V. Anfara, K. Brown, and T. Mangione. Qualitative analysis on stage: making the research process more public. *Educational Researcher*, 31, 7 (2002).
2 For more on "hanging out" with the homeless, see G. Dordick. *Something Left to Lose: personal relations and survival among New York's homeless* (Philadelphia: Temple University Press, 1997).
3 P. Maykut and R. Morehouse. *Beginning Qualitative Research: a philosophical and practical guide* (London: Routledge, 1994).
4 M. Patton. *Qualitative Evaluation and Research Methods* (Newbury Park, CA: Sage, 1990).
5 M. Miles and M. Huberman. *Qualitative Data Analysis: an expanded sourcebook* (Thousand Oaks, CA: Sage, 1994).
6 A. Strauss and J. Corbin. *Basics of Qualitative Research: grounded theory, procedures, and techniques* (Newbury Park, CA: Sage, 1990).
7 S. Seider. Service-learning. In: M. Devins (ed.). *Talbot's Student Planning Book* (Wellesley: Dexter, 2003).
8 J. Maxwell. *Qualitative Research Design* (London: Sage, 1996).
9 Y. Lincoln and E. Guba. *Naturalistic Inquiry* (London: Sage, 1985).

Index

292   INDEX